AMERICA'S
WAY
BACK

Reclaiming Freedom, Tradition,
and Constitution

DONALD J. DEVINE

ISI
BOOKS

WILMINGTON, DELAWARE

TO THE NEXT GENERATION:

Joshua, Robert, William, Matthew, John, Christopher, Kathleen, Jessica, Erin, Megan, Jeffrey, Allison, Jackson, and Madeline

Cataloging-in-Publication data is on file with the Library of Congress

Devine, Donald John, 1937–
  America's way back : freedom, tradition, constitution / by Donald J. Devine.
    p. cm.
  Includes bibliographical references and index.
  ISBN 978-1-61017-063-5
  1. United States—Politics and government—Philosophy. 2. Libertarianism—United States. 3. Tradition (Philosophy) I. Title.
  JK31.D48 2012
  320.51'2—dc23
                        2011051979

Published in the United States by:

ISI Books
Intercollegiate Studies Institute
3901 Centerville Road
Wilmington, Delaware 19807-1938
www.isibooks.org

Manufactured in the United States of America

Contents

Introduction

---◆---

THE CHALLENGE

THE PAST SEVERAL YEARS HAVE been dispiriting for Americans. Economic stagnation, moral exhaustion, and looming bankruptcy have become hallmarks of our time.

Nothing has seemed to work. In 2008, Americans dramatically rejected the actions of Republican George W. Bush's administration by embracing a new, progressive president. Democrat Barack Obama promised a new energy to fulfill the progressive ideal of a responsible welfare state; he would commit the full power and public resources of the national government necessary to resolve America's major problems. But even as the administration produced more "transformational" legislation than any in memory, the economy sputtered, unemployment remained stubbornly high, the federal debt skyrocketed, and the "entitlement bomb" came closer to going off. Obama managed reelection in 2012, but as one of his prominent supporters put it, "The thrill of 2008 had turned into the frustration of 2012." It now was clear that "our democracy seems incapable of fixing the serious problems the nation confronts."[1]

There is a good reason for our failures to solve our economic and cultural problems: few leaders—of *either* political party—understand the *source* of the problems. As a result, their so-called solutions simply have not worked, and yet leaders call for more of the same old techniques—more money poured into more government programs, and tighter controls over the American creative spirit. This persistence in the face of obvious failure reflects a triumph of progressive hope over the real-world experiences of the past century. Welfare-state progressivism has so corrupted modern political thinking that it has obscured the secret of America's success: the

1

U.S. Constitution's capacity to harmonize the twin ideals of freedom and tradition.

There is an inherent tension between freedom and tradition. Indeed, supporters of one over the other often suggest that a synthesis of the two cannot work. It must be one or the other. Traditionalists claim that pure freedom leads to disorder, decline in public morality, and ultimately anarchy. Libertarians, meanwhile, claim that pure tradition is restrictive, authoritarian, and ultimately tyrannical.

But this book argues that each single ideology needs to be synthesized with the other to escape its own limitations. A close study of the American— and broader Western—experience reveals that managing the tension between freedom and tradition has been the very source of our historic creativity and prosperity. Far from being incompatible, freedom and tradition need each other: freedom needs tradition for law, order, inspiration, and energy; tradition needs freedom to escape stagnation, coercion, and decline. The great achievement of the Constitution's framers was in providing a means for synthesizing freedom and tradition. They carefully crafted a flexible system in which powers were separated and a multiplicity of institutions checked and complemented one another.

Unfortunately, few Americans now understand their Constitution as the Founders did. Most schoolchildren learn about the formal separation of powers among the three branches of the federal government. Often overlooked are the Constitution's more extensive checks and balances—especially the way the document explicitly reserves most rights to the people and to the states. In *Federalist* 51, James Madison noted that the Constitution provided "double security" for the people's rights by dividing power "between two distinct governments." The division of powers allowed different traditions and communities, and the individuals representing them, to act freely and creatively. This is the essential aspect of limited constitutional government: it allows most decisions to be made regionally, locally, and privately—not to be forced by Washington.

Today, however, the central government is the major decision maker on most important matters. This change did not happen by accident. Influenced by late-nineteenth-century European thinkers, America's progressive movement proclaimed the superiority of concentrated power over the Constitution's separated powers. Progressives called for a new "science of administration," believing that national experts could solve society's problems better than the old Constitution ever could. As we will see, this fatally flawed belief has led to most of the fundamental problems we are experiencing today.

To successfully confront these problems, America needs a restoration of the constitutional synthesis of freedom and tradition that has regenerated the West, and the United States in particular, so often before. Such a revival will not be easy, not when the progressive revolutions of the past century have so obscured the foundational role freedom and tradition have played. To rediscover the old Constitution, we must take an extended intellectual journey—into public administration, political science, law, philosophy, even the nature of science itself.

A Few Great Men

Several of the great figures of our time inspired this book. One remains a universally recognized historical figure; one continues to inspire academic professionals in economics, politics, law, and philosophy, in all of which he excelled; another was a charismatic public figure and writer; and a fourth—and most important for this book—is hardly recognized today. These four men were Ronald Reagan, F. A. Hayek, William F. Buckley Jr., and Frank S. Meyer.

Professor Hayek was the first to make a deep impression on the world. His 1944 book *The Road to Serfdom* was a rare bestseller for an academic work. Hayek came from a distinguished Austrian family of intellectuals and entered the study of economics as a means to combat the devastation his nation faced after the Great War. He became a member of the informal group of academics in Vienna referred to as the Austrian School, which included his teacher Ludwig von Mises, the philosopher of science Karl Popper, and the great economic historian Joseph A. Schumpeter, who all promoted the virtues of freedom and markets as superior alternatives to the then-dominant doctrine of socialism.[2]

Hayek's 1960 book, *The Constitution of Liberty*, convinced me of the importance not only of his economic insights on freedom but also of his stress on law and the Western tradition as the foundation for the market and for the free society generally. My interest in Hayek inevitably led to Popper, Schumpeter, and Mises, who together helped refine the cosmology, epistemology, and understanding of history, politics, and law that form the basis for this book. Later, I had the opportunity to meet and learn from Professor Hayek through the international professional association of scholars he organized, the Mont Pelerin Society.

In 1955, William F. Buckley Jr. founded *National Review* magazine. He gathered a group of intellectuals of both libertarian and traditionalist bent

who were unified only in opposition to what they considered a threatening communism and a moribund progressive welfare state. Over time, the
creative interaction among the editors and the electrifying atmosphere they
created for others outside that circle produced a "fusion" of the ideals of freedom and tradition that would become the unifying theme for the modern
conservative movement.

No figure was more important to this fusionism than Frank Meyer,
an editor at *National Review* who worked closely with Buckley. Born into
a secular family, Meyer had been attracted to communism at a young age,
becoming a major functionary of the Communist Party USA.[3] After becoming disillusioned and reading *The Road to Serfdom*, he was ready in 1955
to join *National Review*. Meyer was the provocateur of the debate within
the magazine and beyond. He systematized the results through his regular
column, "Principles and Heresies," and other writings—especially his 1962
book, *In Defense of Freedom*. Meyer showed that the synthesis of freedom
and tradition had played the essential role in the rise of Western civilization
and its American offshoot.

While Buckley charmed government officials and wooed the media,
celebrities, businessmen, and the public at large, Meyer won the hearts and
minds of the young intellectuals and activists who would shape the new constitutional conservative movement in America. He was inspirational, iras-
cible, and irresistible, a force of nature. His written and personal insights
infuse this whole book.

Ronald Reagan was a great admirer of this band of theorists and freely
admitted how much they influenced his thinking. Indeed, he saw much of
his role in later life as putting their ideas into practice. His success can be
measured by the fact that two of his greatest critics, Barack Obama and
Hillary Clinton, conceded that he was transformational in both teaching
and achieving his goals.[4] He was a personal and professional inspiration to
this author: I worked for him for more than a decade, at the end as his director of the U.S. Office of Personnel Management.

The years since President Reagan have seen a decline in economic freedom, traditional values, and the constitutional and social institutions supporting them. Still, understanding his successes can illuminate the way
back. Reagan understood the power of both freedom and traditional virtue.
What's more, he recognized that the synthesis of freedom and tradition cannot be sustained simply for pragmatic political purposes. There must be a
deep philosophical commitment to harmonizing both ideals. The political
process is by necessity full of messy compromises. Without a deep commit-

ment to the idea of the synthesis itself, neither freedom nor tradition can long survive.

In *The Constitution of Liberty*, Hayek wrote, "Paradoxical as it may appear, it is probably true that a successful free society will always in a large measure be a tradition-bound society."[5] This book shows how right Hayek's critical insight was, and how, guided by this truth, America can reclaim the freedom and traditions that have made it great.

One

⟫⟩•⟨⟪

NEW DEAL FAITH SHATTERED

I S IT POSSIBLE EVEN ALL these years later to suppress a smile at Ronald Reagan's little joke about the government's relentless attempts to solve all of life's problems: "The nine most terrifying words in the English language are: 'I'm from the government and I'm here to help'"?

President Reagan may have made a joke, but today, Paul Light is serious about the problem—very serious. Light is the endowed professor of public service at New York University, the founding director of the Brookings Center for Public Service, and a senior adviser to the National Commission on the Public Service. Writing in the *Washington Post*, the company-town paper of the federal government, he made a remarkable statement about the American national government. Light was prompted to write when, on Christmas Day 2010, a previously identified terrorist bomber successfully passed airport security, to be foiled only by his own incompetence:

> The systemic failures that led to the attempted bombing of Northwest Flight 253 are, sadly, all too familiar. Substitute the words "Christmas Day plot" for tainted meat, poisoned peppers, aircraft groundings, the Columbia shuttle accident, Hurricane Katrina, counterfeit Heparin, toxic toys, the banking collapse, Bernie Madoff or even Sept. 11, and the failure to put Umar Farouk Abdulmutallab on the "no-fly" list becomes yet another indication that the federal government can no longer guarantee the faithful execution of our laws.[1]

Professor Light is not alone in condemning the federal government's performance. In fact, the loss of faith in the modern welfare state is widespread.

7

The National Commission on the Public Service has issued two reports detailing the government's inability to execute its laws. The reports were endorsed by avatars of establishment welfare-state progressivism: Walter Mondale, Vernon Jordan, Donna Shalala, Doug Fraser, John Gardner, Charles "Mac" Mathias, Edmund Muskie, John Brademas, Derek Bok, Elliot Richardson, Paul Volcker, and dear old Gerry Ford, among many others.[2]

When Professor Light wrote, the widely accepted Pew Research Center surveys provided a detailed picture of the public's opinions about government and how it differed from the climate of opinion in the late 1990s: "At that time, the public's desire for government services and activism was holding steady. This is not the case today. Just 22% say they can trust the government in Washington almost always or most of the time, among the lowest measures in half a century."[3] The decline in support was not just for politicians but also for the experts in the bureaucracy who must make the programs work:

> Favorable ratings for federal agencies and institutions have fallen since 1997–98 for seven of 13 federal agencies included in the survey. The declines have been particularly large for the Department of Education, the Food and Drug Administration, the Social Security Administration, as well as the Environmental Protection Agency, the National Aeronautics and Space Administration, and the Centers for Disease Control and Prevention.[4]

Being an expert on the management of the welfare state, Professor Light thought that much of the problem was simply administrative and could be cured by organizational reform. Some of the problems identified were conventional—too many layers of government for those at the top to understand what was going on below them; too many political appointees undergoing an "agonizing" confirmation process, resulting in too many executive vacancies; and using too many contractors, whom government officials could not supervise well.

But the good professor cited some disturbing facts about the very experts who populate the public service bureaucracy: only a third of federal employees told government pollsters that their promotions were based on merit; even fewer thought poor performers were held accountable; and less than 40 percent believed innovation and creativity were rewarded. This bureaucratic slack, Light noted, "contributed to the Christmas Day incident" and the general decline of government.[5]

This is not how the modern progressive welfare state was supposed to work.

Bureaucracy: The Modern Solution

With government the butt of so many jokes—Reagan also quipped that "a government bureau is the nearest thing to eternal life we'll ever see on this earth"—it is nearly impossible to understand how bureaucracy once was considered the salvation of civilization.

In the nineteenth century, European intellectuals began hailing the "scientific" approach to administration as the solution to the failings of previous regimes. The German economic historian Max Weber captured this approach in his classic *Theory of Social and Economic Organization*. There he argued that the traditional forms of government were no longer appropriate. Ruling authority should not be derived from lineage, as in monarchies or clans, or from the exceptional qualities of a charismatic leader.[6] Weber held that authority should be based on rational rules, not arbitrary personal status or power. He called for bureaucratic authority based on a rational, hierarchical ordering of society. Weber praised the efficiency of a system, whether public or private, whereby logical rules clearly fixed responsibilities among various bureaus and organizations:

> Experience tends universally to show that the purely bureaucratic type of administrative organization—that is, the monocratic variety of bureaucracy—is, from a purely technical point of view, capable of attaining the highest degree of efficiency and is in this sense formally the most rational known means of carrying out imperative control over human beings. It is superior to any other form in precision, in stability, in the stringency of its discipline, and in its reliability. It thus makes possible a particularly high degree of calculability of results for the heads of the organization and for those acting in relation to it. It is finally superior both in intensive efficiency and in the scope of its operations, and is formally capable of application to all kinds of administrative tasks. . . . The primary source of the superiority of bureaucratic administration lies in the role of technical knowledge which, through the development of modern technology and business methods in the production of goods, has become completely indispensable.[7]

A group of self-identified progressive American intellectuals took notice of this new model of efficient organization. In 1886 one such academic, a newly minted PhD, published a pathbreaking article titled "The Study of Administration." Expressing admiration for the efficiencies of the bureaucratic systems "developed by French and German professors," the scholar wrote that Americans should not "be frightened at the idea of looking into foreign systems of administration for instruction and suggestion." Although he conceded that the European system needed to be adapted for American "popular sovereignty" and local conditions and institutions, he declared that the true challenge was to "make public opinion willing to listen and then see to it that it listens to the right things." The "right things" were to turn political administration over to professional experts and let them decide on scientific grounds what was good for society.[8]

Unfortunately, the scholar said, "not much impartial scientific method is to be discerned in [America's] administrative practices." The source of the problem was the U.S. Constitution, which divided power rather than concentrated it. The Constitution's division of powers had frustrated progress in the United States from the beginning, he argued. According to "The Study of Administration," the Constitution's framers were wrong to fear the concentration of power: "There is no danger in power, if only it be not irresponsible. If it be divided, dealt out in shares to many, it is obscured; and if it be obscured, it is made irresponsible. But if it be centered in heads of the service and in heads of branches of the service, it is easily watched and brought to book. If to keep his office a man must achieve open and honest success, and if at the same time he feels himself entrusted with large freedom of discretion, the greater his power the less likely is he to abuse it, the more is he nerved and sobered and elevated by it." The "science of administration" would provide that responsible form of concentrated power.[9]

A little more than a quarter century later, the author of that groundbreaking article became president of the United States. As president, Woodrow Wilson put much of his progressive thinking into practice. In 1912 he announced a New Freedom program that created the central institutions of the bureaucratic welfare state: the Federal Reserve banking system; progressive income taxation; loans to the largest private-sector business of the day, agriculture; the Federal Trade Commission and the antitrust bureau, which marked the beginning of the regulatory state; and more government regulation generally. These measures fundamentally changed American government, centralizing authority on the premise—and promise—that the federal bureaucracy could more effectively deal with modern problems.[10] Wilson, however, was too hemmed in as a minority president with a conservative Congress, and later by the demands of World War I, to implement fully his constitutional reform program.

Progressivism really became the dominant fact of American government with the election of Franklin Roosevelt, who in 1932 pledged "a new deal for the American people," a "new order of competence and courage," a new way of governing that would compassionately guarantee Americans freedom from want and fear.[11] Roosevelt threw the whole power of a vastly expanded government against the Great Depression, beginning the long reign of progressivism in American government and politics, which endures to this day. Progressivism was not a partisan movement. President Theodore Roosevelt was a leading member of the progressive faction in the Republican Party and he ran as presidential nominee of the Progressive Party. Some modern historians trace the effective beginning of the New Deal to progressive Republican Herbert Hoover's programs, especially his Reconstruction Finance Corporation.[12]

By 1960 the progressive welfare state had become, as its most famous theorist, Gunnar Myrdal, boasted, "the widely acclaimed ideal of a whole nation." Americans by then had accepted the progressive dogma that national prosperity and welfare had come into being not "as a result of the unhampered play of market forces, but through public policies, which are all under the ultimate sanction of the state." The American public expected the government to move to solve social ills. But even by that point the people had grown dissatisfied with the government's intrusiveness. "To many persons, the term 'Welfare State' has negative, not positive, connotations," Myrdal wrote. He worried that this public skepticism made people reluctant to grant authorities the central planning power he thought was necessary to make the welfare state work efficiently.[13] Of course, before the 1960s were out, the federal government had massively expanded its bureaucratic power yet again under Lyndon Johnson's Great Society.

Only by the late 1970s, after years of brutal stagflation—an economy fettered by both inflation and stagnation—did the bipartisan faith in the bureaucratic welfare state show signs of weakening. Even then, however, President Reagan's efforts to reduce the burden of government were quickly overturned. His successors once again turned to expert bureaucracy to plan better for the general welfare. Republican President George W. Bush epitomized the commitment to progressive bureaucratic solutions, declaring, "We have a responsibility that when somebody hurts, government has got to move."[14]

Failing the Test

Bush entered the presidency promising to be both empathetic and effective, pledging his commitment to "compassionate conservatism" and to using his skills as the first MBA president to run government efficiently.[15] When asked what kind of conservative he was, he said he was an "efficient-government conservative" as opposed to a small-government conservative, reflecting the progressivism of his hero Theodore Roosevelt.[16]

The national government's response to Hurricane Katrina in 2005 offered the clearest test of Bush's vision and the welfare-state hope in the federal bureaucracy's efficiency. Progressive columnist E. J. Dionne Jr., the man President Bill Clinton credited with inspiring his "New Democrat" politics, noted that the Katrina disaster was "a time when government is morally obligated to be competent, prepared, innovative, flexible, well-financed—in short, smart enough and, yes, big enough to undertake an enormous task." As Dionne put it, the "government is the enemy until you need a friend."[17]

The Federal Emergency Management Agency (FEMA) set up headquarters in Washington even before the storm landed and began planning distribution of supplies and organizing outside assistance from New Orleans. President Bush declared the hurricane a national disaster on Monday, August 29, the day the storm hit the Gulf Coast. FEMA's parent, the Department of Homeland Security (DHS), proclaimed the storm an "incident of national significance" on Tuesday.

But soon it became clear that the federal government was failing this big test. FEMA initiated its new post-9/11 DHS security pass system, allowing only those with the required expertise to enter the affected zone. This immediately became a bar to outside assistance. Florida attempted to send five hundred airboats but could not receive the needed security clearance; a flotilla from Shreveport was halted too. Bush housing secretary Alphonso Jackson complained at a cabinet meeting that his attempts to provide emergency housing had been thwarted by red tape. When trying to send a private helicopter to the scene, a congressman representing the area was told that FEMA was in charge, the Federal Aviation Administration (FAA) was in charge, and the military was. A mayor in his district was put on hold for forty-five minutes. Security forces blocked scores of private rescue boats from docking on the river. A sheriff was told to e-mail a request for help when he had no electricity.[18]

Bureaucratic planning done years earlier was the biggest culprit. The federal government had actually taken control of the Mississippi levees in 1879. Those protecting New Orleans were supposedly designed to deal with a Category 3 hurricane; for a time Katrina was a Category 4. Who decided on a lower level of protection? Why, the federal government, of course, in the form of presidential budgets, congressional appropriations, and Corps of Engineers plans and projects.[19] The Corps expert bureaucracy must look at the entire U.S. seacoast and make decisions on objective needs, and there is not enough money in the world to build against Category 4 storms all along America's thousands of miles of coastline. New Orleans is particularly vulnerable, but many other locations face potential danger—the largest previous disaster was in Galveston, Texas, for example. Bush had actually spent slightly more on levees than Clinton and much more on organizational expertise in the new Department of Homeland Security. But big money and big government did not help.

A larger problem was that President Bush, along with his FEMA director, the governor of Louisiana, the mayor of New Orleans, and many other officials, encouraged the idea that "we are in charge" and all would be all right as long as the government was on the case.[20] The only problem was that big government was not in charge and can never be. Once it is big, it metastasizes into multiple forms. As the *Wall Street Journal*'s Daniel Henninger noted, "Large public bureaucracies, whether the FBI and the CIA or FEMA and the Corps of Engineers, don't talk to each other much." The need to win government appropriations makes agencies responsive to "political whim," while "real-world problems, as the 9/11 Report noted, inevitably seem distant and minor."[21]

But President Bush accepted the progressive argument that expertise centrally directed with sufficient power can solve big problems. His own brother, Florida governor Jeb Bush, criticized the federal government for trying to do too much: "I can say with certainty that federalizing emergency response to catastrophic events would be a disaster as bad as Hurricane Katrina. If you federalize, all the innovation, creativity, and knowledge would subside."[22] Clearly, FEMA and DHS's security controls severely interrupted both local and voluntary efforts to assist the victims, including the major efforts the state of Florida offered. The agency discouraged multiple offers of private help.[23] Foreign donations were halted at airports and ports to secure required State Department and Department of Homeland Security clearance. "Buy America" provisions of labor law were used to deny a large Dutch offer.[24]

Local agencies and the private sector made a huge impact when they were not blocked by federal controls and regulations. Most of the local people who were first on the scene performed rather well, many heroically. They were supported by private resources of an incredible variety. The Red Cross sent thousands of volunteers to help and delivered financial contributions from tens of millions of Americans. Anheuser-Busch contributed 2.5 million cans of drinking water a week. Bristol-Myers-Squibb gave unlimited access to baby food. Eli Lilly sent 40,000 vials of refrigerated insulin. Kellogg sent seven truckloads of crackers and cookies. General Electric gave trailers, modular space, and medical equipment. Cendant donated rooms for emergency workers. Home Depot sent $500,000 for housing repair. Springs Industry sent sheets, blankets, and comforters. DTE Energy sent 100 trucks and 75 tree trimmers. General Motors gave 150 vehicles to the Red Cross. Navistar arranged for its heavy trucks to go to the region. Fifteen airlines donated thousands of trips to send victims to shelters in other cities. The list of private assistance is endless.[25]

In testimony before the Senate Energy Committee less than a month after Katrina, government and industry experts told the surprised politicians that the private regional electricity grid, the natural gas and petroleum gas lines originating in the Gulf, and the local refining capabilities were already back to 80 percent of capacity and would reach 90 percent in a week or so. Meanwhile, government-run water and sewage pipelines and levees in Louisiana and Mississippi were out indefinitely.[26]

The bottom line is that during and after Katrina, the most efficient federal organization, the Coast Guard, rescued only 6,500 people; local governments helped tens of thousands of others; private efforts rescued tens of millions.[27]

Politicians and bureaucrats did not learn the lesson. The solution to emergency efforts was still to exercise firmer federal control, which results in more red tape and more bureaucracy.[28] In October 2005, as Hurricane Wilma approached Florida, Admiral Timothy Keating, the head of the Northern Command, the military body newly created to oversee homeland defense, told Congress that more national resources were necessary. He added that active-duty military forces should be given complete authority for responding to catastrophic domestic disasters.[29] President Bush had already created a new federal procedure, the National Incident Management System (NIMS), to force federal, state, and local officials to work together, all under federal authority.[30] Even while acknowledging that "most often these incidents are managed most efficiently at the local level," NIMS required overall national management, including a national ID that would exclude all nonofficial citizen volunteers, compounding the Katrina error.[31]

State and local officials fought back against federal power. The head of Florida's National Guard, General Douglas Burnett, later summed up the attitude of people on the ground: "Did we need a three-star general from Texas to come to direct our response? No, we did not." Floridians outmaneuvered the feds, ensuring that the NIMS committee was staffed mainly with Florida state officials and was chaired by Governor Jeb Bush.[32]

Unlike Professor Light, most progressives cannot afford to see the deeper problem: the progressive faith in big government itself.

Bush's Fault?

Rather than face the possibility that national planning itself was inadequate to the scope of the problem, progressives sounded a constant refrain: that Katrina was "Bush's fault." Author Greg Anrig wrote a whole book, *The Conservatives Have No Clothes*, to prove that President Bush had a "hostility toward government" that caused the government's efforts to fail.[33] In fact, the president did direct enormous resources toward Katrina, and they were managed by bureaucratic experts, not by political appointees, much less by the president himself. What other resources of the national government could he have thrown at Katrina? His FEMA director could have expressed himself better, but he was essentially correct as far as what the feds possibly could have accomplished: "Considering the dire circumstances that we have in New Orleans—virtually a city that has been destroyed—things are going relatively well."[34]

Contrary to Anrig, budget expenditures clearly show that Bush pretty much accepted the progressive logic. In his first term he increased nondefense discretionary government spending more than any recent president, Democratic or Republican—by 25 percent, or a rate of 6.2 percent per year. His Medicare prescription drug program was the first major new entitlement since Lyndon Johnson.[35] By the end of his second term, Bush had increased discretionary spending *104* percent, compared with only 11 percent during Clinton's presidency. Subsidy programs grew by 30 percent under Bush.[36] Some hostility to active government!

Well, Bush might have spent, but he was hostile to regulation, the progressives responded. For example, in the book *The Wrecking Crew: How Conservatives Rule*, Thomas Frank insisted that Bush showed he really opposed regulation when he said that "government should be market based."[37] Anrig claimed that the Bush administration exceeded even the Reagan years in deregulation.[38] Yet it was the Bush administration that created (with Congress, of course) a whole new regulatory department—DHS—to deal with Katrina-like disasters. The move failed, but not because there was insufficient regulation.

There was plenty of regulation under Bush. It just didn't work.

Was it lack of regulations that led to the widespread problems found at Walter Reed Army Medical Center in 2007? The military provides health care to nine million soldiers, and the Department of Veterans Affairs covers five million more. Two massive bureaucracies baffled patients, to say nothing about the Physical Disability Board process, which took endless time to make a determination regarding return to duty and degree of disability.

Only 22 percent of the most widely used new drugs were available through the Department of Veterans Affairs, and three million seniors had switched to the Medicare program to get its larger choice. The greatest problem was breaking through the multiple regulations of two different bureaucratic systems. The result was that the most deserving of all governmental clients— wounded veterans—were confused and experienced delays in treatment or received little or no assistance.[39]

What could be more important than securing the homeland from terrorist attack? Would this be something President Bush would wish to wreck? In fact, the DHS airport screening bureaucracy received the most funds and management attention, but the results were abysmal. In tests between November 2001 and February 2002, screeners missed 70 percent of knives, 30 percent of guns, and 60 percent of mock bombs. In 2003, testers were able to sneak explosives and weapons past the screeners at fifteen airports nationwide. Between October 2005 and January 2006, homemade bombs were passed through security at all twenty-one airports tested.[40] Making things more difficult, Congress passed bills allowing union collective bargaining over screening matters. DHS secretary Michael Chertoff was reduced to telling Congress that the greatest need was more intelligence about local activities, which could be gathered only if everyone got "to know their neighbors better."[41]

The Bush administration actually increased regulation in almost every field—to record levels, in fact. A comprehensive study by the Competitive Enterprise Institute's Clyde Wayne Crews shows that by 2008 the Bush administration had 79,435 pages of regulations in the official Federal Register—an increase of more than 8 percent over even the Carter administration's all-time high (73,258 pages in 1980). By contrast, the Reagan administration had cut the number of pages of regulations more than 30 percent from the Carter years, to 50,616. A 2008 letter to President Bush signed by both conservatives and liberals (including the Competitive Enterprise Institute and the Environmental Defense Fund) put the matter bluntly: "Your administration has already issued more regulations than any in history." This is hostility to regulation?[42]

"How Much Can Government Do?"

The economic crisis that began in 2008 showed in even starker terms the failure of the progressive welfare state. Progressives hailed the New Deal's interventions for "ending the Great Depression." For decades thereafter it was accepted wisdom that the government had mastered the business cycle and could, through government spending and regulation, protect against any similar catastrophe. As *Washington Post* columnist Robert Samuelson put it, the conceit of modern economics "has been that we had solved the problem of stability. Oh, there would be periodic recessions, but the prospects of a major economic collapse were negligible because we knew how the system worked and could take steps to prevent it."[43]

But on September 29, 2008, the Dow Jones stock prices dropped 777 points, and several major banks appeared to be on the edge of failure. The whole economic system seemed at risk. President Bush undoubtedly had cause to remember the old saw that economists were created by God to make weather forecasters look good.

Even presumed free marketers were on board for government to save the economy in the face of the presumed threats. Before the key congressional vote on Treasury Secretary Henry Paulson's record-shattering $700 billion bailout and socialization of investment-banking risk, the editors of the *Wall Street Journal* declared that "this government intervention is justified" (although they preferred the Federal Deposit Insurance Corporation to the Treasury and the Fed).[44] The editors disparaged the House Republicans who had temporarily defeated the bailout as running "for cover," and they criticized the few free-market economic analysts who opposed the plan as ideologues "safe in their think tanks" who think economic reality is an "academic seminar."[45]

In reaction to the Federal Reserve bailout of Bear Stearns, the generous debt guarantee to JPMorgan Chase, and the opening of direct credit lines to other investment firms, E. J. Dionne Jr. could not contain himself: "Never do I want to hear again from my conservative friends how brilliant capitalists are, how much they deserve their seven-figure salaries and how government should keep its hands off the private economy."[46]

Still, it was clear to the *Wall Street Journal* editors that the government caused the panic in the first place:

- "The original sin of this crisis was easy money," which the Federal Reserve had promoted right up to the present crisis, but especially from 2003 to 2005, creating a "vast subsidy for debt that both households and firms exploited."
- Federal and state regulations created an oligopoly of ratings agencies—S&P, Moody's, and Fitch—that promised to rate the risk on securities accurately. With government protection implied, risk taking increased. Congress's 2007 action to end the oligopoly, unfortunately, came too late.

- In 2004 the Securities and Exchange Commission (SEC) allowed the more regulated finance firms, such as Lehman Brothers and Bear Stearns, to increase leverage rates from the previous ten-to-one ratio up to thirty- or forty-to-one. When the bull market cooled, those firms failed.
- The Community Reinvestment Act of 1977 "compels banks to make loans to poor borrowers who often cannot repay them." In 1993 the Clinton administration rewrote the regulations to force more loans and in 1994 announced a National Homeownership Strategy to push even more poorly financed minority borrowers into mortgages. Spurred on by Congress to issue more and more "affordable mortgages" to those who could not afford them, the government-created Fannie Mae and Freddie Mac bought the "increasingly questionable" mortgages that began the rout. They were allowed to hold just 2.5 percent of capital compared with 10 percent for banks. Wonder why these loans might fail in a crisis?[47]

It is not as if no one foresaw what would happen. In 2005 the normally opaque Federal Reserve chairman, Alan Greenspan, told Congress in the bluntest possible terms: If Fannie and Freddie "continue to grow, continue to have the low capital that they have, continue to engage in the dynamic hedging of their portfolios, which they need to do for interest rate risk aversion, they potentially create ever-growing potential systemic risk down the road. We are placing the total financial system of the future at a substantial risk."[48]

Many suggested that a lack of government regulation had caused the crisis. But as economist Alan Reynolds emphasized, there was no shortage of regulation. Even after Congress repealed the banking regulatory provisions of the Glass-Steagall Act in the late 1990s, the federal government still issued and enforced plenty of regulations—through the Federal Reserve, the SEC, the Comptroller of the Currency, and the Federal Deposit Insurance Corporation (FDIC). Not one of those august agencies exhibited foresight or concern about the default risk among even many prime mortgages, or about any lack of transparency with respect to bundling mortgages into securities. Reynolds summed up the matter well: "People do not become wiser, more selfless, or more omniscient simply because they work for government agencies."[49]

In fact, the experts created the problem in the first place and had no idea how to fix it. The *Washington Post*'s Samuelson wrote just before the bailout vote, "Our leaders are making up their responses from day to day because old ideas of how the economy works have failed them." We were witnessing "the bankruptcy of modern economics," he said.[50] A mere two weeks after the bill passed Congress, Treasury proved Samuelson correct by fundamentally changing the program from buying troubled assets to buying senior preferred stock and warrants of the largest banks, without changing the law.

Even Secretary Paulson acknowledged the limits of government effectiveness. In March—six months before he began pushing for the $700 billion bailout—he had appeared on *Fox News Sunday* and admitted that a correction was "inevitable." He added, "Can we outlaw the forces of gravity? You know, how much can government do?"[51]

Yes, what can the government do? It actually took a decade and a world war to end the Great Depression, despite the New Deal's claims of success. Many economists believe the Federal Reserve's actions may have caused the Depression in the first place.[52] The New Deal regulatory scheme could not avoid or solve the stagflation of the Jimmy Carter years, the $250 billion savings-and-loan bank failure crisis of the mid-1980s, the commercial banking crisis of the late 1980s, or several dozen smaller recessions in between.

Look at the current federal regulatory system. The Federal Reserve was created to regulate banking, which dominated the capital market for most of the twentieth century. Today, however, unregulated hedge funds and broker balances account for half of investment capital. The regulatory system clearly failed in the most recent economic crisis, with some banks receiving government bailouts and some collapsing altogether. By contrast, unregulated or minimally regulated hedge funds and private equity companies received no bailouts—and they survived the crisis. Could the trouble not be the market but the decrepit New Deal regime that tried to tame it?

Entitlement Implosion

Although Americans doubt the federal government's effectiveness, many still expect the government to provide benefits. Popular expectations are costly—nowhere more so than with entitlements. For decades politicians have simply ignored the ticking entitlement bomb. But as the government itself documents, these programs will very soon consume the government's resources and swallow a major share of the economy.

Consider the projected costs of Social Security and Medicare. Simply put, Medicare and Social Security costs are exploding.[53] Their combined costs amounted to about 6 percent of gross domestic product (GDP) in 2000; according to the government's projections, that will jump to more than 20 percent by 2023.

And those projections are optimistic, to say the least. A key promise of the Obama administration's health-care overhaul was that it would save Medicare hundreds of billions of dollars. The official report of the Trustees of Social Security and Medicare takes pains to convey this impression, showing the costs as a percentage of GDP flattening out around 2030 and holding steady thereafter. But in an appendix to the report, Medicare's chief actuary observes that pretty much everything in the preceding two hundred pages is bunk, forced through by a politicized Congress insisting on rosy assumptions. He labels the estimates "implausible," saying that the report's financial projections "do not represent a reasonable expectation for actual program operations in either the short range . . . or the long range."[54]

Even President Bush's failed proposal to substitute private accounts for perhaps 2 percent of current Social Security contributions would have been insufficient to deal with the problem. And his 2003 Medicare prescription drug bill added one and a half times the total unfunded liability of the Social Security program to the Medicare liabilities.[55]

A chart from the Trustees of Social Security and Medicare report presents a precise road map to the coming bankruptcy of the federal government. Entitlement costs already outstrip the revenue generated by these programs—and the gap is growing rapidly. As every politician knows, these programs are unsustainable. The Ponzi-like approach of Social Security promises greater benefits than are actuarially supported by income, but politicians could ignore the issue because the system took eighty years before it went into the red. Lyndon Johnson's Medicare/Medicaid went into the red the same year—in about half the time it took Social Security.

Still, few leaders dare challenge the public's expectations or address the coming financial implosion.

One Last Chance

The profound reality today is that a greatly respected progressive like Professor Light can come to the reluctant conclusion that most of the problem with welfare-state government is fundamental:

Tinkering will not fix these problems. Congress and the president must embrace far-reaching reform in what government is asked to do and how it implements laws. The question is not whether government has an audacious agenda but whether it can convert great endeavors into achievement. One thing is certain. Substantial reform will not happen until Congress and the president acknowledge that the Christmas Day plot is symptomatic of a much larger threat. They merely need to read the two national commission reports to start drafting legislation. Until that happens, the next failure is only a matter of time.[56]

Notice the "in what government is asked to do" part. Since when had a progressive suggested that there was anything government was not supposed to do to help people in need?

The reports of the National Commission on the Public Service likewise suggested that the problems were endemic. As the second report concluded, "There are too many decision-makers, too much central clearance, too many bases to touch, and too many overseers with conflicting agendas. . . . Accountability is hard to discern and harder still to enforce."[57] But even these probing reports did not really give fundamental solutions. Is it possible to cut layers, bureaucratization, centralization, and nasty politics without doing fewer "audacious" things? Even the presumably administrative problems seem to require more radical solutions.

Progressivism entered American politics promising to solve problems through expert bureaucracy if only the national government were given sufficient resources and authority to plan effectively for the general welfare. But over the past century the federal government has been given unimaginable resources and authority, and still the results have been abysmal.

Public confidence in the welfare state was finally shaken in the late 1970s. Americans no longer believed that the government could save them from want and fear. Indeed, the government seemed a major part of the problem. The structures President Woodrow Wilson had set up to regulate trade, banks, business, and agriculture had been added to over the years. Each time the regulatory regimes failed, subsequent presidents and Congresses simply added new regulatory controls and new layers of bureaucratization. This is how we got to the point where Professor Light can conclude that government can no longer meet its constitutional obligation to faithfully execute its laws.

Is it any wonder that the federal government's favorability has been declining for decades (except for a short-lived improvement following 9/11)? Even the poor, the main justification for progressive policies, do not believe that government works for them. A massive study of low-income workers by the Henry J. Kaiser Family Foundation and the *Washington Post* found that 53 percent said government programs that "try to improve the condition of working families" do not have "much impact"; 20 percent said they actually "make things worse." This was not a partisan issue: low-income Americans did not believe any change in political administration would help.[58]

The problem with the modern welfare state is not a lack of resources or regulations. It is more fundamental. Why is it that after such a long record of reform the United States finds itself in a bureaucratic paralysis, near bankruptcy?

To understand why America's Constitution is breaking under the burden of modern progressivism, in coming chapters we will traverse world history and philosophy, the rule of law and human motivation, the nature of science as understood by Wilson's new theory of administration, and more. The solution, as we will see, is not to produce some simple, semiscientific utopian blueprint but to recover the Constitution. And that will require much more moral and intellectual effort.[59]

That effort is essential. Progressives were presented with one final opportunity to make their dream a reality beginning in 2008. Barack Obama sensed Americans' fears and frustrations. President Bush's approach had failed, and the new president promised renewed hope and positive change. With strong majority support in both houses of Congress, President Obama still had time to avoid the spending crash, recast the economy, and redeem the progressive dream.

So what happened?

Two

CHANGE REQUIRES MORE MUSCLE

I T IS IMPOSSIBLE TO EXAGGERATE the excitement that greeted Barack Obama on his inauguration as president of the United States on January 20, 2009. CBS coanchor Maggie Rodriguez opened the *Early Show* the day before by saying, "A new day is dawning here in the nation's capital on the eve of the inauguration of Barack Obama as the forty-fourth president of the United States. . . . Does it get any better, or more beautiful, or more spectacular, than this?" CNN's Jim Acosta set an even higher standard: "Barack Obama has some big shoes to fill, roughly the size of the ones up on the Lincoln Memorial. . . . Obama's inaugural address may be more than the speech of his lifetime. Historians and speechwriters say it could be one for the ages."[1]

After the inauguration, NBC's Andrea Mitchell summed it all up on the *Nightly News*:

> What a day it was. It may take days or years to really absorb the significance of what happened to America today. . . . When he [Barack Obama] finally emerged, he seemed, even in this throng, so solitary, somber, perhaps already feeling the weight of the world, even before he was transformed into the leader of the free world. . . . The mass flickering of cell phone cameras on the mall seemed like stars shining back at him.[2]

Obama shared the optimism. He certainly was not one who had lost faith in government to solve the nation's problems. All that was required, he was convinced, was a renewed commitment to the progressive ideal and sufficient power to carry it out. He had both, with large Democratic majorities in both houses of Congress ready to support his agenda. That agenda was incredibly ambitious, as the new president made clear in his first-year program, titled *A New Era of Responsibility*.[3] Obama announced during his campaign that he would be a "transformational" leader and even used Ronald Reagan as his example for how he planned to remake America: "Ronald Reagan changed the trajectory of America in a way that Richard Nixon did not and in a way Bill Clinton did not. He put us on a fundamentally different path because the country was ready for it."[4] President Obama believed the nation was again ready, but now for a very different course.

The first part of his transformation was to return to New Deal Keynesian stimulus spending and market intervention to force an economic recovery—but to do it with significantly greater power, resources, and programs than his predecessors had employed. By his fourth day as president, he had agreed to an $800 billion stimulus package that House Speaker Nancy Pelosi had devised. This plan aimed not to rescue banks, which would be left to the Federal Reserve, Treasury, and earlier programs, but to revive the economy by directly creating jobs, primarily in the public sector. The program not only was important theoretically but also would satisfy important constituencies such as labor unions, especially public-sector ones where government employees were now the dominant force. The bill specifically required its stimulus-funded work to be performed by union labor, and the president concurrently issued three executive orders to assist union organizing in the federal sector.

Obama demonstrated his ideological commitment in a range of areas. He promised universal coverage for health care. He announced full implementation of existing fuel mileage standards to reduce auto pollution emissions and demanded that Congress adopt California's even stricter requirements. He called for a comprehensive cap-and-trade energy bill to substantially reduce greenhouse gases and combat global warming. Following on President Bush's initial decision, the Obama administration proceeded to nationalize automaker General Motors, with its union workers granted substantial stock control. The government also forced Chrysler's preferred shareholders to lose their investment as it transferred Chrysler ownership to the Italian firm Fiat and its U.S. union workers. President Obama even gratified his allies on the most sensitive of the social issues by overturning the ban on federal funds for overseas groups promoting abortion.

Education would be transformed too. Higher-education Pell Grants would be changed from yearly appropriations to an automatic entitlement and increased by $200 billion the initial year. Private banks were to be forced out of the federally guaranteed student loan business, which would now consist only of direct government lending. The stimulus bill, passed on February 12, 2009, added $98 billion in new spending programs for the Department of Education. The Omnibus Appropriations Act of 2009, signed a month later, included $66.5 billion for education, a $4.5 billion increase over the preceding fiscal year. Together, the stimulus and omnibus packages provided $102 billion more for education—a historic 163 percent increase, topping President Bush's already expanded education spending by one-third.

About the only area in which President Obama was not transformational was the one in which as a candidate he implied he would be most different from his predecessor: defense and foreign policy. His opposition to the Iraq War and his promised change from the "disgraced" policies pursued by President Bush provided the greatest contrast with his leading opponent for the Democratic nomination, Hillary Clinton. Yet early in his administration, when a Turkish student asked the president whether his Iraq policies were close to Bush's, Obama replied, "Well, just because I was opposed at the outset, it doesn't mean that I don't have now responsibilities to make sure we do things in a responsible fashion." To that, the *Wall Street Journal* editorialists responded, "We'll mark that down as a 'yes.'"[5]

In arguing for passage of ambitious domestic programs, the Obama administration warned that if these reforms were not adopted in full, unemployment would rise to an unacceptable 8 percent.[6] The stimulus bill finally allotted $790 billion in new spending and Treasury added $720 billion in loan and asset guarantees. This was on top of the $700 billion Congress had allotted in late 2008 under President Bush for rescuing troubled assets and the $736 billion in Fed bank guarantees. Every principle of New Deal thinking assured that these unprecedented amounts would guarantee a vigorous economic recovery.

Transformational Budget

In 2008 President Bush estimated that the deficit for 2009 would be merely $407 billion. On entering office, President Obama was presented official figures demonstrating that the final Bush deficit would actually be $1 trillion. At 8.5 percent of national wealth, this deficit was the highest ever, excluding the World War II years; in fact, it exceeded the previous high by 40 percent. Two decades before, the entire *budget* had not even reached $1 trillion. It would be difficult to add new programs and spending with such deficits, but Obama was determined to rival FDR and Reagan as a transformational president.

The new president's first priority was to increase the number of government experts to manage the new funds and responsibilities. He began with a request for 100,000 more federal government employees. Professor Paul Light, who was the source of the 100,000 figure, admitted, "I think that is just a start." The Heritage Foundation said the actual number of additional employees under Obama's budget would be nearer to 260,000.[7]

Sensitive to the progressive requirement for expert administration, President Obama assembled a team with impeccable credentials to manage the economic crisis. Federal Reserve chairman Benjamin Bernanke was a graduate of Harvard and the Massachusetts Institute of Technology—where his thesis was on economic crises—and had been chairman of the Economics Department at Stanford, member of the Fed Board of Governors, chairman of the Council of Economic Advisers, and finally Fed chairman under two presidents. The new secretary of the treasury, Timothy Geithner, had served the Treasury Department as early as 1988 and risen to undersecretary; he had been a director at the International Monetary Fund; and at age forty-two he had become president of the Federal Reserve Bank of New York, where he worked closely with Bernanke during the first stage of the financial crisis. For the White House economic team, Obama brought in Lawrence Summers, who had been treasury secretary under Bill Clinton and then president of Harvard University; Summers had also received the prestigious John Bates Clark Medal for economic accomplishment.

A goodly number of experts were needed because the proposed changes were technically very complicated. The first issue was the mortgage glut that was the proximate cause of the crisis. Yet when Secretary Geithner and Housing Secretary Shaun Donovan addressed the mortgage rescue plan early in the administration, it was clear that neither could explain the process. The treasury secretary constantly passed reporters' questions to Donovan, who went over their heads with expert bureaucratese, leading to still further media confusion, less confidence, and nervous markets. It may have been scientifically sound, but reporters could not comprehend who was eligible for the plan and who was not. The details soon changed and kept changing, so they could not possibly explain it to average people.[8] In spite of everything, the real-estate market remained flat.[9]

The budget was the central planning document demonstrating how the administration would solve the economic crisis, but Office of Management and Budget (OMB) director Peter Orszag and Council of Economic Advisers chair Christina Romer had difficulty explaining its logic. Reporters expressed confusion when told that a proposed $634 billion increase in health spending, which was only a "down payment" on additional health expenditures, was actually a cost saving, since reporters were used to treating spending as costs rather than as savings. In response, Orszag referred to "evidence" from studies proving that increased spending now would "pay off over time" with more savings later.[10]

If billions in increased spending wasn't really spending, then the proposed cap-and-trade energy tax wasn't really a tax, the Obama team argued. A reporter asked whether the administration's proposal to tax carbon emissions by businesses would result in costs passed along to consumers, which would in effect be a tax increase—in violation of the president's pledge not to tax those earning under $250,000. Orszag acknowledged that the effort to "address global climate change" would "have some effects on households." But he added, "That's one reason why we are linking the cap-and-trade program to Making Work Pay, which is a tax credit for working families that would provide relief in their budgets over time."[11] So, according to Orszag, cap-and-trade would have "some effects on households," rather than be an increase to taxpayers. The "effects" would be on those using energy, which of course was everyone, down to the very poorest. As it worked out, the cap-and-trade climate bill passed the House, but Democrats in the Senate shelved it after even the left-leaning Greenpeace and Friends of the Earth opposed the bill for containing too many compromises.

Romer, for her part, admitted under questioning that the calculation of receipts and future deficits was based on an estimated 3.2 percent annual growth rate in the year 2010, one-fifth higher than America's long-term average growth—and on even higher growth estimates for 2011 through 2013. One reporter was moved to respond: "We've been hearing these denunciations of the Bush administration for being dishonest in the way they presented the numbers. . . . It appears, though, that you're taking a very rosy outlook for how the economy is going to come out. Isn't that another form of trying to gild the lily, so to speak?"[12]

Whatever the difficulties in explaining the policies, there was no question that the proposals were new, large in scope, and expensive—in a word, transformational. Except for cap-and-trade, the Obama administration and a supportive Congress and Federal Reserve more or less succeeded in translating this progressive agenda into public policy.

Muscle to Move the Economy

While the new administration instituted major new programs to solve the economic crisis, what could its team of experts actually do administratively to muscle the economy forward?

It would be extremely difficult to get tougher than the Bush administration's experts had already been. In October 2008, Treasury Secretary Henry Paulson, along with Fed chairman Ben Bernanke and New York Fed president Timothy Geithner, called together the nation's nine top bankers for a meeting at the Treasury Department. "The executives did not have an inkling" of what was to be discussed, according to a later news report. By his own admission, Paulson "presented his case in blunt terms." He gave the bankers a one-page document that said they "agreed" to sell ownership shares in their firms to the government. He told them they "must sign it before they left."

It was remarkable that such government strong-arming was occurring in twenty-first-century America. It seemed something more akin to what a Third Reich economics minister might have done in 1933. Although Paulson acknowledged that taking this action with the banks was "objectionable," he gave the country's most powerful bankers little room to object. Three of the bankers resisted during the meeting: two, including Bank of America CEO Kenneth Lewis, quietly resisted, while another, Wells Fargo chairman Richard Kovacevich, outright opposed the plan. But, as one observer said, "It was a take it or take it offer." All nine signed before they left.[13]

Nor was that the end of the strong-arm tactics. The most shocking example involved Secretary Paulson's demand that Bank of America buy ailing investment firm Merrill Lynch. As the *Wall Street Journal* revealed months later, Bank of America's Lewis told Paulson he was reconsidering his agreement because Merrill Lynch's losses could pose a grave threat to his own stockholders. Testifying under oath before the New York attorney general, Lewis said that he went forward with the deal only when Paulson and Bernanke told him it was necessary to save the economy—and that he and his board would be replaced if he did not comply.[14] Although Lewis testified that he was not directly ordered to keep the negative information from his stockholders (and other investors), he insisted that this was the clear intent of his regulators' instructions. Paulson, he said, had told him, "We do not want a public disclosure." Paulson and Bernanke took their own advice: they did not inform their own Financial Stability Oversight Board, set up by the Troubled Asset Relief Program (TARP), about the problems with Bank of America and Merrill until the purchase was already a fait accompli.[15]

A Credit Suisse employee later claimed he received a phone call from a Federal Reserve official congratulating the firm for having avoided investments in the subprime mortgage market that had led to the U.S. financial meltdown. Then the U.S. official reportedly asked the Swiss firm to purchase American bank "toxic assets" through the TARP program. When the employee asked why his firm should participate when it had avoided these as too risky in the past, he was told, "Because someday you'll need us." It was not very subtle, but extortion rarely is.[16]

The Obama administration's first attempt to control the banks was more straightforward. The opportunity arose when the administration conducted and reported on the so-called stress tests of the financial health of the banks that had received federal support under the Bush administration. The Treasury Department had earlier said that it did not want the banks to repay the bailout shares, which would end Treasury oversight and supposedly imperil the economy. Not surprisingly, then, the department now ordered even healthy banks to build larger reserves of common stock, making it more difficult for them to repay the government and escape its control. Most of the nineteen studied banks had met the 6 percent legal requirement for reserves, but Treasury now required that they raise more in common equity (rather than preferred stock, which the government had earlier demanded for the bailouts, artificially inflating their relative importance) or borrow from the government in new convertible (to common) preferred stocks. The truly weak banks like Citigroup clearly required additional reserves, but even Bank of America ($3.4 billion in reserves) and Wells Fargo ($1.5 billion) were required to buy common equity.[17]

Wells Fargo "got an especially rough deal," as analyst Richard Bove put it. The previous year the company had raised more than $11 billion to buy struggling Wachovia and take it off the government's hands. "They did the government a massive favor," Bove said. "And the government returned it by saying: 'Screw you. Go out and raise more capital.'"[18] Wells Fargo was well financed, but then the government made it meet a fully unexpected requirement. That surprise requirement could be understood as bureaucratic "payback" to Wells Fargo's Kovacevich (who happened to be a free-market advocate) for his initial opposition to the bailout and his desire to repay the government funds and escape its red tape.

In spite of this new muscle, the economic crisis was now being called the "Great Recession." Clearly, Obama's new economic team needed to do something more if it was to revive the economy.

Market Management

While the previous administration's TARP program to shore up banks remained the leading edge of the plan to prod the economy back to life, the Obama team also adopted a Term Asset-Backed Securities Loan Facility

(TALF) program, extending assistance to small businesses and households by supporting the issuers of asset-backed securities. This effort, too, proved inadequate to "unglue" the markets, so Treasury Secretary Geithner introduced a plan in March 2009 to contribute between $75 billion and $100 billion in capital in a new entity, backed by the FDIC, to encourage purchasing and holding additional loans. Also, because some of the most toxic assets were created in 2005 and 2006, Treasury would empower TALF to buy up older, "legacy" assets as well as newly issued securities. Finally, the plan would create a Public-Private Investment Program (PPIP) to purchase mortgage-backed and other securities using a combination of private money and capital from the government; private investors and the government would share in any profit or loss.[19]

Even with all these new alphabet programs, Treasury met substantial resistance. First, the private sector demanded tough contracts to protect it from the new risks raised by joining these programs. Second, Congress added restrictions on those who agreed to invest in them, such as new limits on hiring immigrants that many opposed. Most important, private firms feared that the government would later change the rules, as it had when it put caps on executive compensation that was contractually required to be paid. "The government is viewed as being unpredictable," explained a partner in a law firm that represented potential TALF participants. Consequently, the program failed to attract enough private capital, forcing Treasury to get even tougher with additional programs.[20]

While still trying to control the toxic asset problem, Treasury was given the additional job of overseeing the U.S. auto industry through a task force managed by longtime political operator Steven Rattner. His solution for General Motors was to give the government 50 percent stock control, the United Auto Workers (UAW) 40 percent, and those already privately invested in the firm (mutual funds, pensions, hedge funds, and normal investors) a mere 10 percent. According to the *Wall Street Journal*, this would give the government an 87-cent return on its dollar investment, the union trust 76 cents, and the "powerful" big money investors merely 5 cents.[21]

The unions did even better at Chrysler: a 55 percent share went to the UAW, 35 percent to Fiat (which was not an investor at all), 10 percent to the government, and nothing at all to the secured creditors (and the pensions and retirees that invested in them), who were legally the priority creditors. The creditors at Chrysler first refused to accept the deal, forcing the auto firm into bankruptcy. But they resisted only as long as no one knew who they were. When the bankruptcy judge forced investors to identify themselves, the number of complainants dropped from twenty to five, and the initial claim of $6.9 billion was reduced to only $300 million. Through political pressure, Treasury officials had successfully reduced the private claims by more than 90 percent. The very next day, the last five capitulated too. "In the end, they just concluded that the political cost to their institutions was too high to bear," explained their lawyer.[22]

What "political costs" were the bankers and investors afraid to bear? The president of the United States himself had decided to up the pressure. At a news conference after Chrysler was placed in bankruptcy against Treasury's wishes, President Obama lashed out—the *Washington Post* headlined, "President Slams Holdouts"—"I don't stand with those who held out when everyone else is making sacrifices." He castigated the secured stockholders as "a small group of speculators."[23] Obama also warned that if the creditors held out, Chrysler could even be forced to liquidate. Who could stand to be rebuked by the most eloquent and praised president in recent times? Even the Republicans in Congress dared not speak for fear of being seen as favoring "speculators." A *Journal* investigative team concluded that the creditors' about-face "was a vivid example of the government's tightening grip on a humbled financial industry." The *Journal* reporters added: "Pulling a trick from the hedge-fund playbook, the government used its leverage as the sole willing lender to Chrysler, either in bankruptcy court or out, to extract deep concessions from some of the country's biggest banks . . . upend[ing] a long-standing tradition concerning rights in a bankruptcy: Senior secured lenders usually get paid in full before lower-priority creditors get anything. Not this time."[24]

Using internal sources within Treasury, other *Journal* investigators discovered that White House chief of staff Rahm Emanuel had earlier decided, "at the president's urging," to become directly involved in Treasury operations after initial Geithner missteps. Secretary Geithner himself implicitly confirmed this by telling reporters, "I had to make a judgment . . . that to do this right we had to have a fully integrated approach" with the White House. Emanuel, of course, was one of the savviest political operators in Washington, most famous for his advice on using a calamity for maximal political gain: "You never want a serious crisis to go to waste."[25]

Emanuel was simply following the lead of previous administrations, which had pushed businesses into poor risks and then blamed them for incompetent investing. Indeed, as the *Wall Street Journal*'s George Melloan pointed out, it was "the federal government's 'affordable housing' endeavors beginning in the 1990s that had allowed and even forced banks to make highly risky mortgage loans" in the first place. Those mortgage loans were later "folded into mortgage-backed securities (MBS)" that were sold worldwide but especially to government corporations Fannie Mae and Freddy Mac. They were backed by a credit bubble the Fed had created to increase mortgage values. When the prices fell, "the MBS market seized up and financial institutions holding them became illiquid and began to crash."[26]

To attain the elusive control of the marketplace that progressive philosophy required, the government was forced to keep pushing harder to force additional private investment and accommodations. Ultimately, the Treasury special inspector general for bailouts warned that he was pursuing twenty pending criminal investigations into potential "fraud" against private bankers (mainly for paying bonuses).[27] In such a threatening environment, it seemed imprudent for private firms—and retirement and charitable funds are the largest investors—to invest capital in any venture that could be second-guessed as risky. If even preferred investors could not receive protection, or if top executives were threatened with punishment, the safest course was not to confront the regulators but to invest in safe if low-yielding government bonds, frustrating the whole plan to "unstick" private investing.

No matter which progressive remedy the Obama economic experts tried, no matter how hallowed the theory, no matter how credentialed the experts, no matter how much force and intimidation they used, they could not reduce unemployment very much, real median household income continued declining, and the economy remained flat.[28]

Health-Care Transformation

No progressive dream had been grander over a longer period of time than the desire to give government the power to guarantee every American equal access to quality health care. The high point of President Obama's promise to transform the United States occurred when, in March 2010, the House of Representatives, with three votes to spare, adopted a wholesale reform of the U.S. health-insurance system, granting national government experts effective control of one-sixth of the economy. Signing the bill three days later, President Obama reveled in the victory. He took pride in "a century of trying" by progressive forces and "a year of debate" that culminated in this crowning accomplishment of his presidency and of the whole New Deal revolution.[29]

By a stroke of the president's pen, all Americans would be required to have government-approved health insurance or pay fines. The greatest claimed benefit was to provide "universal coverage" for all. Actually, under the bill only 80-plus percent of the population would be covered. Of those previously uninsured, half would be added as welfare recipients under the joint federal/ state Medicaid program for the poor, not under Obamacare itself, and the other half would be required to buy insurance through one of the new cooperative exchanges that were supposed to be created by the states. People earning 133 to 400 percent of the poverty level would be eligible for premium subsidies, which would be paid on a sliding percentage of income. Even the most subsidized in exchanges, however, would pay more than they had before, since they paid nothing when uninsured. But individuals who earned more than $43,320 would pay much more—indeed, the full premium.[30]

To pay for the benefits, taxes would increase for higher-income earners. Beginning in 2013, individuals earning more than $200,000 would pay higher Medicare payroll taxes, as well as an additional 3.8 percent tax on all investment income. Tax deductions would be decreased for middle-income earners. Deductible medical expenses would shrink for people who itemized on their tax returns. Present nontaxable health spending account deductions would become taxable over $2,500.

Almost everyone already covered by insurance would pay higher premiums to fund four new requirements. The young would pay higher rates to support their sicker older compatriots. The middle-aged would be required to add expensive "preventive care" coverage (without deductibles or copayments), which would increase premiums. The elderly would have preventive medicine coverage added as a Medicare benefit, and premiums for those earning more than $85,000 per year would be increased to pay for it. Finally, Medicare Advantage enrollees would pay higher fees or have their coverage cut, or both, to help support the new benefits.

OMB director Orszag announced from the beginning that the health reforms would be justified by their ability to control increasing health costs through adopting "best practices." When asked about the $23 trillion in debt (double the total national income of the United States at the time) the administration's programs were projected to accumulate over the next ten years, the budget director replied: "More important than what happens over the next five to ten years [with the total budget] . . . [is] the rate at which health care costs grow" over the long run.

At his initial budget briefing, Orszag had said that adopting "effectiveness research" based on academic studies would produce "efficiencies" that would reduce not only long-term health costs but also the total long-term government debt.

One approach he touted was "boosting primary care physicians," who would reduce long-term costs by preventing more serious illnesses later, even if this step greatly increased the costs of preventive care now. He conceded that a just-issued Dartmouth study did not find that primary care reduced costs, but he countered that "a lot of that variation [in that study] that you see across the United States is correlated with the number of specialist visits that you have and the ratio of specialists to primary care physicians without any corresponding improvement in quality."[31] He did not provide evidence to support his claim.

Orszag then changed the subject to say that reforming the physician payment system would improve medical quality. He added that the "evidence" also showed that community health centers were effective, so spending more resources there would save money and improve quality in the long run too. Reforming health care was becoming very difficult to explain. What was the goal? Was it universal coverage, or preventive care, or primary care physicians or the payment system or community health centers or effectiveness research or saving money?

Some major goals of Obama administration health reform conflicted. Community rating—that is, not allowing insurance companies to charge higher premiums based on preexisting poor health status or high risk factors—had been one of the top progressive goals for the past half century. Another goal was to promote so-called wellness, both to satisfy the progressive altruistic instinct that led it to promote health reform in the first place and to supposedly save money on future treatment. Therefore, the bill allowed higher premiums for people who smoked, who did not manage their obesity, who did not regulate their glucose intake, who did not exercise, and so forth. Unfortunately, propensity in these matters is mostly preexisting, so insurance companies would be able to get around community rating restrictions with higher nonwellness premium increases for those in these categories.[32]

The very top goal of progressive health reform had been to assure that everyone was covered by insurance. Because the young, as a group, deal with many fewer ailments than do the elderly, they often take the (minor) risk of being uninsured to avoid paying premiums. Requiring all to purchase insurance or pay a penalty meant that healthy young people, who tend not to need health insurance, would have to subsidize the elderly, who tend to get sick—costing thousands of dollars per year for mostly low-earning young entry workers. Presumably to offset this, retirees were asked to bear somewhat more of the burden. The result of this conflict was that both groups tended to oppose the plan. A poll by the Galen Institute at the time showed 71 percent of Americans opposed mandating insurance coverage with a penalty for not purchasing it, and 68 percent opposed even minor restrictions on seniors.[33]

Obamacare also inadvertently created incentives to game the system. For example, employers could calculate that it was more practical to pay the $3,000 per-employee penalty for not insuring their employees than as much as $12,000 for insurance. Many individuals, especially young ones, could find it cheaper to pay the yearly $750 penalty than thousands on insurance premiums.[34] They could always acquire insurance once they became ill, because the law required insurers to accept those with preexisting conditions. Consequently, Obamacare income would be lower than estimated. Additionally, although the Congressional Budget Office (CBO) claimed that the bill would save $143 billion over a decade, Congress later increased payments to physicians by $200 billion, offsetting the promised savings. More important, the final law required CBO to make its estimates on the basis of ten years of income and only six years of spending, dramatically underestimating program costs.[35]

Even after passage of the bill, many issues remained unsolved. A Medical Advisory Council would decide later which medical services were "essential benefits" to be covered and which were not. An additional Independent Payment Advisory Board was supposed to decide which kind of treatment was "best" and therefore eligible for reimbursement, sounding awfully close to the word President Obama had banned from the debate, *rationing*. Another board, the U.S. Preventive Services Task Force, would decide which benefits insurance companies would have to offer "free," without deductibles and coinsurance.[36] Moreover, the final bill was compromised to state that findings from "comparative effectiveness research may not be construed as mandates, guidelines or recommendations for payment, coverage or treatment." How, then, could Orszag's promised savings from "effective" treatments be realized? Would the government's experts be allowed to exercise their "expertise" or not?

The first to act was the Preventive Services Task Force. Indeed, during the height of the debate it announced a mammogram study that almost defeated the whole undertaking. The panel recommended that such tests were unnecessary for women below the age of forty. After a near riot of opposition, the Department of Health and Human Services quickly reversed the official findings. It was not a good omen for making effective cost-saving decisions (though perhaps it was good for women's health) that the Obama administration could not resist political pressure against the presumed best available evidence from the expert health-care bureaucracy.[37]

As a result of these difficulties during the debate over Obamacare, three-fourths of Americans worried that a new plan would increase bureaucracy in the health-care system; 79 percent were concerned that access to physicians would be restricted; 83 percent thought the quality of care would be lowered; 82 percent worried that coverage would decline; 84 percent were concerned that the government deficit would grow; and 84 percent worried that their health-care costs would rise.[38]

A transformational program had been adopted but at a very high cost in popular support.

Progressive Discontent

For all the questions that arose after Obamacare became law, the real challenge for progressives had come during the long, fierce debate over the health-care bill. Getting Congress to pass the program required President Obama and the Democratic congressional leadership to compromise many core progressive principles.

In light of the popular opposition, congressional Democrats were reluctant to support a truly principled plan, remembering not only how Hillarycare had led to the Republican takeover of the House of Representatives for the first time in forty years in 1994 but also how, in 1989, elderly activists upset over a new Medicare tax had actually chased the Democratic chairman of the House Ways and Means Committee through the streets (leading to the repeal of the "reforms" adopted the previous year).[39]

Clearly, something more had to be done if health transformation was to become a reality.

According to a perhaps apocryphal story, House Speaker Nancy Pelosi called several of her Democratic members into her office and told them they had to vote for the bill. When one replied that he would lose his seat if he did, she supposedly said that those who were in her office were all there because they had already lost, so they had nothing further to lose and might as well gain some goodwill from the leadership and the president.[40] In any event, the bill did pass the House. The problem would come from the Senate, where sixty votes were needed for passage.

The reformers' top goal was a "government option" health plan competing with private plans, "to keep them honest." This proposal was already a compromise from the progressive ideal of administering a single government health plan for the entire nation. But even the public option met resistance from Democrats, including Senators Mary Landrieu and Ron Wyden; the moderate Wyden introduced a plan without the option. Kent Conrad, Democratic chairman of the Senate Budget Committee, proposed a national co-op institution with state affiliates and looser government controls. But another, more progressive Democrat, Senator Charles Schumer, immediately opposed the alternatives as not regulatory enough.

The Democrats were in a fix. The more power the government had, the more worried the Democratic middle became—but the less control given to the feds, the more concern rose on the Democratic left. Finally, Joseph Lieberman, an independent who caucused with Democrats, came to the conclusion that the public option was "a cost we can't take on," leading to its eventual removal from the bill.[41]

That blow to principle was significant enough, but when the health price tag was estimated at $1.6 trillion, Senate Finance Committee chairman Max Baucus, a Montana Democrat, rejected it outright as impossibly extravagant, demanding something less than $1 trillion. The only alternative was more revenue to offset costs, which came into conflict with President Obama's pledge that no one earning under $250,000 would face increased taxes. The Democratic House leadership responded by proposing a tax for those above $280,000, bringing the top rate to 45 percent, the highest since the 1986 reforms. But even that would pay less than half the cost, so other Democrats suggested either a value-added national sales tax or taxes on alcohol, sweets, and other "unhealthy foods," both costs disproportionately falling on the poor. Eventually, against progressive opposition, the Democrats settled on proposing a large number of smaller tax increases and fees, and the projected total expenditures were set below $1 trillion.

Sufficient money could have been raised by eliminating the existing tax credit on employer-provided health insurance to pay for benefits. But Candidate Obama had opposed the plan, because unions argued that this would adversely affect their members, who had more generous health benefits than the rest of the population. The top seventy unions threatened the whole project if Democrats repealed the credit, calling such a proposal "dead on arrival." Senator Baucus then proposed excluding union health plans from his proposal, upsetting Democrats from nonunion southern states without appeasing the unions. Eventually, union "Cadillac" health plans were excluded from the regulations, at least temporarily.

President Obama personally assured the president of the U.S. Conference of Catholic Bishops, Timothy Dolan, and its Democratic-leaning secretariat that Catholic institutions would be exempted from any provisions against their principles. But later, in 2012, new regulations earned the enmity of Catholics and others for requiring religious hospitals, schools, and charities to cover certain abortion-inducing drugs, sterilization procedures, and contraceptive devices by 2013. In response to the new regulations, Dolan commented: "In effect the president is saying we have a year to figure out how to violate our consciences." An administration attempt at compromise only fanned additional resistance.[42]

Even with extensive opposition in their own party, President Obama and the congressional leadership were able to pass the historic bill with exactly the sixty votes required in the Senate. In celebrating passage of the law, the president claimed that he had "pushed back on the undue influence of special interests. . . . We proved that this government—a government of the people and by the people—still works for the people."[43] Then the congratulations rolled in. The group whose $26.1 million lobbying effort was the most expensive by any industry lobby in history, the Pharmaceutical Researchers and Manufacturers of America, hailed the health package as "important and historic." The second biggest lobby, the American Medical Association, sent cheers too, as did the American Hospital Association, AARP, General Electric, and for-profit insurers led by giant Aetna, whose stock hit a yearly high the following day.[44]

The truth was that the Obama administration had learned from President Bill Clinton's inability to pass comprehensive health reform. Rather than fighting the health industry, the administration had invited its leaders into the discussions. Health-care reform would pass, Obama officials said; the only issue was whether the health industry would have any input in the legislation. It worked—but even with large Democratic majorities in both houses of Congress, it had resulted in a complex, compromised program that would force private health insurers to increase premiums. Not all progressives gave the insurance industry a free ride. According to the *Washington Post*'s E. J. Dionne Jr., when, after the bill passed, a reporter asked a celebrating Nancy Pelosi whether health insurers would raise premiums and blame it on the bill, she warned that "insurance companies should be aware they're not 'automatically included' in the health exchanges the legislation creates." Making the threat more explicit, she added, "Unless they do the right thing, they're not going in."[45]

Soon after the bill passed Congress, progressives received the first sign that insurance premiums would increase dramatically under Obamacare for all who already had employer-covered health insurance, including many with limited incomes. Securities and Exchange Commission regulations required private companies to report greater estimated future costs for their employee and retiree health premiums. Within the first few days, AT&T reported that it would incur $1 billion in extra insurance costs; Deere reported $150 million; Caterpillar, $100 million; AK Steel, $31 million; 3M, $90 million; and Valero Energy, up to $20 million. Consultants Towers-Watson estimated that total write-downs of company value would reach $14 billion, in the middle of a recession.[46] Concerned about the political and economic effects, House Commerce Committee chairman Henry Waxman informed company executives that their "assertions are a matter of concern" because he had predicted lower health premiums. So he threatened hearings to grill those who kept saying premiums would be higher.[47]

Little wonder that self-described "lifelong progressive" Miles Mogulescu, author, attorney, and coproducer of the documentary film *Union Maids*, expressed deep concern that business interests had crafted and supported the Obama program to advance their own private agendas. He wrote, "Voters viscerally sense that the White House and Congressional Democrats may be as concerned with protecting special interests—whether it's drug companies, private hospitals, or Wall Street banks—than they are with protecting the people."[48]

Many progressives were upset to learn that the cost of passage was unequal treatment for the states. Senator Ben Nelson had kept Nebraska from having to pay for the bill's Medicare expansion; Senator Carl Levin had nonprofits in his state of Michigan excluded from the excise tax to be paid in other states; Senator Patrick Leahy had provided extra funding for Vermont; Senator Mary Landrieu had received an extra $300 million for Louisiana; and three states' senators won exceptions to Medicare Advantage cuts that would be imposed on all other states.[49]

The general public likewise did not think highly of the bill. A *Washington Post* poll following the vote found that 48 percent of Americans supported the plan but a 50 percent majority opposed it. Asked about the type of health care they would expect to receive in the long run from the reforms, 18 percent said quality would be better, 35 percent said it would be the same, and 44 percent said it would be worse. A plurality of 49 percent said there was too much government involvement in the program, 35 percent said it had the right amount of government, and 14 percent said there was not enough. Contrary to presidential assurances that the deficit would be reduced and that no one who was satisfied with his or her current plan would be required to change, 65 percent said the deficit would actually increase and 60 percent said everyone would be required to make changes like it or not; the elderly were the most opposed.[50] And the polls only got worse as time went on.

President Obama's energy, resourcefulness, persistence, and commitment of political power in passing the most comprehensive social reform policy since Lyndon Johnson's Great Society were indeed historic. But the comparison could have also served as a warning. The Democratic Party lost five of the following six presidential elections after Johnson's similar accomplishment.

A New New Deal?

President Obama entered office with high expectations but also facing the worst economic downturn since the Great Depression. His New Era of Responsibility program made it clear that he was dedicated to the progressive philosophy that had addressed the earlier economic crisis. Obama persisted in advancing New Deal principles by giving the experts the needed power, especially by greatly expanding credit and stimulus spending. Federal Reserve liquidity hit an all-time high, an incredible 32 percent higher than the previous record, reaching $2.75 trillion. By 2012, Bernanke had kept the borrowing rate at between 0.25 percent and zero for most of the term, and he promised to keep it there almost indefinitely. Plus the Fed had engaged in three rounds of "quantitative easing" in the hope of forcing rates below zero (adjusted for inflation) over the long term. Spending, too, exceeded post–World War II highs, with the total stimulus between 2009 and 2012 reaching $5.1 trillion.[51]

Unfortunately for Council of Economic Advisers chair Christina Romer, just after the stimulus passed Congress, unemployment soared above the 8 percent she said the stimulus was devised to prevent. Soon it reached 10 percent and held just below that level for more than a year; well over three years after the stimulus bill passed, unemployment still had not fallen much below the 8 percent that the Obama administration said was the worst-case scenario. Although sympathetic economists Alan Blinder and Mark Zandi claimed that unemployment would have reached 15 percent without the stimulus,[52] Lawrence Lindsey pointed out, "The striking observation is that after correcting for the higher starting [unemployment] rate, the actual performance of the economy is almost exactly what Romer and Bernstein said would happen if we had done nothing, rather than passing the $800 billion package." In fact, the stimulus had not stimulated and had not prevented higher unemployment.[53] What would Roosevelt do?

President Obama's autobiographical *Dreams from My Father* already showed his basic progressivism topped by his faith in expertise. But Obama had been around long enough—a community organizer cannot miss this—not to trust the progressive experts too far. So he created duplicate roles for White House and cabinet officers, for one to check and catch what the other missed, similar to what Franklin Roosevelt had done.[54]

Yet two sets of experts could just confuse matters more and cause delays, especially on top of a bureaucracy already filled with agencies fighting for turf. Even the best agencies with the most defined missions can battle and block one another—as Defense, State, and the CIA did during the Iraq War, muddling the Bush administration's Iraq policy.[55] Tellingly, the Obama transition used the White House national security adviser as its model for creating the double-check system for domestic policy "czars." What it missed was that National Security Adviser Condoleezza Rice had merely added another element of interests into the Iraq policy mix to further confound the process.

In such a competing bureaucratic system, the resentments in the losing agencies (or in the White House) can become profound. Only the agencies know the real details of the policies and may not volunteer information they think will diminish their power. The agency bureaucrats know how to represent their interests and which congressmen and journalists can be used for political payback.[56] How, then, can the president know whose expert opinion to accept? The double teaming simply placed the president in the middle between conflicting, self-interested, and/or filtered expert advice. Progressivism at bottom offers no guide other than relying on the scientific experts and their power to command. But what happens when the professionals disagree?

Presumably, the wise leader then chooses based on a pragmatic evaluation. But pragmatism requires a context, without which it is simply a muddle. There must be some set of principles from which pragmatism adjusts. President Obama's progressive ideology gave him some presumptions, but its first principle was turning to government expert planners, which represents the essential philosophical paradox of his progressivism: experts often disagree.

By the beginning of Obama's second year as president, things started looking ominous. In January 2010, a Republican shocked the nation by winning the Massachusetts Senate seat previously held by progressive icon Teddy Kennedy after criticizing the economy and the president's plans to fix it. It looked like Republicans were ready to win the House later in the year. President Obama felt it necessary to retrench a bit, blaming the public's mood and the country's problems on "Washington," its "partisanship," its "pettiness," its "same tired battles" and "gimmicks." The president conceded that government could not do everything, saying that Washington seemed "unable or unwilling to solve any of our problems."[57]

Even President Obama seemed discouraged. He would have to find another way.

Three

WHY CAN'T WE ALL AGREE?

N A MAY 16, 2009, radio address to the nation, after months of highly fractious and partisan battles to enact his transformational agenda—for a new stimulus program, for comprehensive cap-and-trade environmental restrictions, for redesigning education policy and its financing, and for a restructuring of the health-care system that would give the government a dominant role over one-sixth of the economy—President Barack Obama asked the majority of the population still disagreeing with him to "come together around common goals."[1] Later, in an attempt to reunite a fiercely divided nation, the president said that he and the Republicans in Congress who had unanimously opposed his proposals agreed on "80 percent" of what was needed for health-care reform.[2]

The "common goals" Obama said must be accepted were his proposals. He did not introduce compromises that met any of the opposition's major concerns. He wanted to win back public support but not at the expense of his programs, especially health-care reform. Yet he truly seemed to want everyone to agree with him, especially as he moved on from general ideals to the more complicated problem of actual legislative programs.

Time and again, Obama expressed the desire to find agreement where others saw obvious, even insurmountable differences.[3] The most extreme example took place early in his administration in a discussion with the Catholic cardinal of Chicago, Francis George, over the contentious issue of abortion. The differences between the two men's positions could not have been starker. Candidate Obama had promised that "the first thing" he would do as president would be to sign the Freedom of Choice Act, which, in the words of the Congressional Research Service, would set as "the policy of the United States that every woman has the fundamental right to choose to bear a child; terminate a pregnancy prior to fetal viability; or terminate a pregnancy after viability when necessary to protect her life or her health."[4] By contrast, Cardinal George had signed a statement declaring that the Freedom of Choice Act "would have lethal consequences for prenatal human life" and "would be an evil law that would further divide our country."[5] So President Obama thought the law was a first priority and Cardinal George thought it was evil. Somehow, though, the president insisted that the two agreed on the issue. After their White House meeting, Cardinal George said, "It's hard to disagree with him because he'll always tell you he agrees with you. Maybe that's political. I think he sincerely wants to agree with you. You have to say, again and again, 'No, Mr. President, we don't agree [on abortion].'"[6]

There seems to be a remarkable human need to think everyone deep down agrees with us. The horrendous case of Army major Nidal Malik Hasan illustrates the point. On November 5, 2009, Hasan was reported to have opened fire at Fort Hood in Texas. Thirteen were killed and forty were wounded.

Many people rushed to insist that these were fellow servicemen and that differences in religion and values were not likely to have had anything to do with the matter. The president told the nation, "We don't know all the answers yet and I would caution against jumping to conclusions until we have all of the facts."[7] The Army chief of staff, General George Casey, directly warned his subordinates not to infer anything from reports that Major Hasan had yelled the Islamic jihadist war cry "Allahu Akbar" (Allah is great) before opening fire.[8] *Time* magazine's Joe Klein denounced "odious attempts by Jewish extremists . . . to argue that the massacre perpetrated by Nidal Hasan was somehow a direct consequence of his Islamic beliefs."[9]

But it was the Army psychiatrists who really took the prize for consensual correctness. National Public Radio's Daniel Zwerdling investigated Hasan's six-year tenure at Walter Reed Army Medical Center in Washington, where the Army officer completed his residency in psychiatry, as well as his fellowship at the Uniformed Services University of the Health Sciences. Zwerdling found that beginning in 2003, "a committee of officials from both places met regularly to discuss pressing topics surrounding the psychiatrists and other mental health professionals who train and work at the institutions." During one meeting in the spring of 2008, he reported, "one of the leading—and most perplexing—items on their agenda was: What should we do about Hasan?" Hasan had been a "trouble spot on officials' radar." Not only had his supervisors "repeatedly given him poor evaluations," but also "both fellow students and faculty were deeply troubled by Hasan's behavior—which they variously called disconnected, aloof, paranoid, belligerent, and schizoid." According to officials, Hasan "antagonized some students and faculty by espousing what they perceived to be extremist Islamic views" and told at least one patient, "Islam can save your soul." By the spring of 2009, some officials wondered whether Hasan "was mentally unstable and unfit to be an Army psychiatrist." Zwerdling reported that one official actually "wondered aloud to colleagues whether Hasan might be capable of committing fratricide, like the Muslim U.S. Army sergeant who, in 2003, killed two fellow soldiers and injured 14 others by setting off grenades at a base in Kuwait."[10]

So why did Army officials not do something? They did. After six years of "trouble" and "repeatedly" bad evaluations, they promoted Nasan from captain to major in May 2009! Why? As Zwerdling explained, the psychiatric staff did not want to appear judgmental and "repeatedly bent over backward to support and encourage him." The psychiatric officials "worried they might be 'discriminating' against Hasan because of his seemingly extremist Islamic beliefs."[11] The more Hasan deviated, the more the psychiatric staff felt it had to prove compassion and pass him.[12] A member of the medical staff told the *Washington Post* that Hasan's teachings on Islam were suspicious but "you don't want to close him down just because it's different."[13]

As good bureaucrats, the psychiatric officials knew that, as Zwerdling put it, "Walter Reed and most medical institutions have a cumbersome and lengthy process for expelling doctors, involving hearings and potential legal battles. As a result, sources say, key decision makers decided it would be too difficult, if not infeasible, to put Hasan on probation and possibly expel him from the program." So what did these bureaucratic officials do? They transferred him to Fort Hood. Why? Zwerdling explained that it was because they knew Fort Hood had the largest contingent of psychiatrists in the Army and that the good ones could pick up the slack for the poor performer Hasan. Some thought, too, that with so many other psychiatrists, maybe someone would decide to help him.[14]

As in government bureaus everywhere, no one would put anything on the record because they did not want to punish "a member of the team." No one would question the dogma that we really are all the same and deep down agree on important matters.

So Hasan was sent to perform soldier readiness evaluations at Fort Hood. Refusing to see obvious differences had deadly consequences.

Historically We Did Agree

President Obama and the expert psychiatrists were by no means the first to claim agreement when many would argue there was none. The need for agreement across presumed differences goes deep into the major world cultural traditions. Christianity incorporates Jewish history and revelation, against the beliefs of Jews. The Qur'an describes Abraham, Isaac, Jacob, Joseph, Elijah, and the other Hebrew icons, as well as Christianity's Jesus, as early Muslim prophets. Marco Polo reported that the great Mongol emperor Kublai Khan considered these prophets plus Buddha, Confucius, and Muhammad as all in agreement, all contributing to his empire's cultural values in one vast religion of mankind headed by himself.[15]

This need for agreement requires an extended explanation if one is to understand why America is in crisis today. Throughout most of humanity's long history, it has been thought essential that human groups agree on most everything. As long as there have been recognizable humans, back to the caves of Chauvet and Lascaux, perhaps thirty thousand years ago, simple survival in a primitive subsistence society often depended on agreement on what needed to be done. Debating the merits of a hunt while the prey was on the move was not practical for early humankind. It was not until surplus arrived that nonconformity became affordable and questioning tribal assumptions became feasible, although even then challengers often demanded that all agree with their own contrary beliefs. Agreement on fundamentals was the basis for all early societies.[16]

The Native American writer Eagle Man called his people those who "were always here." The early tribe, the clan, the native people tended to lead an isolated way of life basically unaware of or wholly hostile to and separated from other peoples. Each group considered itself the only real people in the world. Life was lived within the local tradition, "within the great, complete beauty" of Mother Earth and the Great Spirit that lived in conjunction with them. "Mother Earth is our real mother, because every bit of us truly comes from her and daily she takes care of us," including at the end of life in a "much higher plane beyond." There is individuality but only "provided that individual freedom does not threaten the tribe or the people or Mother Earth." Nature is in an "eternal circle," where everything is "truly holy: we are all related"—land, mountains, rivers, weather, animals, and plant life. All exist in harmony with nature, with all commanded to take only what "you need to exist."[17]

In the primitive spirit culture, infants are born into a family and community and simply accept what they are taught: the rules, tribal customs, sexual practices, religion, and so forth—in a word, traditions. Tradition shapes reality for the child even in the modern world. But as he gradually comes into contact with the outside world, family traditions can be questioned. With communities, too, outsiders can question previously unchallenged ways of living—family relationships, dress, sexual customs, traditional foods, how to pray and work, and even the accuracy of holy stories and founding myths. With little migration, commerce, and communication in the beginning, traditions developed almost complete unanimity of support. But once trade or migration or conquest or all three arrived, things changed.[18] Traders arrived from foreign regions to sell seemingly value-neutral and nonthreatening material goods, but the camels, horses, ships, and armies brought new ideas with them, including the values of work, property, and culture that made the production and marketing of the new goods possible in the exporting nation.[19]

Even before outside influences, individuals differed and restrictions were required to enforce common beliefs. Tribal leaders enforced conformity with social pressure, punishments, and tribal rites up to and including genital mutilation and human sacrifice.[20] With the rise of agriculture, the new centralized leadership in kingship and temple religion regimes developed more sophisticated means of agreement and control.[21] As societies developed surplus, they often expanded through conquest; confronting peoples with different traditions required severe practices to control them. Torture became a defining characteristic among North American Iroquois, intermittent blood sacrifice a practice among Mideast Moabites, and regular rituals of human sacrifice among Aztecs and Mayans.[22] Rome was extremely brutal in extending its borders through war and in enforcing its mores and rules through punishing beatings and crucifixion.[23] Even empires that relied more on moral suasion were not loath to use power and coercion to reinforce teachings or to force agreement to preserve the social order.

Political theorist Frank Meyer—following twentieth-century philosopher Eric Voegelin—labeled all such early civilizations as cosmologically unified societies:

> For the first twenty-five hundred years of recorded history men lived in civilizations of similar styles, a style for which the Egyptian may stand as the type. These cosmological civilizations conceived of existence so tightly unified and compactly fashioned that there was no room for distinction and contrast between the individual person and the social order, between the cosmos and human order, between heaven and earth, between what is and what ought to be. God and king, the

rhythms of nature and the occupations of men, social custom and the moral imperative, were felt not as paired opposites but as integral unities. The life of men in these civilizations, in good times and bad, in happiness and unhappiness, proceeded in harmony and accord with nature, which knows no separation between what is and what ought to be, no tension between order and freedom, no striving of the person for individuation or the complement of that striving, the inner personal clash between the aspirations of the naked self and the moral responsibilities impressed by the very constitution of being.[24]

Although these civilizations often had gods or forces transcending the social order (Egypt even had an official monotheistic god for a short while), such gods were undemanding, remote, and unreliable and presented no challenge to the cosmological consensus.[25]

Following Lord Acton,[26] Meyer argued that only two partial exceptions—or temporary "stirrings"—in human history ran counter to this general tendency toward regimes of cosmological unity and agreement. Breaking the "cosmological veil" occurred when Classical Greece and Judaic Israel "burst asunder the unity of what ought to be and what is" by "separating the immanent from the transcendent, the immemorial mode of living from its previous identity with the very constitution of being." These two civilizations are often viewed as "polar opposites," but in both, "at their highest level, there emerged a clear distinction between the world and the transcendent." More, they both developed "the startlingly new concept of a direct relationship between men and the transcendent" that was "not fully mitigated by the state, the ruler, the culture or the tribe."[27]

It was the philosophers of the Hellenic world, Socrates, Plato, and Aristotle, who "raised to the level of the consciousness this new understanding of the nature of men and their relations to ultimate things," although the lingering cultic agreements constituting Athenian society held back the full import of this new distinction. "It was the contradiction between the inherent Hellenic awakening to the possibilities of the new state of being and the trammels of the inherited old with which the Greek philosophers wrestled. What they created out of their struggles was the first systematic intellectual projection of an independent relationship between free men and transcendent value."[28]

Specifically, Plato's Allegory of the Cave taught of a reality beyond the concrete here and now, a conceptual realm above or behind "reality" as we see it. Humanity—all of it—is lost in the darkness of ignorance so that we can see only a reflection of reality, as shadows projected from a fire to the wall of a cave. The real things are hidden so that we only see the shadows, which we think are real. What people think is real is what they learn through their traditions in various communities. But they see only the shadows of the tradition, not the reality behind it. The "ideal forms," the spiritual *essences*, are hidden behind the apparent reality. The cosmological tradition of the shadows may provide an agreed-upon explanation to people, but it is false. It does not reach reality; it reaches only to the conventions and traditions of a people, which are distorted reflections from the fundamental truth and transcendent reality that exist behind it.[29]

Jews likewise conceived of a reality that transcended normal everyday life. Father Abraham disagreed with the cosmological consensus of his Mesopotamian origins and struck out on his own, following the revelations of his single God to worship only Him and obey His precepts. The history of Israel can be understood as a progressive deepening of the understanding of what this monotheistic God wanted his people to do. This linear rather than cyclical conception of history—which Judaism basically invented—led to Moses, who rejected another cosmological civilization to introduce a new law of life written by this very Deity.[30] This new law created separation "between the cosmos and human order, between heaven and earth, between what is and what ought to be," and between "God and king, the rhythms of nature and the occupations of men, social custom and the moral imperative."

Athens and Jerusalem, however, only partially and temporarily succeeded in breaking their prevailing cosmological agreements. Meyer noted that "neither the philosophy of Hellas nor the prophecy of Israel ever completely threw off the conditioning influence of their social and intellectual heritage."[31] Although God's law in the person of the Prophet Nathan was authoritative enough to challenge the control of its greatest king, David, who repented for his complicity in the notorious killing of his subordinate Uriah, mostly the kings ignored the prophets and followed the ways of the world. In the signal communal choice between God and king, even the Chosen People chose king over God. As the Prophet Samuel reported the words of God, the Jewish people, in choosing a king over the community and turning its back on direct contact with God, rejected not the judges but God himself, who warned against institutionalizing the authority of the state and predicted its oppressions and ultimate failure. But the kings demanded agreement and did rule, at least until a more powerful force overwhelmed them.[32]

As for the philosophers of Athens, they never held even the limited power wielded by the prophets. They represented one or two small schools among several and reached only a small part of the populace and officialdom. Although Athens had some limits on the power of authorities, the voice of the people spoke for its traditional cosmological agreement and could not be successfully challenged. The power representatives of Athens's democratic state killed its greatest philosopher, Socrates, by enforcing the majority's agreed-upon view. Plato failed in his attempted coup to replace both the cosmological agreement and the democratic state. In the end, neither Athens nor Israel was able to escape, and both were conquered by an even more engulfing cosmological unity.

The End of Agreement

With the coming of the Roman Empire, the Western world found itself within an even more powerful cosmological force, one that dominated it for a millennium. In the rest of the world, in China, India, Persia, Mezzo-America, and the rest, it was pretty much the same. Although Rome and others allowed some local practices and mores to survive, they did so as a practical means to more effectively control people by husbanding resources. Disagreement over the empire or emperor and his decrees was not tolerated, and challenges were suppressed brutally. Rome was enormously successful at using power, and it seemed it would exercise control forever. Why did it not? Why do moderns not live under Rome or another cosmological civilization? After thirty thousand years of human history, what changed?

What held the Roman consensus together was the control structure of the civilization, the state, its government, its military. As Meyer put it, the state "was the sanctified symbol of the cosmos," uniting earthly and transcendent realms "in a grand power that left to the individual person little meaning or value beyond that which adhered to him as a cell of the whole."[33] The state likewise represented the center core for every lower social stratum. What happened in history to break through this suffocating unity? It took a direct challenge to that unity in that premier cosmological civilization, Rome itself, aimed directly at the emperor.

From a remote corner of its far-flung empire, a small voice cried out, "Render to Caesar the things that are Caesar's and to God the things that are God's."[34] What could have been of less concern to the power of Rome? Yet somehow this small Jesus movement grew, so that by the Edict of Milan in AD 313, Christianity had become the effective religion of the empire. Despite the fact that Constantine and succeeding Caesars sought to control, suppress, or incorporate the Christian Church within the state, in the words of Fareed Zakaria the Christian Church was "the first major institution in history that was independent of temporal authority and willing to challenge it."[35] With state and religious loyalties divided, the cosmological unity could not be sustained. Both institutions came under pressure, and tension developed between them.[36]

To Meyer, it was "the Incarnation and the Christian doctrine of the person that flows from it" that broke "finally and forever the unity of cosmos and the person." As important as were commerce and its introduction of new ideas, to truly break the agreement required a power that could compete with the state and its sanctifying myths. Only something as mighty as the supposed incarnation of the very transcendent into time seemed able to challenge the overwhelming historic power of the state. Dividing the transcendent from the state desanctified the state and deprived it of its spiritual power, setting the individual as the arbitrator between the two powers.[37]

Once the individual had choice—even if limited to a class or segment of the population—it was impossible ever again to maintain agreement or even control, to subsume individuals totally within a cosmological whole except by pure force for limited periods of time. Once weakness showed, the individual, recognizing his freedom and power, took advantage, organized, and even revolted. As a consequence, a limited form of government arose in Europe, and its effects spilled out to the remainder of the world over time.[38] Ever since, world time has been divided into years before and after the advent of that liberation, creating a new "common era" distinct from the separate cosmological ones that ruled before.

By no means did all see this lack of agreement and division of control as positive steps. Indeed, the idea that God had set man so free from human control was positively frightening to many. The man considered the first modern philosopher, Niccolò Machiavelli, blamed Christianity for dividing power and so weakening the European state that it became extremely difficult to control anarchy and preserve the social order, especially to preserve public authority. Machiavelli wrote, "The mode of living today, as a consequence of the Christian religion, does not impose the necessity of self-defense that existed in ancient times," when, he believed, unified power could control events with guile and force. Christian mores considered guile and force generally immoral, did not sanction destruction of towns and pillaging to fund wars, and did not justify such force as lessons to those who might attempt to rebel from public authority. As such, Christianity hampered the degree of state power Machiavelli thought essential to effective government.[39]

The great social theorist Jean-Jacques Rousseau blamed Christianity for creating a "double power and conflict of jurisdiction" between church and state that had "made all good polity impossible in Christian states." For "all that destroys social unity is worthless, all institutions that set man in contradiction to himself are useless." He recommended philosopher Thomas Hobbes's solution for a "restoration throughout of political unity."[40] Whereas Hobbes required the consolidation of power directly under a single ruler, Rousseau argued that a "general will" representing all the people was required to force a new cosmological agreement for modern times. Machiavelli, Rousseau, and Hobbes all concurred with Meyer that Christian ideals and institutions were responsible for ending agreement and loosening control. The first three considered this as undermining social order, whereas Meyer regarded it as a beneficial tension that resulted in individual freedom and social creativity.

Unquestionably, this new division of power and ideals resulted in a type of society very different from any seen previously. Meyer noted:

> The characteristic concepts, institutions, and style of the West, where they stand in the sharpest contrast to those of other civilizations, are shot through and through with tension. And this is true from the most matter-of-fact levels of existence to the most exalted. Everywhere, impossible contradictions maintain themselves to create the most powerful and noble extensions of the Western spirit. At the most mundane level, the economic, the Western system takes leave of hard matter, etherealizing money, the very foundation of production and exchange. The Gothic cathedral, thrusting to the heavens, denies the weighty stone of which it is built, while rising from the center of its city it affirms the beauty of materiality. The doctrine of the Lateran Council, central to the philosophical tradition of the West, proclaimed, after a thousand years of intellectual effort, the pure tension of the Incarnational unity, in radical differentness, of the material and the transcendent. This is the mode of the West at its highest and most typical.[41]

While a dual loyalty freed the mind from unitary control, it was the concrete institutionalization of the loyalty in the church that created an alternative power structure that could confront the state. Indeed, the church's founder taught this alternative structure to be at least somewhat independent of Caesar's. In theory, "two sets of tensions" were arraigned around church and state, but rulers by no means automatically accepted the Christian ideal of separation. Even supportive ones such as Charlemagne insisted on naming bishops and supervising what they taught to assure agreement with state wishes. The church slowly limited his successors' power. As the church won rights from the state, however, other institutions began to claim similar prerogatives. Local parishes and monasteries demanded and won some independence from bishops. Lords won reciprocal rights from kings and knights. Towns, boroughs, ports, and cities wrested rights from nobles. Guilds and merchants won privileges from municipalities and monarchies.[42]

The English Magna Carta of 1215 made these multiple tensions formal, listing the rights of all these institutions and individuals and making even the monarch subject to the "customs and liberties" of the realm.[43] There was no single place for power to reside other than in the individual and the institutions and traditions with which he identified. This rough tension between church, state, and society lasted nearly a millennium. Agreement was merely spiritual but often had concrete effects. Although only a very broadly defined creed was required for agreement to be in communion with the church, by the reign of England's Henry II the church could humble even the monarch, demanding public penance for the murder of Thomas Becket.[44] The monarchs continually resisted this decentralized diversity that limited their dreams of grandeur, but they depended on the wealth generated by the freedom this diversity created. They found it difficult to collect taxes, their subjects often demanding further concessions, as in the Magna Carta itself.

This limited monarchical power and unprecedented if limited degree of freedom in medieval Europe unleashed a creativity ignored by most modern historians. Historian Jean Gimpel rightly recognized that the Middle Ages introduced "machinery into Europe on a scale no civilization had previously known." Moreover, this historic level of productivity turned out to be "one of the main factors that led to the dominance of the Western hemisphere over the rest of the World."[45] Gimpel added:

> In the medieval era of growth, there were at least three . . . key groups: the landlords, who among other achievements built the 5,634 water mills of the [medieval English] Doomsday Book, the Cistercians, who built the model farms and factories, and the bourgeois or self-made men, on whose ingenuity depended the financing of the expanding textile and other industries.[46]

The waterwheel was the primary engine of economic development for the three groups leading this first industrial revolution. The Chinese adopted the waterwheel for field irrigation, but only European civilization mastered it for general manufacturing to make its manual labor significantly more productive. Slavery, which had declined ever since the fall of Rome under pressure from the church, became superfluous and did not return to the West until the Age of Discovery.[47] Prosperity brought substantial freedom to towns and cities. Although peonage in rural areas hardly is consistent with modern concepts of freedom, even Karl Marx considered it an advance from the slavery and despotism of ancient times, then still existing in the rest of the world. As a result, notes Oxford historian Chris Wickham, "between the early Middle Ages and the beginning of the fourteenth century, the population of Europe grew consistently, perhaps tripling in size." The continent enjoyed a general prosperity unknown to the rest of the world.[48]

The Utopian Temptation

Then a crisis occurred that threatened everything. Between 1347 and 1350, the Black Death hit, taking one-third to one-half of Europe's population. This plague was, in Gimpel's words, "the worst catastrophe Western civilization has suffered."[49] Christian piety had neither prevented the catastrophe nor provided the remedy, provoking a frantic search for a more worldly solution. As the devastation created the conditions for change, the new wealth to support a smaller population gave different barons the resources to slowly restore order and unity under their royal power. The accompanying rise of Protestantism provided an alternative moral order to sanctify the challenging royal claimants. As a result, dynastic power struggles came to dominate Europe, consolidating states (the Hundred Years' War) or increasing dynastic reach (the bloody Thirty Years' War). Although religion provided support for the wars, the churches were severely weakened when the Treaty of Augsburg (1555) and later the Treaty of Westphalia (1648) granted monarchs full control over their subjects' religious denomination. Cosmological agreement was restored as national populations became unified under established churches, either Catholic or Protestant, under the firm control of the state.[50]

In spite of Westphalia, dynastic wars continued without abatement. The Thirty Years' War, often called a religious conflict, was actually a continuation of the Bourbon-Hapsburg dynastic struggles, as proved by the fact that Catholic France was on the supposedly Protestant side of the conflict. Religion became so weak that as early as the sixteenth century, Henry VIII of England could confiscate the monasteries and bring the church and much of the nobility under his power with hardly a murmur from the Catholics (except in the north). In France, Francis I won religious control by suppressing the Calvinists and bringing the Catholic hierarchy firmly under his command. Before this nationalization, popes had been influential actors in a range of states; afterward, popes such as the worldly Gregory IX were selected for expertise in dynastic power politics as they looked inward to the security of the Papal States.[51]

Such a radical historical change, ending centuries of divided power and tension, required a utopian justification. English court theorist Robert Filmer provided just such a justification. He idealized the monarch as the divinely blessed sire of the nation, requiring the same degree of obedience as one's father, on earth and in heaven. The king was to bring the nation's divided "family" under the protective hand of the loving father to maximize agreement, order, and national greatness.[52] The weakened religions were in no position to argue against the sacrilegious claim of the "divine right of kings." But the illusion that monarchical unity and centralization represented strength was revealed when, in 1704, the "Sun King," Louis XIV, lost the Battle of Blenheim to a motley alliance led by English shopkeepers who had emerged in a second industrial revolution.

As the great analyst Montesquieu was shocked to discover, power separation, tension, individualism, and commercial productivity were the keys to future success, much as they had been before the monarchical centralization.[53] Once Europeans, or a critical number of them at least, had tasted freedom and dreamed sublime ideals, cosmological unity could not prevail under the divine-right kings who attempted to speak unambiguously and authoritatively in a single voice in a complex and divided world. But a divine right of kings was not the only possible utopian solution, as Meyer explained:

> A clear vision of the naked confrontation of individual men with transcendence created a yawning gap in human consciousness. It was something of the effect of eating the fruit of the Tree of the Knowledge of Good and Evil. On the one hand stood the perfection of transcendence, and on the other the imperfection of human existence. The temptation was enormous to close that intolerable gap, to grasp that understood transcendent perfection and by sheer human will to make it live on earth, to impose it on other human beings—by persuasion if possible, by force if necessary.

Meyer added that "the effect of this temptation was portentous for the future, because of its continuing impact upon both the Hellenic and the Judaic traditions, the twin sources from which our Western civilization derives so much of its content." The effects could be seen, he said, in Plato's *Republic* and *Laws*, which developed "the concepts of molding human life." Centuries later, the utopian temptation became evident in "such polities as Calvin's Geneva or Spain of the Inquisition or Cromwell's England." The utopian desire "to impose a pattern of what the imposers considered perfection" became "secularized with the passage of time" and in the process grew "ever more rigid, total, and terrible, as in the all-powerful Nation of the French Revolution or the Dictatorship of the Proletariat of the Communists." Meyer continued:

> The Utopian temptation arises out of the very clarity of vision that tore asunder the cosmological world-view. Released from the comforting, if smothering, certainties of identification with the cosmic order, men became aware of their freedom to shape their destiny—but with that freedom came an awesome sense of responsibility. For the same leap forward that made them fully conscious of their own identity and their own freedom made them conscious also of the infinite majesty and beauty of transcendence and of the criterion of existence that perfection puts before human beings, who in their imperfection possess the freedom to strive to emulate perfection. A yawning gulf was opened between infinity and finity.[54]

This still is our problem today. The hope for perfection is infinite and the freedom to reach for it is unbounded. Once one glimpses the ideal of perfection (no matter how one defines perfection), realizes how far reality is from that goal, and has the freedom to grasp for the ideal, how can one not use all one's strength try to close that gap and achieve agreement on a more utopian ideal?

Plato's *Republic* had opened the gap, and although the power of the Athenian cosmological state had suppressed his compelling vision of perfect justice in the utopian republic, the dream lived on.[55] Rousseau's more popular utopian vision required a new rational, secular religion under control of a unified general will led by the state to provide agreement and legitimacy and keep internal order.[56] One version was actually established in the French Revolution by Rousseau's radical admirers Robespierre and Saint-Just. Revolutionary France rejected the old tradition absolutely, outlawing Christianity, tearing up its calendar dated from Jesus's birth, and making secular deism the established nonreligion of the state. Unfortunately for the revolutionaries, Napoleon Bonaparte had another idea. He reintroduced the calendar and the church, though he brought all these institutions under state control.[57] But Rousseau's ideal of the utopian democratic state survived as well.

Napoleon's third legitimizing utopianism was based on a love of nation that would be inspired and guided by a divine-like secular leader and supported by the popular will. The Napoleonic Wars spread nationalism every-where. By 1850, historian John Lukacs writes, the "ancient states had become nations," which then constituted "the main instruments of historic change" for modern times, coming to "dominate everything else."[58] This secular nationalist utopianism inspired the bloody unifications of Germany and Italy and the secular war of nationalisms that was World War I. That war, in turn, prepared the way for Adolf Hitler and his version of secular national-ism, which provoked World War II. As far as reach of power was concerned, the most successful modern utopian ideology was socialism, which V. I. Lenin transformed into an organized communist political vanguard that in different forms dominated Russia, China, central Asia, eastern Europe, and beyond for much of the twentieth century and endures in milder forms today.

As Meyer observed about such utopias, the results of trying to return to cosmological unity were catastrophic. From the fall of Rome to the dynastic wars of the fourteenth century, a period of more than eight hundred years, decentralized medieval Europe lost perhaps two million lives from war and conflict, half of them from the Crusades, which were actually many different wars spread over almost two centuries. From the beginning of the Hundred Years' War to the Battle of Blenheim, or four hundred years, the divine-right dynastic utopias killed more than the whole medieval period in half the time. During the divine-right period, the Hundred Years' War alone cost two to three million lives while the later Thirty Years' War lost seven mil-lion more people in one-third the time. The modern secular utopians killed even more in a mere two centuries. The French Revolution and its wars led to 800,000 killed, and the Napoleonic Wars totaled almost two million dead. World War I nationalism resulted in fifteen million deaths, and Nazi Ger-many's and Japan's World War II totaled fifty-five million. Communism's Soviet Union cost fifty-five million of its own citizens' lives as it launched its utopian dream.[59]

Agreement on American Tradition?

Why is this history relevant to Americans? Do the dreams of Plato, Rous-seau, Napoleon, or Lenin matter today? After all, that was Europe, which, Meyer concluded, had reached toward but "never achieved" breaking fully from the suffocating unity of cosmological thinking.[60] But America is differ-ent, exceptional, is it not? Did not John Winthrop declare it a chosen people in a "city upon a hill"?

Yet as Meyer also pointed out, America, too, had been "tempted always by the false visions of Utopianism." The fight "against Utopian corrosion is the continuing history of the United States since its foundation, a struggle which continues to this day and which is not yet decided."[61]

America was truly exceptional in that before the competing powers lost their struggle with the divine-right states in Europe, the old tradition of Magna Carta rights, transferred by English colonists, became deeply rooted in its colonial beliefs and institutions. Indeed, these rights and freedoms emerged in purer form in America, because they did not have to contend with the strong counterforces of nearby monarchy, customary feudal pre-rogatives, established clerical power, conflicting common and traditional law, and deference to authority and time-honored classes—all of which frustrated the actualization of these rights in the motherland. Consequently, a "first new nation" with a more vibrant tradition of liberty developed across the vast Atlantic Ocean.[62]

Back home, England had transformed from decentralized medievalism to a centralized monarchy under Henry VIII and Elizabeth. But disputes over monarchical succession, religious disagreements, and parliamentary power issues at home and wars abroad continued through the whole colonial period, forcing the mother country to follow a policy of benign neglect that deprived governors of revenue, making them dependent on local support. In the colonies of North America, power became divided between a monarch-appointed or proprietary governor, an executive-appointed but mostly local judiciary, and a less powerful but not defenseless local legislature. The result was a balance of power, as under the Magna Carta's, that kept local rights in tension with state, private, and church obligations. There were established Anglican churches in Virginia and the South, monopoly Puritan congregations in New England, and various degrees of religious and civic toleration in early Rhode Island, Maryland, and Pennsylvania. Besides the English, there were Dutch in New York, Swedes in Delaware, French in New England, and Spanish in the South. A certain sense of freedom prevailed amid diverse local traditions.[63]

In the mid-eighteenth century, when Great Britain attempted to bring its colonies under the same centralized divine-right utopianism it had established in the homeland, it found power much too diffuse even to collect American taxes to pay for their own protection from French and Indian incursions. These separate colonies resisted uniform treatment, what with their different religions; different agricultural, manufactured, natural, and traded goods; different property distributions and laws; and different divisions of political power. Trying to force unity led the colonists to resistance, revolution, and ultimately independence under a new constitutional order.

As Meyer put it:

The men who settled these shores and established an extension of Western civilization here carried with them the heritage of the centuries of Western development. With it they carried the contradiction between the driving demands of the Western ethos and the political system inconsonant with that ethos. In the open lands of this continent, removed from the overhanging presence of cosmological remains, they established a constitution that for the first time in human history was constructed to guarantee the sanctity of the person and his freedom. The establishment of a free constitution is the great achievement of America in the drama of Western civilization.[64]

Although its adoption was seriously contested, soon thereafter the Constitution became an unquestioned article of faith in the new United States. Here was something all Americans could agree on. But it was a minimalist type of agreement. The central government was limited to a handful of enumerated responsibilities so that citizens were required to agree only on a few matters and were free to disagree on much of the rest. The different state, regional, religious, and material interests existing in tension pretty much went their own way, solving problems voluntarily, locally, and individually, as the French social analyst Alexis de Tocqueville described so well in his monumental book *Democracy in America.*[65] As Tocqueville noted, even with the control of the central government light and almost all governmental activity local, "the interests of the country are everywhere kept in view; they are the object of solicitude to the people of the whole Union, and every citizen is as warmly attached to them as if they were his own."[66]

Although the Constitution prevailed over many difficulties during the early years, slavery and its extension could not be resolved. A utopian court overturned Congress's attempts to resolve it, and an ambitious president with a nationalist vision engaged in a war with Mexico that added potential new slave states, stoking fears on all sides. With the election of Abraham Lincoln, the Republican Party seemed able to unify the North and West against the South's traditions and institutions, very much including slavery; the South then demanded a separation that the others were unwilling to grant. After a half million military and perhaps twice as many civilian casualties, slavery was eliminated and a new constitutional unity of sorts was reestablished. The Thirteenth Amendment ended slavery, and the Fourteenth and Fifteenth Amendments limited the states, but there was general agreement not to enforce them too finely. At least on the surface, constitutional agreement had weathered the conflict and American diversity and exceptionalism had survived, but at some cost to its federal system.[67]

The tension between the unifying ideal behind the new amendments and the actual continuing division and decentralization led many to see the constitutional separation itself as "a serious imperfection," where the "federal government lacks strength because its powers are divided," as Woodrow Wilson put it.[68] Inspired by the centralized regimes of the Europe of his day, Wilson sought to concentrate power in the executive and a subordinate professional bureaucracy, which would enact a scientific plan to serve the common good. The progressive ideal would thereafter unify power under the cosmological principle of scientific administration.[69] When the great progressive "world revolutionary," as Lukacs labeled Wilson,[70] became president, he was extraordinarily successful in establishing a retinue of expert agencies to help override the checks, and he was able to fund it with a substantial progressive income tax. During World War I, he controlled the railroads, supervised food production, assisted the growth of unions, managed industrial production, regulated unpatriotic speech, and insisted on the ideal of international self-determination that shattered the old empires of Europe.[71]

The end of the war saw a "return to normalcy" decentralization under Presidents Warren Harding and Calvin Coolidge, but that was soon followed by a revival of progressive centralization under Herbert Hoover and Franklin Roosevelt. As the 1929 Depression continued into 1938, however, voters retaliated by electing eighty Republicans to the House of Representatives, allowing the opposition party to win enough seats to form a coalition with conservative southern Democrats that ended effective progressive control. Twenty-five years later, in the aftermath of President John Kennedy's assassination, large progressive majorities in Congress enacted an ambitious Great Society civil rights and welfare agenda under President Lyndon Johnson to complete what they considered the Fourteenth Amendment's promise of social equality. But thereafter, the traditional party balance returned and even turned further right, frustrating any comprehensive progressive program.

Now reformers came to view the long history toward progress as breaking down into a "deadlock of democracy,"[72] at least until Barack Obama entered the White House. Through it all, progressives remained convinced that it was necessary for Americans to agree on only one critical matter: to solve America's problems, the people must be convinced to support the planned, neutral, rational solution arrived at by the nation's top scientific minds and adopt it into law. The experts would work under two democratic political parties—Republican and Democratic—but within an overall agreement that both parties should defer to expert opinion once it had arrived at the most scientific solution.[73]

In the early days of his administration, President Obama had made the hope explicit: "The days of science taking a backseat to ideology are over."[74] Was it too utopian to ask all Americans to agree only on turning away from outdated traditional thinking and allow modern science to create a better world for them? Would that not be a truly rational American exceptionalism that all could agree on?

Four

———⟫∘⟪———

SUPERSEDING TRADITION?

A MERICA REMAINED TRADITIONAL AND PAROCHIAL well into the twentieth century. Ninety percent of government employment and two-thirds of its spending was local, and private society was lightly regulated, with only foreign policy, interstate commerce, and a few miscellaneous others run by national political officials and their small, patronage-based staffs, all essentially under one roof. A national civil service law was not even adopted in the United States until 1883, and the majority of federal employee positions were not covered by it until World War I.[1] The professional, scientific bureaucracy envisaged by the nineteenth-century Europeans and Americans who designed the modern welfare state simply did not exist.

For most of history, abstract science was pretty much confined to the ivory tower. Technology was far more important, as many minor practical adjustments proved their worth by improving traditional technological processes incrementally over time. While technological improvement would remain important, perceptions began to change radically in the eighteenth and nineteenth centuries, when Antoine Lavoisier in oxygen research and Louis Pasteur in bacteriology demonstrated that science could have direct practical effects. Once science took the lead, it captured the imagination everywhere. By the end of the nineteenth century, science seemed to be leading traditional knowledge in almost every field of public endeavor.[2]

Politics became political science. Governing became the science of public administration. Social life became the sciences of sociology, anthropology, and psychiatry. In the United States, Professor Woodrow Wilson was in the forefront of creating these new scientific disciplines and professional associations to spread the new public philosophy.[3] "The modern idea is to leave the past and to press on to something new" was his forward-look-ing view.[4] Wilson was especially prominent in the leadership of the pub-lic administration movement, where in his seminal work on the subject, he concluded that what was needed for the future was centralized "impartial scientific method."[5] Even civil service reform was merely a "prelude to a fuller administrative reform," a "moral preparation" for making it "unpar-tisan" and "businesslike."[6]

President Wilson and later Franklin Roosevelt led the United States toward a more bureaucratized, exam-selected, educated, and scientific per-manent civil service. Under President Roosevelt a professionalized civil ser-vice became the dominant force in the making and execution of policy. With its new power, however, bureaucracy soon became a policy target, with tradi-tional politics laying every misstep at its door. The issue of inept bureaucracy helped Republicans win a congressional majority following World War II and the presidency in four of the following six elections. In 1976, Democratic presidential nominee Jimmy Carter broke the streak by running mainly on a program of reforming the civil service, to make a mostly discredited bureau-cracy work once again.[7]

President Carter did in fact totally restructure the national bureaucracy with the Civil Service Reform Act of 1978 (CSRA). Although it emphasized leadership from top political appointees to make the bureaucracy more responsible, the reform centered on a new rationalized performance-man-agement personnel system—including merit bonuses for career executives—that would reward good work and have consequences for poor performance. The old system had ended up rating more than 90 percent of employees as satisfactory; almost no one was rated superior or fired.

Right from the beginning, however, politics overwhelmed the rational design. As a result of pressure from his labor allies, President Carter was forced to add a union bargaining system into his act alongside the one based on performance. That conflicting system still exists in a somewhat modi-fied form, with the unions in a critical position to frustrate professional administrative procedures. Moreover, during his final days, President Carter approved a consent decree to end intelligence-based civil service exams because minorities did not perform well on them.[8]

It was left to President Ronald Reagan actually to implement the CSRA. The attempted introduction of pay for performance and other such reforms provoked America's most aggressive era of public-sector union activity, with numerous job actions and work stoppages across government. The air traf-fic controller union, especially, had negotiated concessions on pay and work rules that went well beyond the traditional scope of union benefits. But, in a rash move, the union struck against the government. President Reagan dismissed them all. Although there have been no governmental strikes and few restrictive job actions since, union opposition continued to frustrate the effectiveness of the reforms that were enacted, and the consent decree against intelligence tests remains in force until this day.[9]

In an attempt to mollify this aggressive public-sector workforce, President George H. W. Bush downgraded the remaining performance standards and much of the legal superstructure with it. The 9/11 attack spurred new reform efforts to add performance management back into the new George W. Bush administration. Donald Rumsfeld at the Department of Defense, Tom Ridge at the Department of Homeland Security, and Andrew Card at the White House all supported using the Reagan-Carter political/performance model to exempt work schedules, equipment utilized, training, length of temporary reassignments, promotion rules, and overtime, among other functions, from being bargained by a union or appealed as a prohibited civil service practice when matters of security were involved. Proposals were introduced for Department of Defense civilians (the military are in a different system) and Homeland Security, but both were blocked in Congress and were later abandoned under the Obama administration.[10]

The American civil service bureaucracy has developed into a very strange amalgam of administrative models planned by no one. For half of the bureaucracy, a dual CSRA system of both civil service and union bargaining rules holds sway. Some performance enhancement followed the Carter-Reagan performance reforms, but seniority and work-to-the-rule have predominated since then except at the highest executive levels. For the other half of government, specifically at the Departments of Defense and Homeland Security, new systems have been promised but none have emerged in the face of fierce union opposition. In addition to this structure of two million civilian federal employees stand twelve million private contractors performing national government work. State government bureaucracies likewise implement federal laws. With tight budgets, contracting has appealed to both political parties because privatization saves money—30 percent or more, in most studies—and results in more efficient work. But private and state contracting enormously complicates the operations of a supposedly rationally hierarchical civil service system.[11]

What is clear is that the progressive ideal of a neutral, scientific bureaucracy has been badly tarnished in modern times. But to progressives, this administrative disarray is simply evidence of the need for even greater efforts to infuse scientific principles into bureaucracy reform. Although neither party has proposed any comprehensive reform in recent decades, the hope for a true scientific administration remains strong, especially in the key policy areas of the environment, education, and controlling global warming.

Planning the Environment

Once upon a time, a young progressive idealist was moved by the first Earth Day to devote his life to saving America's land through rational government planning of the environment. He was inspired to attend forestry school to learn the science and then joined the U.S. Forest Service, anxious for a career to serve the nation.

Early on, Randal O'Toole saw that the Forest Service was allowing vastly more timber to be harvested than was prudent according to scientific forest management principles. The reason was that to grant more resources to the service, in 1930 Congress passed a law allowing income from such sales to go directly to pay the service's administrative costs rather than having to be approved through the annual appropriations process. This incentive encouraged the great overcutting the new recruit observed. In an effort to control this waste, in 1976 Congress required the 120 national forests to create rational timber management, land-use, herbicide-spray, and wilderness plans that had to be integrated into regional and finally a national program to scientifically allocate timber and other resources and at the same time protect the environment.[12]

The problem, as O'Toole explained in his revealing book *The Best-Laid Plans*, is that the forests were so vast and complex that only guesses of their size and composition could be made. Many agency plans calculated timber at values fifty to one hundred times what private companies were actually paying for it, and/or estimated tree growth at faster rates than possible, and/or planned for trees as tall as 650 feet—nearly twice the height of the world's tallest. The plans did result in lower timber harvests, since many forests held only three-quarters or even two-thirds of the plan's supposedly fantastic yields, but now most of it was sold well below cost. The plan took eighteen years to complete, cost $1 billion, but made no economic sense. One Forest Service planner explained: "There is never enough time to do it right but always enough time to do it twice."[13]

Government bureaucrats did what they were given incentives to do. If the real incentives were to cut trees, they would cut and cut until there was nothing left. If after that abuse, Congress gave them incentives to conserve, they would let trees grow and grow until fires broke out everywhere, turning these trained timber experts into reconstituted firemen without time for timber cutting or conservation. As that aberration became apparent, the incentives would change again. The foresters started by harvesting too many trees, but then the incentives changed and conservation went overboard. Intrigued by the results at his own agency, O'Toole expanded his study to include all government land planning. He found the same results in parks, transportation, energy, urban renewal, and land use generally.[14]

Still committed to rational environmental policy, O'Toole came to the conclusion that national planning is impossible—no one can deal with such vast complexity. If the politicians try to force the bureaucrats to balance two, three, or more goals, the bureaucrats become immobilized by the complexity, so they plan and plan and plan—and delay and delay—until the plan implodes. Like the Forest Service, other government planners have to make up the data—and garbage in, garbage out, as the computer guys say. O'Toole believed that if government agencies were given only a single, precisely defined mission, they could be reasonably efficient. Incentives would need to be designed to complement the mission, not conflict with it. Performance criteria would need to be set to evaluate agency progress. Agencies would be required to compete with other government and private alternatives.[15]

O'Toole concluded that the best planning is localized—and optimally privatized to get close to the complex reality, to relate supply and demand, and to minimize red tape. Government decision making must be kept simple and devise market proxies if it is to perform even reasonably well.[16] Government lacks the signals of the price system that allow the market to sort out complex phenomena and respond to it. Revenue-producing agencies should be funded only from user fees, and agencies that do not produce revenue should be placed in a competitive setting to introduce at least some market discipline into bureaucratic processes.[17]

Yet O'Toole's has been a voice in the wilderness: environmental administration has become more centralized, bureaucratized, and regulatory than ever.

The lesson most of the experts learned from these environmental failures was the same as from the economic crisis—that these were failures of market and decentralized decision-making and required more government regulation to fix them. A 2008 newspaper headline told the story: "Unraveling Reagan: Amid Turmoil, U.S. Turns Away from Decades of Deregulation." The turning was coming even from the "Republican heirs to the legacy of President Reagan," such as Securities and Exchange Commission chairman Christopher Cox, who had been a White House adviser to Reagan.[18] If anything, in spite of its failures, regulation seemed more popular with administrators than ever.

Bureaucracy and Complexity

On the day of President Obama's greatest regulatory triumph, the signing of his "transformative" health-care bill, reality responded with a nasty bump. As a consolation to the many progressives who had demanded a single government-administered health plan, congressional leaders had added a provision that would turn the student loan program—which had previously offered both private and government loans—into a totally federal program. The president was severely embarrassed when those who went to the government website that was now the only source of information on student loans found an announcement that the site did not exist.[19]

Before his celebrating White House staff could drain their champagne glasses, the president had come face to face with the essential problem of bureaucracy. It is relatively easy to pass a program. It is very difficult to manage one in the complex reality that is American public administration. Reading the classic book on the subject—Ludwig von Mises's *Bureaucracy*—could have given the president a warning. Governmental management is much more difficult than private management because there is no market-equivalent device that tells top management what is going on below.[20]

Mises demonstrated that private managers have a signaling device through their profit-and-loss bottom line that tells them whether they are successful, whether the business is making a reasonable return on investment or not. In fact, every subordinate unit in the organization can be studied to find whether it is making a profit or not, allowing the top executive to emphasize the productive and eliminate what is not, thus maximizing resources. Although private managers can miss the signals and bookkeeping can have errors, there is a measuring device that runs through the whole organization, no matter how many layers, that allows the CEO to measure success without having to know the details of what is taking place below.

Government has no equivalent. Although there is bookkeeping galore, it merely tells what is spent and on what. It gives no signal when to spend more or less because there is no equivalent for profit or demand. Indeed, its records encourage a perverse response. If a problem gets worse after money is spent to alleviate it, the usual reaction is that even *more* funds should be spent to solve the problem in the future. Moreover, there is no means to track objectively what subordinates are doing or whether they are successful. The only signals from the depths of the bureaucracy to the executive at the top come from immediate supervisors, who report subjectively through complex appraisal systems how well they think an employee is doing.[21]

Roy Ash, former director of the Office of Management and Budget and cofounder and president of Litton Industries, used to explain how much public-sector management differs from that of the private sector by asking private CEOs: "Imagine you were the chief executive officer of your company and that the board of directors was made up of your customers, your suppliers, your employees and your competitors and that you required a majority vote on everything. Wouldn't you conduct your business in a different way than you do now?"[22]

A wide range of groups and people have a say in what America's government does: its customers (the public, its suppliers), the businesses that contract with and are regulated by the government, its employees (the public-sector unions and civil service associations that work for it), and even its competitors (the opposing political party working through Congress). Since all have some power, government officials and bureaucrats usually make some attempt to accommodate everyone. Decision-making is impossibly compromised by competing interests and tends not to work either to satisfy anyone or to solve the problem at hand.[23]

The idea of President Obama's health care for all may have been sublime, but when it emerged from Congress things were a bit more complicated. When the government's chief actuary was able to look at the details, he found: fourteen million people would actually lose their employer coverage by 2019; tens of billions of dollars in new fees and excise taxes would "generally be passed through to health consumers in the form of higher drug and devices prices and higher premiums"; the new long-term care insurance program would face "a significant risk of failure"; estimated reductions in spending "may not be fully achievable"; 16 percent of all hospitals, nursing homes, and other providers treating Medicare patients could be operating at a loss by 2019 and could "possibly jeopardize access to care for beneficiaries"; a significant portion of those newly eligible for Medicaid would have trouble finding physicians who would see them; and the increased demand for Medicaid services could be difficult to meet.[24]

Likewise, President Obama's "sweeping overhaul" of the finance system was aimed at preventing a repeat of the 2007–8 crisis. A new Financial Services Oversight Council would be established to identify which financial firms might cause a future "systemic" risk to the economy, and council members were given additional powers to require reports and control capital levels, reserves, and types of investment risks such firms may incur. The council would consist of the treasury secretary (as chairman), the Federal Reserve chair, the comptroller of the currency, the Consumer Financial Protection director, the Securities and Exchange Commission chair, the Federal Deposit Insurance Corporation chair, the Commodities Futures Trading

Commission chair, and the Federal Housing Finance Agency director. The Treasury would have the final word in case of deadlock.

One may notice that these were precisely the agencies and leaders that failed to see the previous crash developing. In fact, they were—along with Congress, which would continue to oversee the process—the main sources of the problem, in that they created incentives for quasi-government bureaucracies Fannie Mae and Freddie Mac to guarantee mortgages people could not afford to pay. If these experts could not anticipate the problems before, or know how to solve them after, how could they possibly do so in the future? As the *Wall Street Journal* noted at the time, the laws of administration are unlikely to be changed by rearranging the deck chairs.[25]

When President Obama signed the Dodd-Frank Wall Street Reform and Consumer Protection Act, the law included something called the Volcker Rule (named after former Federal Reserve chairman Paul Volcker), which was intended to prevent banks from using customers' federally insured deposits to make risky investments for the banks' own benefit. Congress, naturally, did not define the rule in law but left it to the bureaucrats. When the government bureaucracy finally issued the rule, it did not offer a definition but instead discussed the rule in the form of 1,347 questions. Businessmen objected that they could not comply with a rule that simply asked questions. The regulators themselves conceded in the rule that "the definition of what constitutes a prohibited or permitted activity . . . involves subtle distinctions that are difficult both to describe comprehensively within regulation and to evaluate in practice."[26] But businessmen could still go to jail for not complying.

The basic progressive assumption about bureaucracy is that political science experts can control the social world just as physical scientists control the material world. But how valid is that assumption? The millions inconvenienced by the Icelandic volcano eruption affecting air traffic and weather as these reforms were being enacted—much less the 92,000 killed and 300,000 injured in the Haiti earthquake, also in 2010—might question how well physicists actually control nature. But the more fundamental reality is that the social world is infinitely more complex than the physical.

The great Nobel Prize–winning economist and philosopher F. A. Hayek had long warned against such a simplistic assumption. He pointed out that scientists have estimated there are 10^{56} physical atoms in the whole solar system—but there are that many interneuronic interconnections in a single person's mind in a few minutes of intense cortical activity. A single person in a seventy-year lifetime collects one thousand times as many bits of information as he has nerve cells. Interactions with one other person multiply the interrelations vastly, and the complexities of three hundred million people interacting (let alone seven billion) worldwide are simply unimaginable.[27] Hayek labeled the progressive assumption that this level of complexity could be controlled by some magical "scientific" formula a "superstition," which in this case is a belief that a select group of people knows more than it actually does, that this group has mysterious knowledge of how the world really works.[28]

Neanderthals Teach Science

The great skeptic H. L. Mencken's final report from the famous Scopes evolution trial in Dayton, Tennessee, comes roaring down to us as sharply edged as ever after more than eighty years:

> Let no one mistake [the trial] for comedy, farcical though it may be in all its details. It serves notice on the country that Neanderthal man is organizing in these forlorn backwaters of the land, led by a fanatic, rid of sense and devoid of conscience. Tennessee, challenging him too timorously and too late, now sees its courts converted into camp meetings and its Bill of Rights made a mock of by sworn officers of the law. There are other states that had better look to their arsenals before the Hun is at their gates.[29]

Mencken contrasted unsophisticated traditional thinking against modern scientific understanding. He had earlier concluded: "No principle is at stake at Dayton save the principle that school teachers, like plumbers, should stick to the job that is set before them, and not go roving around the house, breaking windows, raiding the cellar, and demoralizing children." None of those involved had the sense to stick to what they actually knew when scientific and educational matters such as evolution were being discussed.[30]

A more recent case on teaching evolution suggests that things have not changed much—except that Neanderthal man has switched sides. In 2005 U.S. District Court judge John E. Jones III presided over a similar case from equally obscure Dover, Pennsylvania. Judge Jones could have avoided making a Hun of himself either by declaring the case moot—the school board that had required a statement in its biology textbook claiming evolution was only a theory rather than a fact, and that "intelligent design" was an alternative explanation to Charles Darwin's, had been defeated in the prior election—or by ruling that the board decision was biased by religious prejudice. The new school board had already announced it would appeal only if it lost the case, so Jones knew he could not be reviewed by a higher court. He was presented with a once-in-a-lifetime opportunity to demonstrate on a world stage his intellectual and scientific superiority to the boobs.[31]

The distinguished member of the Schuylkill County Bar, educated to the highest academic levels as a Bachelor of Arts at Dickinson College and, comfortably again, at its School of Law, let hubris unleash his pen. Jones did not merely decide a case of law; he chose to define biology, science, and rationality itself, constitutionally, legally, once and for all, for all time—demonstrating rather conclusively that absolutely nothing had been learned over eight decades.

What gave Judge Jones his superior powers? He conceded that his analysis must deal with "complex if not obtuse" matters, but he claimed that "after a six-week trial that spanned 21 days . . . no other tribunal in the United States is in a better position than are we to traipse into this controversial area."[32] Yes, he did say *traipse*, and that he learned it all over the momentous span of six weeks! Surely his extensive scientific background—as the former chairman of the Pennsylvania Liquor Control Board and before that as solicitor of the great metropolis of Pottstown, Pennsylvania—granted him the scientific expertise to resolve these matters definitively.

The twenty-one-day wonder's first target was the comparatively easy subject of biology. He acknowledged that a few serious scientists had found problems with evolution, citing gaps in the record and life forms that did not seem to evolve from lower bodies. But he concluded, "Just because scientists cannot explain today how biological systems evolved does not mean that they cannot and will not be able to explain them tomorrow." Judge Jones thought this obvious truth disposed of the case, but the notion that scientists *would* someday be able to solve the problems of evolution was a belief based on faith, not on the empirical science he earlier claimed was the only standard for an idea's worth. Although any scientific theory deserves the liberality of this assumption, it is clearly based on cosmology rather than empirical observation.[33]

In evaluating the alternative intelligent design theory favored by the first school board, the judge again retreated from empirical standards. He simply declared, "Intelligent design is a religious view, a mere re-labeling of creationism and not a scientific theory. It is an extension of the Fundamentalists' view that one must either accept the literal interpretation of Genesis or else believe in the godless system of evolution."[34] This sweeping statement ignored the fact that even many traditionalist Christians who believe in intelligent design do not view Genesis literally in every regard and that

Christianity's largest denomination, the Catholic Church, accepts evolution and design as likely parts of the explanation rather than either/or. It also ignored the consensus of evolutionary science itself, which has devised the cosmological idea of the Big Bang as part of its explanation—a bang that by definition is anything but evolutionary.[35]

Judge Jones did not hit full stride until he defined science itself. "Science has been limited to the search for natural causes to explain natural phenomena," he wrote, opining that the scientific revolution was explicitly about the rejection of "revelation" in favor of empirical evidence. This certainly would have been a revelation to the devout Isaac Newton, one of the most important leaders of that revolution, or to Brahe, Copernicus, Kepler, Leibniz, Napier, or most of the rest of the pioneers who believed in both science and religion.[36] But the judge moved bravely on: "Science has been a discipline in which testability rather than any ecclesiastical authority or philosophical coherence has been the measure of a scientific idea's worth." Science, he said, is a discipline that avoids any search for "meaning" or "purpose." He claimed that "the essential ground rules" are those that "limit science to testable, natural explanations."[37]

The judge's admirers were correct to note he had given a "clear definition of science."[38] Yet to anyone familiar with philosophy of science, it obviously was a most particular definition of science, one called logical positivism. This was the dominant view in the late nineteenth and early twentieth centuries and still tends to be the view of establishment institutions like the National Academy of Sciences, which in Judge Jones's case played the role of the Holy Office experts against Galileo (who also was a devout believer). But many have challenged this particular definition—and religionists are not the only ones to dispute it. For example, the philosopher Karl Popper, who was not a believer in God, wrote *The Logic of Scientific Discovery* in the early twentieth century to critique positivism from a strictly logical point of view.[39]

The key to understanding Judge Jones's value-based approach to science is his use of "testability." Popper was the first to rigorously demonstrate that science cannot prove theories but only attempts to falsify theories. Testing to prove theories is logically impossible. New evidence can falsify a theory but can never confirm one, since new evidence can always overturn the earlier findings, as Judge Jones himself noted.[40] No theory is ever proven but is always open to dispute. Logically, this must include evolution.

The judge was also on shaky ground in claiming that science was limited to natural causes to explain natural phenomena. He recognized the need for logic, which even positivists like A. J. Ayer recognized was not material but analytic. More important, Popper claimed that all science rests on cosmology, which defines the point of view, the motivation, the methodology, and the types of problems scientists find worthy of study but are not material themselves.[41]

But the judge did not seem aware that his claims were controversial. The cosmology or cosmologies that structure science cannot be tested empirically—logic cannot, mathematics cannot, the scientific method cannot, Big Bang cannot. Interestingly, Big Bang was rejected by the leading evolutionists of the 1960s for the same reason intelligent design is today: the explanation left a place for God outside the theory. But Big Bang proved irresistible to scientists as part of a more rational explanation, and most evolutionists rely on it today.[42]

Likewise, in the 1970s, it became increasingly impossible to ignore the scientific evidence that Darwin's "fittest" did not always survive. If some events outside evolution as Darwin used the term were recognized, however, some secularist scientists feared leaving room for the unwashed to introduce an outside creative force. The truth is that no one follows pure Darwinian evolution today except those who have little or no idea what scientists actually believe. The fossil record shows innumerable species that died out even though they seemed more fit than those that survived. So evolutionists were forced to recognize outside catastrophic events such as meteors that overruled evolution to some extent and killed off normally superior species.[43]

Both Big Bang and catastrophism would be heresy to Darwin, and his followers violently rejected these concepts when they were introduced. They are a normal part of science today, taught in most textbooks. Will intelligent design be taught in the future? Who knows? What is clear is that some keepers of the scientific tablets—especially those for whom Darwinian evolution has become a metaphysic (note the strange capitalization of Big Bang)—will continue to reject any additions.[44] The Judge Joneses of the world will persist in following lagging conventions and the mob will assist them. But reality has a way of intruding, and establishments are not always successful, especially over the long run.

Most interesting are the parallels between the earlier and recent controversies. Like Tennessee, Pennsylvania passed a law requiring adherence to the current orthodoxy—creationism in the 1920s but evolution today. The Dover school board tried to skirt a state law that forced the orthodox view—except this time it was the *scientifically and popularly* orthodox view. When popular emotion was whipped up, the mob threw out the dissenters.[45] In both cases, the popular theory was made into law and forced on a minority that held an alternative view. In both cases, the law was made the ass, manipulated to favor the majority public position over the minority one.

As in the past, the more rational position will probably prevail over the longer term. What is certain is that intelligent design is not simply a religious dogma, as it is supported by nonreligionists (several of whom appeared before Judge Jones, although he chose to ignore or misrepresent them).[46]

One thing is sure. Mencken would be unsurprised that human nature had not changed. Only the Hun had changed sides. The "fanatics devoid of sense," the Neanderthals, and sworn officers of the law were still abusing the Bill of Rights, only now they were led by a federal judge and his antediluvian image of science.

Science Speaks on Climate

To lend authority to his sweeping claims about science, Judge Jones relied heavily on leading scientific associations. Those same associations put their full prestige on the line in October 2009, when the presidents of eighteen different scientific organizations wrote all members of the U.S. Senate before the legislators voted on a momentous cap-and-trade bill to control global warming. These experts lectured senators on the proper decision to make:

> Observations throughout the world make it clear that climate change is occurring, and rigorous scientific research demonstrates that the greenhouse gases emitted by human activities are the primary driver. These conclusions are based on multiple independent lines of evidence, and contrary assertions are inconsistent with an objective assessment of the vast body of peer-reviewed science. Moreover, there is strong evidence that ongoing climate change will have broad impacts on society, including the global economy and on the environment. For the United States, climate change impacts include sea level rise for coastal states, greater threats of extreme weather events, and increased risk of regional water scarcity, urban heat waves, western wildfires, and the disturbance of biological systems throughout the country. The severity of climate change impacts is expected to increase substantially in the coming decades.

The letter made sure to include the following note: "The conclusions in this paragraph reflect the scientific consensus represented by, for example, the Intergovernmental Panel on Climate Change and U.S. Global Change Research Program."[47]

But soon evidence emerged suggesting that the scientific climate change community was manipulating that consensus. The evidence came out with the dramatic leak of thousands of e-mails from and to scientists at the University of East Anglia's Climate Research Unit—a major advisory body to the United Nations Intergovernmental Panel the experts cited in the letter to the Senate. The controversy over the e-mails, and the larger question of whether scientists were manipulating data to make the case for climate change, forced the Democrat-led Senate to shelve the once overwhelmingly popular climate control legislation. Although the British university later claimed it was vindicated because a parliamentary committee investigation could not prove the Climate Research Unit distorted the data or interfered with peer reviews, Parliament still found the scientists' approach deeply troubling. The British newspaper *The Guardian* reported:

> MPs today strongly criticized the University of East Anglia for not tackling a "culture of withholding information" among the climate change scientists whose private emails caused a furor after being leaked online in November. The parliamentary science and technology select committee was scathing about the "standard practice" among the climate science community of not routinely releasing all its raw data and computer codes—something the committee's chair, Phil Willis MP, described as "reprehensible." He added: "That practice needs to change and it needs to change quickly."[48]

The worldwide scientific community went on the attack against its critics. On May 9, 2010, 255 members of the U.S. National Academy of Sciences wrote an open letter saying they were "deeply disturbed by the recent escalation of political assaults on scientists in general and on climate scientists in particular." The signers conceded, "There is always some uncertainty associated with scientific conclusions; science never absolutely proves anything." But they added: "When someone says that society should wait until scientists are absolutely certain before taking any action, it is the same as saying society should never take action. For a problem as potentially catastrophic as climate change, taking no action poses a dangerous risk for our planet." The scientists characterized those who disagreed with them as being "typically driven by special interests or dogma, not by an honest effort to provide an alternative theory that credibly satisfies the evidence."

But what is a legitimate "scientific consensus"? Is the consensus itself scientific or is it but a subjective judgment of scientists that can be influenced not only by scientific opinion but also by ideology, the availability of government grants, professional honors, promotions, and the like—that is, by "special interests and dogma"? As philosophers of science from Popper to Thomas Kuhn have noted, this consensus is not only subjective but is also one awaiting overthrow. The National Academy of Sciences letter conceded the point: "This process is inherently adversarial—scientists build reputations and gain recognition not only for supporting conventional wisdom, but even more so for demonstrating that the scientific consensus is wrong and that there is a better explanation. That's what Galileo, Pasteur, Darwin, and Einstein did."

Still, the climate change community would brook no dissent. The country's leading organization of physicists, the American Physical Society (APS), went even further than the 255 members of the National Academy of Sciences. The APS issued an official policy statement that declared, "The evidence is incontrovertible: Global warming is occurring." So much for the inherent "uncertainty associated with scientific conclusions."

In fact, many scientists expressed doubts about the "scientific consensus" on global warming. Nobel Prize–winning physicist Ivar Giaever resigned from the APS because he could not support the society's policy statement on climate change. He wrote, "In the APS it is OK to discuss whether the mass of the proton changes over time and how a multi-universe behaves, but the evidence of global warming is incontrovertible?"

In early 2012, sixteen prominent scientists, representing institutions including MIT, Princeton, and Cambridge, signed an editorial entitled "No Need to Panic about Global Warming." They wrote, "The lack of warming for more than a decade—indeed, the smaller-than-predicted warming over the 22 years since the U.N.'s Intergovernmental Panel on Climate Change (IPCC) began issuing projections—suggests that computer models have greatly exaggerated how much warming additional CO_2 can cause." They added, "Although the number of publicly dissenting scientists is growing, many young scientists furtively say that while they also have serious doubts about the global-warming message, they are afraid to speak up for fear of not being promoted—or worse."[49]

A George Mason University study found that only 19 percent of television meteorologists not subject to academic pressure believed that climate change was a result of mostly human causes.[50] Many in the public are skeptical too. A Gallup poll in 2012 found that 42 percent of Americans believed that global warming claims were exaggerated. Back in 1997, only 31 percent of Americans had been skeptical of such claims.[51]

The United Nations Intergovernmental Panel has also come under scrutiny for downplaying uncertainty about global warming. An independent investigation conducted by the InterAcademy Council, a consortium of national scientific academies, called for "fundamental reform" at the Intergovernmental Panel. The panel's 2007 report had stated that climate change was "unequivocal" and that the panel had "high confidence" that climate change could cut Africa's agricultural output in half by 2020. But the InterAcademy Council noted that the panel had a "weak evidentiary basis" for the claims, and the investigative report concluded that the panel had not consistently followed its own rules for measuring uncertainty, leading to "unnecessary errors." The InterAcademy Council demanded a conflict-of-interest policy for future UN climate leadership.[52]

For all the questions about data collection and manipulation or about professional or ideological dishonesty, the deeper question is whether any conclusions and policy "actions" the scientific climate change community proposes are scientific statements at all. As Popper argued, science cannot "demonstrate" any theory but can only falsify.[53] Of course, people can learn from eliminating false theories and can infer that other theories that have survived numerous attempts to falsify them seem more valid. But an inference by fallible people does not "demonstrate" that a theory is correct. Classical physics took a mechanical view, seeing nature as a clock to be understood and manipulated through knowledge of simple components. But that view began to be questioned as an adequate explanatory model as early as 1900, when Max Planck concluded on the basis of his empirical tests that radiation was emitted in discontinuous quanta. By the time Albert Einstein universalized quanta for all radiant energy and Werner Heisenberg suggested that light consisted of both waves and particles, the idea of single, simple explanations of phenomena had been discredited.[54]

Real-world prediction cannot be the goal of science. That is because sciences conducts its empirical testing in ideal environments—closed systems such as "vacuums," "frictionless planes," test tubes, and so forth. Only in these environments, which are designed to be infinitely simpler than the real world, can science explain in any precise sense. As the mathematician philosopher Michael Scriven put it, "We know of no important quantitative law in optics, acoustics, thermodynamics, magnetism, gravitation, etc. which is held to be exact" when related to real phenomena.[55] For example, the mechanical relationship between weight and distance posits the unreal assumptions of weightless, perfectly rigid, and frictionless beams; the law of falling bodies assumes the unreal condition of a vacuum; and the kinetic theory assumes an absolute temperature and zero volume for gasses. Even

Euclid's "obviously true" assumption that a straight line is the shortest distance between two points is not true over long distances on a curved globe like the earth, and the older mechanical paradigm made a distinction between an abstract physics that explained and an engineering that actually manipulated reality.[56]

Real-world prediction is even more difficult in the other sciences. Chemical formulae by no means fully describe real substances, and in biology predictability is not even seen as relevant in explaining animal behavior.[57] In these cases, the much higher degree of complexity makes description and explanation more difficult and requires probability rather than mechanical assumptions. Indeed, as physical science becomes more complex, it is moving toward the less deterministic probability logic that mathematician Blaise Pascal expected more than three hundred years ago.[58] As philosopher Richard Rudner put it, it now appears that "an adequate rational reconstruction of the procedures of science would show that every scientific inference is properly construable as a statistical inference."[59]

The problem with probability is that no definite decision based on empirical testing can be made, because critical probability levels can be adjusted to make hypotheses impossible to reject or accept. Of course, the belief that these sciences can be "reduced" to the accuracy of mechanical physics still is widespread, especially in more popular treatments, but even if they could be reduced to physics, it would probably be to modern uncertainty physics rather than to simple mechanical physics. In either case, the problems of measurement remain.[60] When one measure is claimed to cause another, that claim actually is an inference, since such statements are not empirical but are of the if-then form. It will always be possible that some unknown forces are disturbing a given causal relationship or are leading us to believe a causal relationship exists when in fact it does not. Therefore the only way we can make causal inferences at all is to make simplifying assumptions about such disturbing influences.[61]

Science once seemed direct: keep proving theories and sooner or later everything will be explained. The old mechanical view of the universe conceived reality as a dark box consisting of everything that was not known; knowledge would eventually illuminate all of the darkness. The more modern view is that the box has no boundaries. As our scientific knowledge illuminates areas of darkness, the edges of the unknown push ever outward. That is to say, as science learns more, it learns that its areas of ignorance are expanding. If this is true, scientists could never know everything precisely— or even come close.[62]

Even those who argue that the "scientific method" is procedural and objective do not deny, when prodded, that there are "pragmatic aspects of explanation" that go beyond the method itself.[63] It seems, though, that this "pragmatic" area—that is, back in the real world—is where people make the actual decisions about whether a theory can be acted on.[64] There is not some objective entity known as "science"; there are only flesh-and-blood scientists, who decide whether the experimental results should be published, how published results will be reviewed, and, therefore, whether they will be taken seriously by other scientists. Professional criteria are used in the evaluation, but it also seems as if personal commitments to ontologies, methodologies, measuring instruments, and even animosities, ideologies, and idiosyncrasies influence decisions. As the editor of the most prestigious British medical journal, Richard Horton, put it: "The stakes are so high. A single paper in *Lancet* and you get a chair and you get your money. It's your passport to success."[65] Galileo was opposed by scientists in clerical garb who were invested in Ptolemaic science; they had the credibility to carry the argument against him, but they also had reputations to lose if other scientists came to accept Galileo's views.[66]

Although abuses are inevitable, there is no alternative to having those in the science make judgments. As long as there are several disciplines and the freedom to start new ones, there is enough openness to allow for innovation. Yet it is essential that people who make real-world decisions be aware of the limits of science. When scientists predict real-world events, they are no longer scientists but fallible prognosticators. When they propose practical solutions, they are no longer scientists but engineers. No scientist has ever been responsible for a defective bridge. Scientific bridges are abstract and cannot fail. Only engineers build bridges that fall—or predict weather hundreds or thousands of years in the future when real-world climate forecasters have trouble with tomorrow's weather.

Scientists slip from science into dogmatic advocacy even when they provide policymakers with executive summaries of their reports. The language of scientific reports is complicated, but more important for the purposes of policy advocacy, it contains many necessary scientific qualifications. The authors of the leaked memos conceded that they "simplified" findings to influence the politicians. Daniel Botkin, an early climate change scientist turned skeptic, noted that climate scientists can say "period, end of story" about their conclusions to silence skeptics. But that, Botkin said, "isn't science," which requires humility that some other explanation remains possible.[67]

When no less an authority than Nobel Prize–winning scientist Steven Chu, President Obama's secretary of energy, spoke on global warming to the scientists at the Oak Ridge National Laboratory in early 2010, he was frank enough to admit, "We don't understand the downward trend [in temperatures] that occurred in 1900 or in 1940. We don't fully understand the plateau that's happened in the last decade."[68] In other words, such data suggest that it is not getting systematically warmer, but our dogma tells us otherwise and we have faith that warming will be proved in the long run. Unfortunately, his policy prescriptions were not as nuanced as his scientific honesty.

The Necessity of Tradition

The whole progressive "promise of American life," as leading progressive theorist Herbert Croly, titled his book of reform, was based on applying scientific insights to rationalize social life.[69] The government would reform society by identifying hoary traditions, applying reason to discover the problems with them, rejecting them, and allowing a professional and neutral scientific administrative bureaucracy to determine and implement rational solutions. This dream foundered on both practical and scientific grounds. Science was not as amenable to real-world application as the progressives assumed, and when their engineering approximations were put in service, they tended not to work. Einstein and crew aimed at only overturning over-simplified mechanistic science, but in the process they exposed the limitations of public administration.[70] The final insult was that even the scientific deus ex machina the progressives relied on rested on the parochial tradition it sought to supersede.

Science, being an organized pursuit, must have some beginning, some axioms or assumptions on which it is founded, and which exist *prior to* science. Philosopher Edwin Arthur Burtt called them the "metaphysical" foundations of science.[71] Although some argue that science's general beliefs can be inductively justified through observation, the modern reliance on mathematics even for "observation" forces science away from the empirical. Summarizing Einstein's views, author Lincoln Barnett wrote that "with every improvement in its mathematical apparatus the gulf between man the observer and the objective world of scientific description becomes more profound."[72] Two of the twentieth century's leading mathematicians, Alfred North Whitehead and Bertrand Russell, held that all knowledge ultimately was based on instinctive beliefs.[73]

What are these beliefs that precede science? There seem to be four: that there is a real world, that this real world has recurrent regularities, that these can be abstracted and their essences operationalized, and that these data can be described and causally explained. All four must be considered assumptions, because at least since the eighteenth century, philosophers have questioned them all, especially whether one can prove the existence of a real empirical world or whether real essences can be causally explained. And since the time of Aristotle, scientists have recognized the importance of positing theoretical first principles that are not proven, because testing all assumptions in an infinite regress is impossible.[74]

But it seems necessary to go even further. Scientific assumptions are not meant to be true in any real-world sense. As we have seen, even some of the most fundamental theories of physics apply perfectly only in ideal conditions—that is, within closed systems such as test tubes or vacuums that are less complex than reality. Thus, scientific theories are based not only on assumptions but on assumptions that are absurd under the canons of common sense.[75]

Such simplicity is required so that some rather than no knowledge may be obtained. Even logic is not absolute. Thus, Nietzsche called Aristotle's logic simplistic, since to hold by the law of identity that A = A (at all times) ignores change. Likewise, he argued that to hold by the law of noncontradiction and the law of the excluded middle that A cannot be B and non-B or that A is either B or non-B is based on the belief that there can be precisely equivalent things, while in fact A cannot be B or non-B; it is A. Moreover, Nietzsche called mathematics primitive because it would never have been developed if ancients had not thought real-world lines were actually straight and circles round—assumptions that the microscope showed to be false.[76]

The most widely used scientific methodological framework is that of causality, but it has been widely criticized as misleading. Morris Cohen held that after logically excluding the last "remnants of primitive animism" from causality, one is left only with the idea of "regular sequence," or things following one another without the necessity implied by causality.[77] It is reasonable to reply that causality is deeply rooted in commonsense tradition, that it seems more reasonable than noncausality, and that one should therefore choose "the vastly credible over the vastly incredible."[78] Formally, causality has the status only of a traditional assumption, but it is a tradition without which science cannot be conceived.[79]

Radical empiricism, hoping to free science from this subjectivism of the initial intuition, has argued that investigation should begin with the empirical and proceed to analysis without further encumbrance. Yet it can be replied that no one has shown how this can be done without a prior concept and a theoretical context.[80] Consequently, most science tends to assume that it is possible only to devise indices that the investigator assumes to be concrete representations of concepts rather than isomorphic measures of the empirical phenomena. By assuming an "epistemic correlation," the empiricist may incorrectly choose an index that actually stands for another concept as data itself retreat into "patterns inside of patterns."[81]

Where do hypotheses come from if not from the commonsense beliefs of the tradition (or the questioning of them) or from prior science that derived from them? A hypothesis is meaningless in purely objective terms—as if it could stand in space, somehow existing by itself. It seems meaningful only as an investigator's personal assertion that he believes something influences something else and that he means to show some audience why he so believes. And if this is true, then the roots of science are subjective and value-dependent.[82]

At the end of the day, science, as the great Alfred North Whitehead argued, is merely rational debate.[83] By definition, debate is open-ended. Authorities use science to make the world appear more rational, but, as Rudner put it, is it not time to discard "the slightly juvenile conception of the cold-blooded, emotionless, impersonal, passive scientist monitoring the world perfectly in the highly polished lenses of his steel rimmed glasses" for a more realistic view?[84]

This more sophisticated view need not fall into a nihilism that ends up believing nothing and/or accepting everything.[85] As Richard Weaver put it, "There is a difference between knowing an absolute and knowing an absolute absolutely. It is even more certain there is a difference between knowing an absolute and applying an absolute absolutely."[86] It seems reasonable to restore science to its more modest role as one aspect of reason and to conclude that beliefs can be accepted as both the most reasonable explanation (and, thus, to all intents true) and possibly wrong and subject to further correction. Once into the area of concrete action, any engineering conclusion must be judged by practical consequences.

Every scientist should know the limits to empirical analyses and the differences between science and engineering. Yet a good deal of social analysis—especially in the field of policy, as the National Academy of Sciences letter demonstrates—proceeds as if assumptions did not underlie theory, as if data directly proved hypotheses, and as if the scientific answer was also the engineering decision that the policymaker or citizen must implement.

Where do the "metaphysical" assumptions of science come from? Where does a belief that there is a real world, that it has recurrent regularities, that these can be abstracted and measured and causally explained, come from? Every one has been questioned by many traditional cultures and many modern philosophers. Ancient cultures saw continuity between the physical and the metaphysical world, believing that they were intertwined with ghosts and spirits that could influence material events. Plato strongly argued that the apparent world is not the real one. Since it is possible to argue against these assumptions, one can never rest one's defense on absolute principles or data. Eventually, it seems, it is necessary to retreat to the common sense of a tradition for justification (such as when Samuel Johnson kicked the rock to refute Berkeley). In the case of science, the commonsense assumptions seem to have emerged from only one very parochial tradition, that of western Europe as it developed from ancient Athens to the early Middle Ages and on to modern times.[87]

The only rational conclusion seems to be that science itself depends on tradition. As Popper finally concluded from a purely secular rationalist perspective:

> As scientists we want to make progress and this means we must stand on the shoulders of our predecessors. We must carry on a certain tradition. From the point of view of what we want as scientists—understanding, prediction, analysis and so on—the world in which we live is extremely complex. I would be tempted to say infinitely complex if the phrase had any meaning. We do not know where or how to start our analysis of the world. There is no wisdom to tell us. It only tells us where other people started and where they got to. It tells us that people have already constructed in this world a kind of theoretical framework—not perhaps a very good one, but one that works more or less; it serves us as a kind of network, as a system of coordinates to which we can refer the various complexities of the world.[88]

If science, which is organized rational criticism, depends on tradition for its assumptions and beginnings, then tradition is even more essential for our untidy real-world lives, Popper argues:

> We should be anxious, terrified, and frustrated and we could not live in the social world did it not contain a considerable amount of order, a great number of regularities to which we can adjust ourselves. The mere existence of these regularities is perhaps more important than their particular merits or demerits. They are needed as regularities and therefore handed on as traditions, whether or not they are in other respects rational or necessary or good or beautiful or what you will. There is a need for tradition in social life.[89]

Naïve science once assumed that tradition would suppress human creativity and freedom not only in the scientific field but also in the real world. It turns out that tradition—at least one tradition—has been essential to science's development and in fact is required as a place to begin both scientific and social life. This does not mean that tradition should be followed simply for the sake of social order. But tradition is the necessary place to begin and end. It is the repository of both scientific and practical understanding. Moreover, the conclusion that science does not speak directly to the real world but must be interpreted through traditions by fallible individuals implies that those who claim the authority and support of a purely objective science—especially in the realms of power and politics—should be greeted with some skepticism.

Five

---∞◆∞---

WHY FREEDOM?

T HERE IS NO AREA WHERE one desires more scientific certainty than in protecting one's health and food safety. The Food and Drug Administration (FDA) was one of the first federal regulatory agencies, created more than a century ago with a mere dozen inspectors. Today it proudly announces that it regulates one-quarter of every consumer dollar spent. Its mission is "protecting the public health by assuring the safety, effectiveness, and security of human and veterinary drugs, vaccines and other biological products, medical devices, our nation's food supply, cosmetics, dietary supplements, products that produce radiation, and regulating tobacco products." The FDA's two hundred programs represent a daunting scope of operations.[1] The agency's official history calls food and drug regulations a "pillar of the Progressive era."[2]

Always looking for new fields to conquer, in the fall of 2007 the FDA released a revolutionary new pharmaceutical warning label. Larry Lesko, director of the FDA's clinical pharmacology office, announced that the label for the immensely popular anticlotting blood thinner warfarin would caution that a lower dose "should be considered for patients with certain genetic variations." The agency traditionally issued universal warnings, but it announced this new approach to allow the government to begin tailoring cautions directly to individual vulnerabilities. To that point genetic warnings had been posted for only a few limited-audience drugs; warfarin was the first mass test. Research had been approved to extend the model to many other popular drugs, including Prozac, metformin, and albuterol. "If the potential wasn't huge, we wouldn't be doing it," the director boasted in announcing the FDA's more proactive role.[3]

Notice that Director Lesko said "potential." Professor Ann Wittkowsky of the University of Washington warned as the FDA's warfarin decision neared: "It would be irresponsible and potentially harmful to suggest that [genetic] testing be used, or even mentioned, in the label. It is fascinating science, but it is not yet ready for prime time."[4] One problem was that only certain variants of specific genes seemed to affect safe dosage. A 2002 study of the gene CYP2C9 found that some (but not all) variants apparently led people to retain warfarin in the body, which increased bleeding. A 2005 study of the gene VKORC1 also indicated that people with certain variants of the gene responded differently to warfarin, though the findings were ambiguous.

But even if variants of some genes appeared to make a difference, how big a difference did they make? No one knew. The FDA was not able to recommend how much lower the dosage should be for those with the genetic variations. There is a computer estimate of dosages when the genetic factors are evident, but it is only one guess and is not accepted as authoritative.[5] As Dr. Wittkowsky put it, gene research is not yet ready for such sophisticated dosage decision-making for individuals.

Add to that the problem that the genetic tests took ten days to perform. Physicians could follow the older seat-of-the-pants method in the meantime, or they could wait for the test results, with increased risk to patients from delayed treatment. Even once they had the test results, it was still a hit-and-miss decision based on the experience of the physician, because, again, the tests did not reveal what dosage was appropriate for individuals.

In addition, the warfarin genetic tests cost between $300 and $500. Critics were concerned that patients would avoid the inconclusive tests because of the cost and then sue the doctors and/or drug companies if problems developed. Doctors would then refuse to recommend warfarin, which had been used as an effective, low-cost generic thirty million times that year alone and for many years before.

Drugs are complicated things. Warfarin started as a rat poison. A military recruit tried to commit suicide with it, but his use of a low dose prevented blood coagulation, which led scientists to realize it could be useful as a human drug. When President Dwight Eisenhower became the first American to be given permission to use it after his heart attack in 1955, warfarin became the most popular anticlotting agent in history. Yet too small or too large a dose can cause too much clotting or too much bleeding and become a threat to health. Doctors try to balance a person's body size and age and test blood pressure frequently (often daily at the beginning) to get the dosage right. It is an art, not a science, as warfarin was the second most likely drug to send a patient to an emergency room, after insulin. Yet many more patients would suffer and even die without warfarin—or insulin—so physicians try not to let the perfect be the enemy of the good and keep adjusting dosage. There are dangers any way one proceeds: after all, warfarin did begin as a rat poison.

Therapy adds more complexity. Arthur Nienhuis, the president of the American Society of Gene and Cell Therapy, agreed that "gene therapy holds a great deal of potential" (there is that word again). He said that ,after a decade of failure, a dozen children were now living normal lives after receiving gene injections. But he admitted that, in a few cases, gene therapy caused leukemia. That July, a thirty-six-year-old, generally healthy Illinois woman with rheumatoid arthritis received a gene injection in her right knee to relieve local pain and died from an otherwise mild fungus and virus that became virulent and ravaged her organs and blood, consuming her whole body. "It's a major mystery," concluded Kyle Hogarth, who headed the University of Chicago Medical Center, the hospital where she expired.[6]

The FDA has received the greatest criticism for regulating so-called incurable disease drugs. The agency for years insisted that experimental drugs for these patients meet the highest standards, called Phase IV testing, to obtain a full FDA approval. These standards required thousands to be tested in "controlled experiments" where some patients received a full dose and some little or no dose at all. Controlled experiments make sense in many situations, but when patients in the control group will die without treatment, many object. In 2003, when the patients' advocacy group Abigail Alliance tried to save little Abigail Burroughs's life by lobbying for a new expedited approval procedure for terminally ill patients, FDA bureaucrats defended the existing system for its efficiency, specifically mentioning the colon cancer drug Eloxatin. That drug had been placed on an accelerated list, but the FDA did not actually approve it until 2003, by which time fifty-six nations had already done so, France as early as 1996.[7]

Even relatively simple drugs create difficulties. In 2005, under political pressure, the FDA took action to rein in the use of a wide array of popular painkillers. The only painkillers the FDA would not say posed long-term high risks were aspirin and acetaminophen (Tylenol), even though the FDA had not tested their risks. The agency put less widely used drugs such as Celebrex, Vicodin, and Percocet under scrutiny and regulated them to one degree or another; some drugs, such as the pain reliever Vioxx and the arthritis drug Bextra, had to be withdrawn from the market in spite of positive results for many over a number of years.[8] John H. Klippel, the head of the Arthritis Foundation, supported the FDA's intentions but pointed out that the agency's actions left patients in a "serious quandary" in determining how to balance safety and alleviating the pain of suffering. Too much regulation, Klippel said, placed an "undue burden on the health-care system."[9]

What about applying objective science in the refereed academic journals to settle questions once and for all? In 2003 *The Lancet* published a study demonstrating that two high-blood-pressure medications were dramatically more successful when used together than when either was used alone. Almost immediately the study reached number two on *The Lancet's* all-time most-cited papers list. In 2006 several investigators first questioned *The Lancet*, but it took until 2009 for the prestigious scientific journal to issue a retraction for what turned out to have been a totally fabricated study. During the six-plus years before the study was retracted, it affected the health of more than 100,000 patients who used the drug combination and an additional 36,000 who enrolled in follow-up studies.[10]

In fact, retractions have soared in recent years as they have received more popular scrutiny. An exhaustive investigation of research papers published in the top scientific journals found that the number of retractions increased fifteen-fold between 2001 and 2010, while the number of papers increased only 44 percent in that time. Of ten major areas studied, the greatest number of retractions occurred in medicine (from 87 between 2001 and 2005 to 436 from 2006 and 2010), biology (from 69 to 277), and chemistry (from 5 to 147). The time taken to issue retractions jumped from five months in 2000 to thirty-one months in 2009. Of course, the retractions typically receive less emphasis than the original findings.[11]

Worse, the results of many scientific original studies cannot be replicated. The pharmaceutical company Bayer reported that it had to stop nearly two-thirds of its early drug research projects because its experiments could not replicate the results of studies published authoritatively in academic journals. Stanford University's John Ioannidis could not reproduce sixteen of eighteen gene studies and concluded, "We have to take it [on faith] that the findings are OK."[12]

But the FDA regulators are always covered. The bureaucrats give the warnings, and it is up to the physicians, drug companies, medical professionals, and patients to deal with the results. If the companies are sued because of the vague warnings or irreproducible results, that is their problem. In the case of the warfarin warning, the FDA even explicitly told the media to notice that the government did not directly recommend that doctors actually conduct the tests.[13] Whatever this new policy actually was, it was not any more scientific than the old seat-of-the-pants process. The only absolute was that the government was safe whatever happened.

The FDA concedes that it was created in a political atmosphere where "muckraking journalists such as Samuel Hopkins Adams exposed in vivid detail the hazards of the marketplace" and that the picture of private abuse "Upton Sinclair captured in *The Jungle* was the final precipitating force" in creating an FDA.[14] But the government cannot guarantee perfect safety any more than the market can. In July 2007, China executed the head of its state food and drug administration, Zheng Xiaoyu, for allowing tainted lead paint, juice additives, toothpaste, and pet food to enter the marketplace.[15] A bullet to the bureau chief's head may promote some kind of responsibility, but even this extreme regulation cannot solve the problem. The complexity inherent in these decisions makes perfection impossible. If an error is made in the private sector, at least someone can be sued. The principle of "sovereign immunity" in the United States protects government bureaucrats from being responsible to nongovernmental oversight.

Why should people who are dying not be able to decide freely by themselves what risks they should take? Certainly they should be made aware of the best research available, but when the evidence is in, why should government rules force the choices individuals must make when results are usually ambiguous? Is it even moral to force half of terminally ill people in a test to take placebos when the testers know the result will be their death? Why even have a monopoly FDA? Why not use several private research firms on the model of the private, international Underwriters Laboratories to provide an alternative opinion and leave the choice to the individual? When it comes to pain and life and death, why is bureaucracy superior to freedom of choice?

Bureaucracy, however, did have a solution for the problem of negative scientific views about FDA decisions. In 2011, in return for granting reporters scoops on decisions before announcing them officially, the FDA told journalists they could not at the same time report outside scientific opinions—in other words, they couldn't report the views of scientists who disagreed with the FDA opinion. Although scientists could still disagree with official decisions, no one else would know there was any opposition because the media could not report it. Scientific consensus was magically restored in one bold move.[16]

It is impossible to make these things up.

Markets and Complexity

For all its zaniness, Lewis Carroll's *Alice in Wonderland* is chock full of wisdom about the difficulties of rationalizing and controlling behavior. "One day, Alice came to a fork in the road and saw a Cheshire cat in a tree. 'Which road do I take?' she asked. 'Where do you want to go?' was the cat's response. 'I don't know,' Alice answered. 'Then,' said the cat, 'it doesn't matter.'" It is often difficult to know where one should be going.

The progressive justification for scientific governmental regulation is that expert bureaucrats can plan society better than the market. But national government planning just does not seem to work. The government's own trustees for its largest programs—Medicare and Social Security—say these very popular programs will go into insolvency in a mere dozen years. Even the essential function of national defense, the next largest program, gets tied down in red tape and long chains of command against small, highly motivated units; the United States does well in fighting other large bureaucracies, but its bureaucratic administrative problems become manifest in conflicts like those in Vietnam, Iraq, and Afghanistan.[17]

As we have seen, the Department of Homeland Security's airport screening results have been abysmal, and during Hurricane Katrina its big-government bureaucracy frustrated outside relief efforts. At the Agriculture Department, meat and poultry are inspected every day, but inspectors still miss half of all food-borne illnesses in the United States.[18] The prestigious Robb-Silberman Commission found that the once-fabled FBI is so sunk within Department of Justice legalistic rules that it is unable to fight terrorism effectively.[19] The Department of Veterans Affairs has a backlog of nearly one million claims for disability benefits, and the national government cannot even bury its heroes in their proper graves at its most hallowed ground in Arlington Cemetery.[20]

The regulation of air-traffic control is a key responsibility. Between 2007 and 2011, the number of Federal Aviation Administration (FAA) air-traffic controller errors nearly doubled to 1,900 instances, including 50 in the most serious category. The FAA's inspector general told Congress that every day there are probably three to five hundred more close calls between airplanes than the FAA reports.[21] In 2010, the FAA took action against a half dozen controllers for fatigue-related cases. In one case a United Airlines jumbo jet passed within a few hundred feet of a private plane. In another incident the same year a controller placed two airplanes on the same runway, almost causing a disaster.[22] In 2011, a controller was found asleep on the job. Upgrades to equipment are frustrated by bureaucratic errors and political delays, putting U.S. efficiency far behind that of the many nations that have privatized their air-traffic control systems.[23] To solve the problem, the FAA decided to drop the phrase "controller error" and instead designate such errors as "mandatory occurrence reports." Honest.[24]

Perhaps the limits of bureaucratic absurdity were met following the tragic British Petroleum (BP) deep-water rig explosion in mid-2010. After ignoring the gigantic oil spill surging throughout the Gulf of Mexico for nine days, President Obama recognized the political dangers that had so damaged his predecessor over Hurricane Katrina and went furiously into action, pledging "every single available resource," including the U.S. military, to contain the spreading spill. A month later—after the spill had gone from 1,000 gallons a day to 100,000 and repeated BP measures to contain the flow had failed—the president visited again and blamed the government regulatory body in charge, firing his own political appointee.[25]

Secretary of Interior Ken Salazar outdid his boss, threatening to "push BP out of the way" and have the government take over the whole problem. But a subordinate, Coast Guard commandant Thad Allen, pointed out the absurdity of Salazar's statement when he asked, "And replace them [BP] with what?"[26] In fact, the government did not have any resources to do the job. Attorney General Eric Holder opened an investigation against the oil company executives that ultimately resulted in criminal charges.[27] All that was missing was the Queen of Hearts saying "off with their heads."

A central government bureaucracy, as the great economists F. A. Hayek and Ludwig von Mises taught so well, simply does not have the expertise or the on-sight, localized, detailed information necessary to make decisions in the face of overwhelming complexity.[28] And as the wonderful teacher Leonard E. Reed tried to explain to generations of students, no one person or corporation knows how to make even a simple pencil. No individual or group knows how to grow and harvest the right Oregon trees most efficiently; manufacture the saws and vehicles for the fabrication; grow and produce the hemp to bind it; run the logging camps; create and manage the railways to ship the wood to California; apply the skills to the millwork within the thickness of less than a quarter inch; run the waxworks and paint kilns; provide the power and oil; mine the graphite in Ceylon; ship and mix it with the clay from Mississippi; press and lacquer it together; clasp it with brass from copper and zinc from mines around the world; top it with rubber from the East Indies; and distribute and sell it around the globe.[29]

Only if each individual and group concentrated freely on what they knew intimately from specific experience could human social life work, much less be efficient. No oversight bureaucracy could know such details, and the person at the top would not have the slightest idea how to make a pencil or anything else. Neither can the person at the top of a private business, but he has to know only his specialty and delegate the rest to those he can evaluate by whether they contribute to his bottom line or not. That is why specialization of labor is the basis for any sophisticated private economy and why markets are indispensable.

Imagine if the government or some central authority tried to create a plan to transport people from home to work each day. It would be a catastrophe trying to arrange millions of schedules, assigning routes and times, allowing time for refueling, substituting for those late or with sick children, deciding when to purchase new automobiles, choosing what type of cars or buses or trains to use, and on and on. Yet somehow, without such a plan, everyone gets up every morning on his and her own and gets back and forth quite well, thank you. Or what if government tried to assign dwellings to everyone that would be appropriate and fair for all? How could it decide who would live in what type of housing, where, with what type of furnishings, with what other people, using what colors and landscaping? Yet somehow it all happens freely.

The founder of modern economics, Adam Smith, made this insight the foundation of his new science. Before Smith, power and preference were thought to be the necessary elements to direct social life. But he argued that modern life is too complex for some central authority to plan and force effectively. Social order succeeds when partiality and restrictions are removed:

> All systems either of preference or of restraint, therefore, being thus completely taken away, the obvious and simple system of natural liberty establishes itself of its own accord. Every man, as long as he does not violate the laws of justice, is left perfectly free to pursue his own interest his own way, and to bring both his industry and capital into competition with those of any other man, or order of men. The sovereign is completely discharged from a duty, in the attempting to perform which he must always be exposed to innumerable delusions, and for the proper performance of which no human wisdom or knowledge could ever be sufficient, the duty of superintending the industry of private people, and of directing it towards the employments most suitable to the interest of the society.[30]

Only individuals who are actually consuming or producing have the detailed knowledge of their own particular circumstances to solve the innumerable problems required or to decide what they prefer to make or purchase. Because each individual acts freely, Smith continued, by directing that industry in such a manner as its produce may be of the greatest value, he intends only his own gain, and he is in this, as in many other cases, led by an invisible hand to promote an end which was no part of his intention. Nor is it always the worse for the society that it was no part of it. By pursuing his own interest he frequently promotes that of the society more effectually than when he really intends to promote it.[31]

Government was necessary but only for a few key responsibilities:

According to the system of natural liberty, the sovereign has only three duties to attend to; three duties of great importance, indeed, but plain and intelligible to common understandings: first, the duty of protecting the society from violence and invasion of other independent societies; secondly, the duty of protecting, as far as possible, every member of the society from the injustice or oppression of every other member of it, or the duty of establishing an exact administration of justice; and, thirdly, the duty of erecting and maintaining certain public works and certain public institutions which it can never be for the interest of any individual, or small number of individuals, to erect and maintain; because the profit could never repay the expence to any individual or small number of individuals, though it may frequently do much more than repay it to a great society.[32]

Local and regional governments were the best for the third function, for most public works and institutions are close to the people in such matters as education and transportation maintenance. Charitable giving and care were too complex even for these local bureaucracies and so were best left to individuals, churches, and other voluntary associations. By keeping government functions few and intelligible, government could focus its resources to perform its necessary duties in a reasonably efficient manner, while the people could solve life's other problems themselves or with their neighbors and would be left with a large measure of freedom.

Smith did allow a limited role for national government in the economy. It could require banks that did business with the government to extend it credit in emergencies, but only up to the amount of taxes expected to be paid in the "year or two before it comes in," which amounts would have to be paid back during recovery.[33] The government could likewise assure that insurance companies had sufficient capital before they were granted charters.[34] This limited role could justify such actions today as the Federal Reserve's extending credit to the U.S. Treasury (and of course private banks) but clearly not at the levels of 2008–9 and not forcing private firms to participate. As Smith noted, "no human wisdom or knowledge could ever be sufficient" to know how to do more in an efficient way or even well.

This limitation was seen very clearly when the Obama administration proposed new rules to assure there would "never again" be a repeat of the 2008 economic crisis. The "historic" financial reform bill passed into law in mid-2010 was to correct for a presumed "lack of regulation" that allowed the abuse that caused the economic crisis. Of course, as we have seen, the finance sector was already one of the most controlled of any business sector, and to develop the new rules the reform would use precisely the same institutions that had failed to head off the crisis.[35] One supposedly new problem was that the interbank lending rate measure was being abused, but both British and American regulators had earlier refused to take action after being alerted to the fact by private banks that were following the rules.[36] New regulations were requested to control very complicated investment devices called derivatives, which were believed to have been a major cause of the crisis. Yet neither the Federal Reserve nor the Securities and Exchange Commission (SEC) had ever been forbidden from regulating derivatives. Both simply chose not to consider them as necessary to their regulatory duties.[37]

No one can possibly know how to regulate something as complex as the nation's whole economy. So why are so few willing to follow Smith and let the market sort it all out freely? The market responds to how self-interested individuals and groups act in the economy through an extremely large number of free decisions. The market can readjust itself through these demands, but the problem is that no one can predict or control the specific results. Will the market discipline investors or traders or short sellers or corporations or pension funds or unions or employees or regulators—or me? Market freedom will restore prosperity, but apparently most people prefer a world they think someone can control in their interest to the uncertainty of numerous free decisions by their neighbors that will have unforeseen but generally positive effects.

Even most serious supporters of the welfare state concede the efficiency of the market in handling complex decisions.[38] They just want to help it out with a bit of regulation here and there to make it work even better. This is a chimera. There is no Wizard of Oz who knows how, when, and where to stop and start. No individual or group has the detailed knowledge necessary to organize and control this mass complexity.

Do Markets Really Work?

How about market failure? What about depressions? Does not everyone, including the *Wall Street Journal*, now believe that government needs to regulate the market in the face of a serious economic crisis? Did not Democrat Franklin Roosevelt need government regulation to solve the Great Depression of the 1930s? Didn't Republican Richard Nixon rely on wage and price controls to curb the raging inflation of the 1970s? Didn't another Republican, George W. Bush, use massive government regulation and bailouts in 2008—to say nothing about Barack Obama's even greater reliance on regulation—to solve the most recent economic crisis?

But let's look at the record. In truth, Roosevelt did not "solve" the Great Depression by throwing government resources at the problem. In 1932 he actually campaigned against the incumbent president, Republican Herbert Hoover, by calling for a *less* regulatory approach—balancing the budget, adopting hard money (including the gold standard), and decentralizing programs to the states. Hoover clearly did not take a laissez-faire response to the Depression. In his memoirs he explained that he specifically rejected Treasury Secretary Andrew Mellon's "leave it alone" free-market solution in favor of his own "economic modernization" regulatory approach. Hoover took many progressive governmental actions to quell the Great Depression: using the financial power of the Federal Reserve, jawboning business on wages and state governments on welfare, undertaking massive federal building and reclamation projects, forcing repatriation of 500,000 Mexicans to open jobs for Americans, pushing through a massive national tariff to encourage purchase of U.S. products, and instituting the New Deal prototype Reconstruction Finance Corporation.[39]

None of it worked. The failed Hoover lost to Roosevelt in a landslide in 1932. But after taking office, Roosevelt did not back off from his predecessor's regulatory approach. On the contrary, he threw the whole power of the government against the Depression. Still, nothing worked—not the Fed credit expansion, not the "pump priming" stimulus spending, not the alphabet soup of regulatory agencies. The Depression continued for a dozen years after the government began its interventionist approach, and the U.S. economy did not recover until World War II.[40]

In spite of this record, and numerous recessions in between, most intellectuals, journalists, and politicians are still enthralled by New Deal mythology. The New Deal may have failed to solve the Great Depression, but the morality play of "greedy businessmen dispatched by virtuous progressive government experts to restore the public interest" retains its power to attract votes. Sure enough, Presidents George W. Bush and Barack Obama copied the FDR plan almost exactly when another economic crisis developed—and sure enough, vigorous recovery eluded them for years.

There are only three times in history that the stock market lost 20 percent or more of its value in a two-day period—1929, 1987, and 2008. In 1929 and 2008, the president took the standard course and threw the whole New Deal playbook at the economy—and in each case failed to fix the problem. What about 1987? So-called Black Monday brought a somewhat sharper decline than in 1929. But as Michael Reagan quipped, "My Dad did nothing; and it worked!" President Ronald Reagan, rejecting those in his administration who recommended even closing the stock markets, followed an Adam Smith, hands-off, let-the-market-seek-its-level approach—and the economy quickly healed, under the economic logic that markets cannot go up until potential buyers think prices have hit bottom.[41]

Reagan was successful with a market approach in 1987, and "leave it alone" worked after Reagan's inherited first recession in 1981 too, with a little help from lowering taxes and government spending. Earlier, Andrew Mellon had implemented President Warren Harding's "return to normalcy" from Woodrow Wilson's tax and regulatory regime to produce the post–World War I recovery. He was probably correct, too, in his advice to President Hoover in the 1929 crises to let the market seek its own level, advice that Hoover rejected. Most earlier presidents had also let the market work. Allowing freedom to readjust the complexity is the way the market should operate. The proof is that no one remembers the 1987 crisis today. Smith did not promise that there would not be crises, only that the market could right itself if allowed to readjust. Nothing else works and only delays recovery, as the Japanese have proved: after nearly two decades of stimulus efforts, their economy is still stagnant, and Japan now has the highest government debt in the world, at 210 percent of its total wealth.[42]

Do nations that rely on more government regulation do better or worse than those that rely on freer markets? Empirically, there is little question that market or capitalist economic freedom is very highly correlated with per capita wealth and the successful elimination of poverty. In 2012 the statistical correlation between economic freedom and economic prosperity among the countries of the world was robust ($r = .65$, $R^2 = .42$), and it has been so annually since 1995, when these data were first collected.[43] The historical continuity is confirmed by the fact that two-thirds of the most economically free nations are European countries or their former colonies. The United States was tied for fourth in economic freedom and was second in wealth per person The data are unambiguous: freedom works, at least to provide economic prosperity.[44]

What Makes Freedom Work?

Economic freedom and prosperity are also highly correlated with political freedom. Freedom House, a bipartisan research institute (one of its founders was Eleanor Roosevelt), measures the degree of political freedom in the nations of the world. Only 29 of the world's 217 countries achieve a rating of 1.0 in political freedom, the best ranking on the Freedom House scale. These most politically free nations are the same Western nations with high economic freedom scores. Most of the next most free (1.5 score) are Western too, with Japan, Taiwan, and South Africa also qualifying as highly free nations. All these nations tend to be among the world's wealthiest.[45] Although it is not certain whether political freedom produces economic freedom or vice versa, it is clear that the two are closely associated.

What besides freedom is necessary for economic success? A World Bank–sponsored study measured other indicators to see why some nations were growing economically and some were not. Surprisingly, the degree of democracy in a nation (called "voice" or popular voice) did not correlate with growth in wealth at all and was only weakly related to political freedom. Much more important than voting or democratic participation or level of education was whether a nation had a strong rule of law. This seemed particularly important for developing nations, where too much democracy actually held them back from prosperity as leaders took rash actions to please the people rather than following the law to protect individuals and their property.[46]

Philosophers as far apart as Karl Marx and John Locke were clear that the legal rules essential for markets concern property. Both agreed that private property was essential to the rise of markets and that all that was necessary to end capitalism was to eliminate private property. Ancient Greece and Rome provided greater legal and moral protection to property than "barbarian" states, and this was at least somewhat responsible for their greater economic prosperity. The Hebrew Bible likewise emphasized protection of private property. Property law survived to some degree even after the fall of Rome and was reinforced by the fact that literally every piece of property in Europe had to be defended in the disorder that followed.[47]

Property rights became more secure in western Europe as nobility, church, manors, guilds, and cities gradually acquired and defended them against relatively weak national governments. The Eastern Roman Empire, meanwhile, did not have such strong mediating institutions, and property rights were much more tenuous.[48] Classicist and military historian Victor Davis Hanson has even given credit to the tenacity of private property ownership for the military superiority of the West. Acknowledged, secure, and independent ownership resulted in the West's more dogged, imaginative, and technologically superior military institutions.[49] Private property became even more secure in the West as it received additional protection from the universalist moral and legal codes developed in the monasteries and spread throughout Europe by a universal canon law. By the eleventh century, Europe had begun to outpace the rest of the world economically.[50]

Why did Muslim states, for example, not grow economically beyond a certain point? Islamic law prided itself that there were detailed rules to cover every aspect of life. Even when there was no rule covering a specific case, all decisions had to be derived from some existing rule.[51] This was true for economics as well, where detailed regulation of commerce was characteristic. As authoritative decisions accumulated, people had less flexibility to adapt to new conditions. There was no moral right to private property, leaving all wealth under the control of Allah's regent, the state. Property was distributed by the all-powerful caliph or sultan and recalled to the state upon death. Because there was no incentive to care for property that could not be transferred to future generations, Muslim lands that had been fruitful often literally turned into deserts because no one had an interest in the long-term development of specific properties.[52] Islam's state property regime survived for five hundred years under the Ottomans, but the complexity of modern communication and markets started to overwhelm its brittle and unproductive hierarchical system. It finally broke down in the twentieth century.

Most of the world followed the Ottoman centralization rather than the West, so the gulf between poor and wealthy nations began to widen. Even within the West, the Anglo-American nations that emphasized decentralized, common-law-based private property proved to be more successful than continental European countries whose comprehensive civil law systems finely regulated how property could be used and transferred. As *Wall Street Journal* columnist David Wessel has observed, these legal decisions made so long ago still affect the greater success of the pragmatic United States and Britain, which have larger stock markets, more shareholding citizens, and greater economic prosperity than the rest of Europe. They have also affected how the West as a whole has prospered compared with the rest of the world.[53]

Second only to the rule of law as an influence on how well nations develop economically is the amount of government spending. The World Bank study showed that the greater the percentage of total national income government spent, the more prosperity for the general population was frustrated. This finding indicates that government spending takes away from what the private sector could spend more efficiently. Government's innumerable regulations apparently confuse and discourage innovation, especially by the entrepreneur, who is the human engine of market capitalism.[54] Census data from 1976 to 2005 show that all the new jobs netted in the United States came from start-up firms, with entrepreneurs creating some 300,000 new firms each year.[55] For total employment to increase, these new firms must prosper. As *Washington Post* economic columnist Robert Samuelson noted, "It is all about risk-taking. The good news is that the entrepreneurial instinct seems deeply engrained" in the United States even during the Great Recession, since many people want to be "their own boss" and "crave fame and fortune." The bad news is that "political leaders seem largely oblivious to burdensome government policies" that restrict this entrepreneurial creativity.[56]

The World Bank study even demonstrated that government spending does not lead to redistribution of income to the poor, contrary to the promises of socialists and progressives. The "distribution effect" of government spending is negative, in fact, highlighting that most welfare-state spending actually goes to the middle class in popular health, education, and retirement programs, not to the poor. The wealthy are often blamed, but the top 1 percent of income earners in the United States at the height of the boom in 2007 earned 19.6 percent of the income but paid 41 percent of the income taxes, about the same as in pre-boom 1999. Surprisingly, an authoritative study from the Organization of Economic Cooperation and Development found that "taxation is most progressively distributed in the Unites States . . . and least progressive in the Nordic countries [notably Sweden], France and Switzerland," the more progressive Western nations.[57]

Given all these data, it seems as if rule of law is required to provide legitimate order and to secure property, which can advance economic freedom and the development of markets, which can lead to prosperity, which in turn can allow political freedom. Too much governmental regulation and centrally controlled spending can frustrate this progression. Only a few nations, twenty-nine in number, have been able to follow this free path to success, the most flourishing—on rule of law, political freedom, market freedom, and economic prosperity combined—being the United States.[58]

Perils of Freedom

The evidence that economic and political freedom leads to prosperity and other valued outcomes is overwhelming. Even the *Communist Manifesto* conceded the revolutionary nature of market capitalism and the fact that "the bourgeoisie, during its rule of scarce one hundred years, has created more massive and more colossal productive forces than have all preceding generations together." Of course, Karl Marx did not think this was sustainable. His idea—taken from the economist David Ricardo—that there was a predetermined "many buyers, many sellers" form to the market led him to predict that over time there would be fewer and fewer sellers and, ultimately, overproduction, crisis, and the collapse of capitalism.[59]

To the economic historian Joseph Schumpeter, however, there was no form to the market whatsoever. The market was simply the result of the free decisions made under its general rules, predominantly those against coercion and fraud, no matter the number of buyers and sellers. Schumpeter argued that the most important type of competition was not even between existing firms within narrow industry markets. The most important competition for wagon makers came not from other wagon makers but from a new product, the automobile; adding machine or typewriter manufacturers faced their stiffest competition with the advent of computers.[60] Schumpeter called this process "creative destruction," which he regarded as the engine of the market. Unless old structures could be swept away or severely modified, better ways of doing things could not break through. A free market would allow new efficient ways and ideas to "destroy" (peacefully and freely) old ways and ideas.[61]

The whole point of the market is that no one person or group can control it. The resulting market freedom cannot be ordered or predicted. Left alone, competition will drive out the inefficient and outdated, producing more efficient means that create more wealth and prosperity for the overwhelming proportion of the population. Markets are the opposite of the stability of Ricardan "perfect competition." Rather, the essence of market freedom is to produce change: freedom and capitalism have no peer in creating new products and wealth. In government, by contrast, bureaus are rarely eliminated and have even been labeled "immortal" by the experts in the field.[62] Peter Drucker argued that this is one of the great benefits of the market over government: growth requires elimination of past failures, and no one loves businesses enough to care when they pass away.[63]

But while increasing wealth, liberty, life expectancies, and living standards, the market can also undermine valued traditions. Creative destruction constantly sweeps away old things and ancient ways. Because free choice often had unexpected consequences for culture and community, there was a price for the new prosperity. Prosperity, not collapse, was capitalism's weakness, as market rationality and the calculating attitude this engendered led people to question whether the desire to take risks or the traditional moral restraints that underlay the rule of law were themselves rational. The only force powerful enough to resist was the national government, so communities, firms, and social institutions often ran to it to escape the changes. But taming the hyperrationalized market increasingly fettered it, protecting less rational (but valued) traditional relationships that were inefficient. As these governmental regulations multiplied over time, they undermined the flexibility and growth that gave the market its very legitimacy.[64]

The enormously influential nineteenth-century thinker Ralph Waldo Emerson condemned the traditionalist resistance as a threat to freedom. Community traditions suppressed individual freedom by enforcing conformity, he argued—not only through raw state power but even by simple communal pressure on feelings of empathy. All human behavior must come freely from one's own individual beliefs, Emerson insisted. Freedom must liberate the individual from all constraints of family, community, and tradition, leaving him as the highest value, over all social and moral norms. To be a free individual, one must not follow the community, the crowd: "Is not a man better than a town?" Even mother and father were shunned in favor of individual freedom. Indeed, "no law is sacred to me but that of my nature." Sympathy must be replaced by "truth and health in rough electric shocks." "Nothing is at last sacred but the integrity of your own mind." "Obey your heart" is the only moral rule.[65] Both the means and ends of life are individual freedom.

Emerson and his associate Henry Thoreau rejected every governmental moral claim against the individual. Government "can have no pure right over my person and property but what I concede it," proclaimed Thoreau. No force, no God, no community, no neutral judge, no majority, no outside standard, no separation of powers could justify state action against the individual's will. It was not even necessary for abuse to be substantial to justify refusing obedience to the state. Thoreau objected to a tax of a few cents, refusing to pay it on principle. Any action the state took without the consent of every individual was unjust and need not be obeyed. "That government is best that governs not at all" was Thoreau's motto.[66]

The philosopher Friedrich Nietzsche took these objections to their logical conclusion. Since the only reality is "man," the individual, society is nothing but individual men and women. Yet, being weak, most will tend to be captured by social institutions. Only the superman can face this hard reality to throw off all society, all institutions, all myths, all external values, all comforting traditions, all cultural lies, even all class restrictions. Man is alone, without God or his rules or his governments. The superman must express himself. He is a "free spirit" who transvalues all values in himself, the only measure of everything. Even the value of pity, of mercy, is only manipulation by formal religion and society, especially through Christianity, as its means to suppress the creativity of the superior person. The superman is the only ideal end for the free, creative, uninhibited, individualistic spirit of modern man, as well as for the iron leaders required for the radical changes necessary to root out the existing powers and the societal inhibitions they support.[67]

If Nietzsche is correct, then could his nemesis Thomas Hobbes also be correct that when free individuals are restrained by nothing but themselves, the result must be a "war of all against all," making the lives of all individuals "solitary, poor, nasty, brutish, and short"? Does a powerful central state—indeed a leviathan—become the necessary countersolution for rational individualists who value social peace over a dangerous freedom?[68] Is individual freedom as the only goal self-destructive in the long run?

How Freedom Worked

Most Americans would recoil from the extremes of Emerson, Nietzsche, and Hobbes and point to their own exceptionalism to demonstrate what represents true freedom. The place to begin is where everyone else does, with the remarkable French aristocrat Alexis de Tocqueville and his masterful study of social life in the then newly established United States.

In trying to explain how America was different from every other nation, Tocqueville asked, What prime force causes social activity in different countries? In his native France, if one wanted some major or even minor task to be performed, one went to the high officials of the national government. If they approved, it was done; if the government opposed it, nothing happened. In England, if some action was to be considered, one went to its socially conscious aristocracy. If this powerful elite favored the idea, it happened; otherwise it did not. In America, he discovered, if some matter was to be accomplished, it would be up to the people who raised the idea to freely organize to undertake the task themselves:

> Americans of all ages, all conditions, and all dispositions, constantly form associations. They have not only commercial and manufacturing companies, in which all take part, but associations of a thousand other kinds—religious, moral, serious, futile, extensive, or restricted, enormous or diminutive. The Americans make associations to give entertainments, to found establishments for education, to build inns, to construct churches, to diffuse books, to send missionaries to the antipodes; and in this manner they found hospitals, prisons, and schools.

If it be proposed to advance some truth or to foster some feeling by the encouragement of a great example, they form a society. Wherever, at the head of some new undertaking, you see the government in France, or a man of rank in England, in the United States you will be sure to find an association.[69]

Liberty, then, immediately became communal as well, since individuals founded free associations. With no hereditary nobility and a wide franchise, there was a certain but by no means precise equality between citizens that made them feel part of the community and willing to act voluntarily to support it. Tocqueville believed that this widespread and free participation in formal and informal associations constituted democracy in action—direct civic action was much more important than was mere voting participation. The only effective government Tocqueville discovered in America was local government, which was similar to a voluntary association in its spontaneity and limited powers. Local government had much less expertise, he conceded, but it was more effective because it was present in the community and knew local circumstances, and everyone—or a sufficient number, in any event—willingly chipped in.[70]

Associations and local government performed much more work than state and national government combined. While each person first attended to his individual business, mainly farming, at bottom success rested on individuals' pitching in and doing what was needed for neighbors when the situation demanded it. Paradoxically, this limit to central power made the national government stronger, not weaker, in the hearts of its countrymen. The national government, doing little to help the citizens, also did little to force or oppress him. The American government, being less intrusive in people's lives, could be loved that much more.

Tocqueville's America was both individualistic and communal; it supported freedom and tradition; it respected individual property and neighborliness; its people were entrepreneurial and conservative—all at the same time. Tocqueville found individualism, but it was individualism within a communal setting. It was not Emersonian individualism without family obligation, sympathy for neighbor, or loyalty to town. Often living in sparse rural areas, individuals and families were forced to rely on themselves. But they also freely helped neighbors. Even the most isolated individuals relied on neighbors, towns, and voluntary associations to do what could not be accomplished alone.

Still, Tocqueville was not sanguine about America's future. Democracy meant that political power resided in the people, who in time would be tempted to call on their government "to secure their gratifications and to watch over their fate" rather than do it themselves or with their neighbors. Freedom could survive only if most people continued to take care of themselves and if strong property rights supported their independence. But most people would rather pursue their daily "petty pleasures," and democratic leaders would indulge them in their ways, not daring to correct them for fear of being turned out of office. In providing more and more benefits, the government would make people more and more dependent. Popular rule would override any divisions or limitations placed on it. Great and small fortunes would be swept away to fund this welfare state so that no independent leadership could stand against the popular tide.[71]

> Their taste for physical gratifications must be regarded as the original source of that secret inquietude which the actions of the Americans betray, and of that inconstancy of which they afford fresh examples every day. He who has set his heart exclusively upon the pursuit of worldly welfare is always in a hurry, for he has but a limited time at his disposal to reach it, to grasp it, and to enjoy it. The recollection of the brevity of life is a constant spur to him. Besides the good things which he possesses, he every instant fancies a thousand others which death will prevent him from trying if he does not try them soon. This thought fills him with anxiety, fear, and regret, and keeps his mind in ceaseless trepidation, which leads him perpetually to change his plans and his abode. If in addition to the taste for physical well-being a social condition be superadded, in which the laws and customs make no condition permanent, here is a great additional stimulant to this restlessness of temper. Men will then be seen continually to change their track, for fear of missing the shortest cut to happiness.[72]

Tocqueville thought the American balance between individualism and community responsibility, liberty and law, and freedom and tradition would last some time, and it did. He warned that the terrible stain of slavery and its ultimate elimination might precipitate an undermining of law, a resort to force and limitation of freedom, and it did.[73] By the early twentieth century the wealth produced by freedom and the market turned America into the world's most prosperous nation. But by then the old "laws and customs" had eroded. The restless pursuit of materialistic happiness seemed to be the only true freedom to many individuals.

Although Tocqueville thought traditional law and custom were essential to create and sustain procedural freedom, more Americans came to see these as hindering their freedom. Following Emerson, they saw freedom as the goal rather than the means toward happiness. Laws and custom may promote economic freedom and prosperity, but they also tell the individual what he or she should not do. To more and more Americans in the twenty-first century, this seemed not to be freedom at all.

Six

---⇒◆◇⇐---

RULE OF LAW

FOR THE FIRST TIME EVER, in 2010 the United States slipped from being rated "free" to only "mostly free" economically in the authoritative Heritage Foundation/Wall Street Journal *Index of Economic Freedom*. That year, the U.S. decline in freedom was the largest percentage drop of any major nation's. In the Chrysler and General Motors expropriations, freedom of contract was undermined; government overregulation, overtaxation, and overspending increased generally; and freedom to invest, the soundness of money, and financial security all declined. Corruption increased too. The United States declined even further over the next two rating years.[1]

As reported in the previous chapter, after analyzing forty years of data from just about every nation, World Bank researchers found that having a sound rule of law was the number-one prerequisite for freedom and economic prosperity. To understand America's decline, we must look deeply into the idea of rule of law.

The philosopher who most influenced American ideas about society and government, John Locke—following a long Western tradition—made rule of law the defining characteristic of a sound, free, and prosperous society.[2] To Locke, individual freedom was first because it came directly from a Creator who made man free even to reject this God and his commands. No lesser authority or power could take life, freedom, or property from the created without the individual's consent; these were moral rights that could not be altered by circumstance, time, power, or government.

Contrary to Emerson's ideal, however, Locke did not portray man as an isolated individual. Rather, man was born into a family, and that created social obligations, ones that did not end fully even on maturity.[3] To protect himself, his family, and his possessions, man was soon forced into communities of families that required customs, laws, and understandings so social life could proceed in some peace and safety. All were created morally equal with equal rights, but as the world filled up, accidents, oversights, trespasses, and outright coercion took place among neighbors, and life and property became "very unsafe, very insecure."[4]

Once having consensually entered political society for safety's sake, man saw his freedom limited. It became freedom only under the law set by the community. Disagreements arose, especially over property in land, animals, food, and the rest. These required legal standards, a very particular rule of law that respected each man's nature. The first requirement, Locke held, was a prior "established, settled, known law, received and allowed by common consent to be the standard of right and wrong and the common measure to decide all controversies between them." Once common standards were made into formal laws, they must be administered by a representative institution that "neither must nor can transfer the power of making laws to anybody else." Formal rule of law was "to govern by promulgated, established laws, not to be varied in particular cases but to have one rule for rich and poor, the favorite at court and the countryman at plow."[5]

The modern theorist F. A. Hayek, often called a libertarian, argued that there simply is no such thing as pure laissez-faire freedom—a society or market with no rules. Coercion and fraud are almost universally seen as requiring control, and in the modern world this control comes from state legislation. There must be legislation to establish property rights, what cannot be contracted (for example, slavery), when contracts can be broken or properly infringed, and how they are to be adjudicated. Although fewer statutes make it easier for citizens to know the law so they may obey it, and make it easier for government to administer, there must be some authoritative moral standards. Law is even more fundamental than legislation, being based on historic community traditions. When legislation agrees with the informal rules, it can be better understood, it is considered legitimate, and it is more likely to be obeyed.[6]

Hayek and Locke agreed that the essential quality of rule of law was to produce the conditions for societal freedom and order by ensuring that all are treated fairly and equally under set rules. On this point they departed from many other commentators, beginning with Plato, who insisted that it was not enough to apply fair rules equally but that the *results* must be fair too. Locke and Hayek argued that predetermined results were inconsistent with the dignity of individual freedom, which cannot be forced in advance of decisions. The only requirement is that rules do not unfairly favor one individual, group, or interest above another. Fair rules are like those in baseball: if the rules are agreed on beforehand, the same for all, and fairly enforced, the result is fair even if the resulting score is 20–0. Applying a single fair standard to all equally should be considered the "rule of law." It is a difficult standard to meet. Most nations at most times create special provisions advantaging particular nationalities, races, classes, interests, religions, genders, ages, and groups over others.[7]

Locke's understanding of the rule of law was incorporated into early American law and ruled during our country's worldwide rise to prosperity and predominance. Yet it was not universally accepted even then. The Platonic accusation echoed through time for its lack of guaranteed fair results. Even more, many no longer considered God and his law, and the traditions derived from them, as credible foundations on which to secure liberties. To these, law must be based on human foundations, which necessarily meant on the most sacred secular symbol, the national state. Government rather than the Creator would become the repository of rights and freedoms. This contrary view had its roots in the philosopher Thomas Hobbes and was systematically formulated in the nineteenth century by Jeremy Bentham, both of whom argued that law was simply any procedurally proper command of a sovereign backed by force.[8]

In this view, the law should not be set by any religious revelation, ancient custom, or tradition of the people but should be based on reason—on what would be good for the largest number of society as determined by the most reasonable in it. Rule of law then meant that the law ruled: the commands of a nation's legal political institutions must be obeyed. Law was what the wise rulers, legislators, and judges said it was because these official conclusions were the best for the safety, good, and freedom of the people as a whole. The citizen may be able to give advice on the composition of the law, but his real responsibility was to obey—or suffer the consequences of noncompliance—for the sake of the common good.

By the twentieth century this strictly utilitarian view was modified somewhat by progressive legal positivist theorists such as H. L. A. Hart, who conceded that there must be some normative sense to the law. But in Hart's view, the norms to be followed were those of the ruling legal authorities, not those based on customary understanding. These authorities would take an "internal view" of the evolving "official" beliefs of the governing political order and apply it to changing circumstances so that the law best expressed the current good of the people, even if the people did not recognize it as such. These decisions still "generally must be obeyed," and they "must be effectively accepted as common public standards of official behavior by its officials." As with the pure utilitarians, law was to be based on the social facts of reality as interpreted by the legal authorities, not on any independent moral rules or rights or traditions such as those in customary, natural, or divine law.[9]

The problem, of course, is that social facts and officialdom change and therefore so do official standards about what the law and freedom are. Also, official opinion can differ from the standards valued by the public, as Hart conceded. Interpretations of law can be changed at will to conform to the "facts" as officials see them. Hart even allowed officials, as a means to achieve the supposedly higher public good, to justify decisions by appealing to public senses of duty and obligation without believing in such morality. There can be no stability or predictability to the law; no higher power or ideal can be appealed to. Official opinion must be superior to public opinion because it is more informed and rational. If popular views, laws, or customs conflict with the official opinion, public elites, especially in the courts, have the right to overrule them.[10]

Imposing law against the public will seems a strange doctrine for a society presumably based on freedom and popular consent. Yet this view underlies most modern U.S. law. It claims the right of judges and lawyers to decide the law in the face of public opposition when the people are wrong. This view of the rule of law as changeable is precisely why Alexis de Tocqueville predicted that "inquietude," anxiety, and restlessness of temper would undermine the true rule of law as he understood it, which was based on set standards and principles. If there are no set principles, law can end up meaning anything, justifying any conduct, or making any interpretation valid as long as public authorities say it is the law.

Consider the 2004 conviction of media personality Martha Stewart. She had heard that ImClone stock had "something going on" and had asked its CEO what it was. Without receiving a satisfactory answer, she told her broker to sell her shares. No traditional law court would have had a problem with this type of decision to protect oneself in the face of uncertainty. Stewart was charged with insider trading—that is, taking advantage of private, insider knowledge of company events to dispose of stock before its value fell. Such activity did not even become a U.S. crime until the 1960s, when under evolving legal positivist thinking, bureaucrats broadened the meaning of a general antifraud provision.[11] Insider-trading regulations remain vague, so much so that until 2012, regulators excluded Congress and its staff from that rule. (Congress finally included its members under the regulations after news reports exposed how senators and congressmen were being treated less severely than the public, and how some had in fact profited from confidential information they received as lawmakers.)[12]

Despite the murky nature of the regulations, prosecutors could not convince a sympathetic judge to accept the insider-trading charge against Martha Stewart. When that charge was dismissed, prosecutors claimed that Stewart had not told the truth to investigators, although that was based on the word of a single employee at her securities firm who could have been prosecuted himself if he did not testify against her. His testimony against the rich and famous personality did convince a jury she had lied but only because Stewart was denied the right to raise the commonsense point in response: the prosecution did not have evidence that an underlying crime ever occurred, so why did she have to answer questions in the first place? As the economist Alan Reynolds noted at the time:

> Martha Stewart has been convicted of conspiring to cover-up a crime she was not accused of having committed—insider trading. She was convicted of "lying" but never charged with perjury. Martha Stewart was also convicted of "obstructing justice" without any explanation of how the prosecution of anyone but herself could have been obstructed by her first attorney's explanation of what motivated her to make a perfectly legal sale of ImClone stock.[13]

Martha Stewart's prosecution was meant to send a message that the wealthy and successful must follow the securities laws. But she was not convicted of violating those laws. The Stewart case shows what can happen when public officials have so much leeway to say what the law means, without widely understood standards. The classic "insider trading" prosecution occurred when two railroad yard employees saw men in business suits poking around nearby flatcars, concluded that their company was for sale, and sold their company stock.[14] What is wrong with that?

Although the rich and famous can hire expensive lawyers, even they are often easy game, for envy is a widespread human failing, as Tocqueville warned for democratic societies. In fact, the Stewart prosecution was instigated by a political leak followed by a formal letter from the House Energy and Commerce Committee, whose members were angry because she chose not to testify before them.[15] Without firm standards of what constitutes illegal conduct, ambitious officials can ignore the rule of law and court public approval instead.

Law in the United States Today

A nation's tort system to settle injuries against persons or property is the center of any civil legal system. *Washington Post* columnist Sebastian Mallaby was blunt in assessing the state of civil law in the United States today: "The tort system is an abomination." It is "unpredictable."[16] In the most comprehensive study available, the actuarial consulting firm Tillinghast-Towers Perrin estimated that by 2003 the tort system cost $246 billion—that's $845 in costs for each American per year. As a share of gross domestic product (GDP), America's tort system was the world's costliest; the second highest-spending country, Italy, had legal overhead almost one-quarter lower. But the "shocking thing," as Mallaby wrote, was that less than half of those hundreds of billions of dollars went to injured plaintiffs. An incredible 54 percent of the total went to administrative costs, with 33 percent going exclusively to the lawyers.[17]

The greatest problem the study discovered was that "the location of the trial, the composition of the jury and the depth of the defendant's pockets—not just the size of the injury"—determined how much the defendants were awarded. This "haphazard nature of the tort payouts undermines the potential salutary effect on corporate behavior" that is the larger purpose of a civil justice system. Court settlements are meant to compensate for injuries to individuals and affected parties—the greater the injury, the greater the payout remedy, supposedly. The social benefit is that companies adjust their behavior to avoid future injuries to employees and customers and thus to escape future damage payments. But if settlements are haphazard rather than based on "known standards," or if judgments hit the richest party nearby even if not at fault, companies or medical doctors do not know how to change their procedures to avoid additional customer or patient injuries in the future.[18]

Tort law abuse is alarming enough, but the increasingly capricious nature of criminal law is even more so. The University of Michigan Law School and the Center on Wrongful Convictions at Northwestern University School of Law recently compiled a National Registry of Exonerations to list all known exonerations from criminal convictions in the United States since 1989. This registry now contains 891 case files of the estimated 2,000 legal exonerations as a result of pardons, dismissals, acquittals, or certificates of innocence during this period. DNA evidence has resulted in 37 percent of exonerations, 63 percent in cases of accused rape.[19]

The results are disturbing. A 56 percent majority of homicide exonerations resulted from findings of misconduct by police or other legal officials.

The leading contributing causes to these miscarriages of justice, 66 percent, were perjury or false accusation—mostly deliberate misidentifications (44 percent). Some of those exonerated were falsely implicated by a codefendant who confessed. Homicide exonerations represent 76 percent of all false confessions in the data. Juveniles and the mentally disabled were, respectively, five times and nine times more likely to falsely confess than adults without known mental disabilities.

Or consider sexual assault exonerations. These resulted overwhelmingly (80 percent) from cases with mistaken eyewitness identifications. Some 53 percent of all sexual assault exonerations resulted from mistaken eyewitness identifications involving black men who were accused of raping white women. The study suggests this huge racial disproportion (about 10 to 1) is probably caused primarily by the difficulty of cross-racial eyewitness identification. Many sexual assault cases also include bad forensic evidence (37 percent). Like adult rape exonerations, robbery exonerations overwhelmingly involve cases with mistaken eyewitness identifications (81 percent). Child sex abuse exonerations are even more troubling, primarily resulting from fabricated crimes that never occurred at all (74 percent).

The report concedes, "Even 2,000 exonerations over 23 years is a tiny number in a country with 2.3 million people in prison and jails." The problem is that we do not know how many others exist, and logic suggests there must be more. "If we could spot them easily they wouldn't happen in the first place."[20] Moreover, 83 percent of the exonerations were for the serious crimes of murder and rape, but these represent only 2 percent of crimes. Surely, criminal actions that receive less publicity have similar problems. It is difficult to know. The Center on Wrongful Convictions will not even investigate if a prisoner has less than ten years to serve, given limited resources, the time necessary to gather the facts, and the greater stakes involved elsewhere.

Targeting the "Quick Hits"

A rash of business failures in 2000 left many investors and employees in a particularly bitter mood. The Houston energy trader Enron was especially fast and loose with contracts, and it quickly became the emblem of all that was wrong with corporate practices. Given the extent of Enron's corporate fraud and the attention the scandal drew, it is easy to forget that the legal case against involved prosecutorial overreach. When Enron failed in 2001, government prosecutors won plea agreements from the company's chief financial officer, who apparently was the mastermind behind the scheme, and his spouse (who was assistant treasurer) by threatening a longer sentence for the wife than the one-year term she finally received. The chief executive officer and the lead accountant were also charged, even though the main issue against the higher-ups was the mushy area of "conspiracy" to hide fraud rather than criminal fraud itself.

Charging these officials directly responsible apparently was not enough for the prosecutors. They also went after Enron chairman Kenneth L. Lay, who was better known, richer, and more sophisticated and so made a more popular target even though he had left company management to the CEO and returned to the chairmanship only after problems developed. John C. Coffee Jr., a Columbia University law professor, said Lay was "a distant, hands-off manager who had resigned and come back" and was unlikely to have known the details of the fraud. Lay apparently did tell stockholders and employees that the company was doing better than it was and encouraged purchasing stock, stating that he was doing so himself, which he did. Even though he and his directors personally lost an incredible $250 million on their purchase and sales of stock, he was still charged with conspiracy to defraud stockholders.[21] Lay's wife, Linda, was threatened with prosecution to pressure him to settle. Even though she actually had made money, unlike him, she was not finally charged. The technical accounting evidence was confusing to the lay jury, and, of course, a company chairman and the CEO must have "conspired" (means "agree together") on something.

The chief executive officer of failed Tyco, L. Dennis Kozlowski, was another unsympathetic businessman who faced prosecution. Kozlowski first won by hung jury but was convicted the second time, after the jury heard about his spending $2 million on a birthday party. In many of the cases against business, the government prosecutors settled with the defendants on whom they had the most proof of guilt in return for testimony against the more rich and famous. While the testimony of an obviously guilty party would seem to be tainted, it was sufficient for a jury that could never comprehend spending a million dollars on someone's birthday.

Another chief executive to face the wrath of the prosecutors was Bernard Ebbers of WorldCom. A *Washington Post* investigative report found that the government's "best evidence" against him was the testimony of the admittedly guilty company chief financial officer, who had made a deal with prosecutors to testify that Ebbers ordered him to fix the books. Witnesses like this are seen as "tutors" who can lead juries, according to Fordham University law professor Daniel Richman. Ebbers did not use e-mail and there was no written evidence, but that did not make much difference in a "his word against yours" courtroom world of a little guy (and his more invisible lawyer) against a rich, pushy CEO, regardless of the truth. Richard Scrushy of HealthSouth was also convicted of conspiracy on the word of a guilty defendant who had made a deal.[22]

Between 2002 and 2006, the Department of Justice Corporate Fraud Task Force convicted or plea-bargained into jail 82 chief executives, 85 corporate presidents, 102 vice presidents, 36 chief financial officers, 14 chief operating officers, and 1,000 managers, relying heavily on conspiracy and other such vague charges. Under its "Principles of Federal Prosecution of Business Organizations," prosecutors could rule that a corporation was not "cooperating" with an investigation if it refused to waive its attorney-client privilege in regard to employee conversations or if a company paid attorneys' fees for its employees. Threatened with becoming targets of the investigation, most firms were intimidated enough to "cooperate" against their employees, making it more expensive for the latter to defend themselves. It is no wonder the Justice Department task force was able to rack up so many trophies. The only problem was that in a case against the accounting firm KPMG, federal judge Lewis A. Kaplan ruled that the task force's main weapon, its "Principles of Federal Prosecution of Business Organizations," violated the Sixth and Fourteenth Amendments and dismissed the charges.[23]

Even vindication is expensive and morally exhausting. In 2005 ten former WorldCom directors settled a class-action suit by paying more than $18 million each from their own pockets—they were ordered not to use directors' insurance—representing one-fifth of their collective net worth. A few days later, ten former Enron directors agreed to pay $13 million each of their own money to settle a shareholder suit. The settlements were made in spite of a federal judge's ruling that there were no grounds to seek redress from the Enron directors on fraud or insider-trading charges. None of the directors was shown to have participated in or known about the frauds involved in the cases. But they were easy targets, including the wife of a former U.S. senator.[24]

At the same time, obvious frauds like Ponzi operators Bernie Madoff and R. Allen Sanford were reported to authorities numerous times but were never charged. Madoff survived an incredible four complaints to the SEC over the years as he was bilking billions of dollars from numerous investors using a not very sophisticated means.[25] Sanford was even more mysterious, since numerous people inside his operations had reported him. Sanford was investigated in 1997, 1998, 2002, and 2004, and SEC investigators actually referred his case to the enforcement division for running a Ponzi scheme. Each time, Sanford simply did not submit the requested information and the SEC declined to act. In 2010, when the SEC inspector general asked the

SEC enforcement staff why they had not prosecuted cases such as Madoff and Sanford, they admitted that senior staff did not seek Ponzi investigations because they were difficult to prove and time consuming to prosecute. Instead, they preferred "quick hits" like "Wall Street cases."[26]

Targeting unsympathetic celebrities for merely questionable business decisions while ignoring flat-out crooks: this is a legal system with no set standards other than political theater. Since even insurance cannot be relied on to protect one beforehand, corporate executives are placed in risky positions, legally and financially. This must affect the risks entrepreneurs will be willing to take and, therefore, affect business profitability, worker income, and societal prosperity, to say nothing about violating the rule of law. Is it any wonder that the U.S. economic freedom score declined? But if one was running a Ponzi scheme that any common-law jury would understand as defrauding ordinary investors, one appeared safe. Indeed, the SEC inspector general believed the agency's leadership announced an investigation against high-flying Goldman Sachs specifically to divert public attention away from its Sanford incompetence.[27]

If law is unpredictable and unknowable beforehand, it threatens property, creates disorder, breeds disrespect, and cannot be obeyed, so that any concept of rule of law is undermined. When a Stanford law professor like Robert Weisberg can say, "It is hard to remember a major fraud case that went to jury trial that led to an acquittal" (actually, Richard Scrushy was acquitted but was recharged and convicted later); when the rules favor the prosecutors, lawyers, and officials; when most convictions are by plea bargains rather than trials; and when a judge rules that the major prosecution principles are unconstitutional, there is something seriously wrong with America's rule of law.[28]

Prosecutorial Abuse

It is in the cases of the most unsympathetic defendants that the most flagrant prosecutorial abuses come to light. Who could be a less appealing figure than former Illinois governor Rod Blagojevich, who boorishly tried to sell Barack Obama's Senate seat for political or economic gain? U.S. Attorney Patrick Fitzgerald could act immediately after Blagojevich proposed the deal because he had already placed wiretaps on the governor for suspicion of unrelated questionable behavior. Within days, the U.S. attorney announced to a roomful of reporters that Blagojevich was engaged "in a political corruption crime spree," that he "has taken us to a new low," that his actions were "appalling" (Fitzgerald used this word several times), and finally that his "conduct would make Lincoln roll over in his grave."[29]

The problem was that, as former top Justice Department official Victoria Toensing noted, "the governor's maneuvering to sell the Senate seat most likely had not yet crossed the line to become criminal" at the time when Fitzgerald held his colossal media conference announcing his indictment of a sitting governor.[30] U.S. Department of Justice guidelines require that prosecutors not go beyond the specific public facts when making announcements of indictments. The guidelines state that a "prosecutor shall refrain from making extrajudicial comments that pose a serious and imminent threat of heightening public condemnation of the accused." What could Fitzgerald have said that would have been more prejudicial than what he actually intoned into every living room in America? As Toensing concluded, this was unethical conduct and deserved public condemnation.[31]

U.S. attorneys are likewise expected to "exercise reasonable care" over the law enforcement officials used for an investigation, as Toensing also noted. Yet, at the same media event, FBI special agent Rob Grant volunteered a question, asking no one in particular whether Illinois was the "most corrupt state in the United States." Answering his own question, he said that if it is not the worst, "it's one hell of a competitor." He gratuitously added that his agents were "thoroughly disgusted and revolted by what they heard" as they listened to the wiretaps. Even if Grant's agents were this sheltered, it is hard to argue that his language was not prejudicial.

While Fitzgerald was effusive with prejudicial comments, he was evasive on the central question of why the wiretaps were set in the first place. The wiretaps apparently started with a complaint from a person who was perturbed that she could not secure a low-level state contract. Thereafter, the investigation meandered widely over an incredible five years until it finally landed with a bug in the governor's office. That this was a rather circuitous route perhaps explains why Fitzgerald did not give a direct answer. He had bent the guidelines before. To quote Toensing:

> In his news conference in October 2005 announcing the indictment of Scooter Libby for obstruction of justice, he compared himself to an umpire who "gets sand thrown in his eyes." The umpire is "trying to figure what happened and somebody blocked" his view. With this statement, Mr. Fitzgerald made us all believe he could not find the person who leaked Valerie Plame's name as a CIA operative because of Mr. Libby. What we all now know is that Mr. Fitzgerald knew well before he ever started the investigation in January 2004 that Richard Armitage

was the leaker and nothing Mr. Libby did or did not do threw sand in his eyes. In fact—since there was no crime—there was not even a game for the umpire to call.[32]

Fitzgerald himself explained that he had two reasons for holding the Blagojevich press conference so soon. First, he said he did not want to wait until a replacement for Senator Obama was already seated. Yet he could have privately told the Senate to hold up the nomination. Second, he said that he "laid awake at night" worrying that the editors of the *Chicago Tribune* would be fired under pressure from Governor Blagojevich before he could act. This seems even more unlikely, since the U.S. attorney was already working behind the scenes with the newspaper.[33] Was Fitzgerald just promoting himself? As an old bureaucratic insider, he undoubtedly knew that the first leaker earns the media's favor and is protected by that status.

As any student of the bureaucracy could tell the legalists, this strategy is especially helpful to guarantee one's own job security. Once a federal prosecutor brings a case, only the most foolhardy president or attorney general will dismiss him. There is a long history of U.S. attorneys publicly announcing a case and successfully enhancing their job tenure. A few clever ones have used the publicity to run for higher office. If top U.S. officials even thought of appointing a replacement, as a new administration otherwise would be free to do, any prosecutor who wanted to keep his job could merely whisper "obstruction of justice" and be safe in his job forever. Rather than receiving any condemnation, Fitzgerald survived well into President Obama's administration.

Such an easy and crass target as Blagojevich would surely be convicted of something. Yet in 2010, after two years, thousands of taped telephone calls, and a five-week trial in which the defense did not call a single witness, the former governor was not found guilty on any of the twenty-three serious counts; he was convicted on only one matter—not surprisingly, of lying to the FBI about crimes of which the jury did not convict him.[34] Federal prosecutors brought Blagojevich to trial a second time after meticulously analyzing what in the original case had been convincing to jurors and what had not. Learning from their mistakes, this time they managed to convict him of conspiracy to solicit bribes but not of soliciting bribes itself.[35] Should legal procedure not count as long as a foul-talking tough guy gets his due? If the main charges against Blagojevich weren't persuasive, his personality apparently was enough to convince the jury to judge him guilty of *something*, such as the old favorite, conspiracy.

Public corruption is illegal, but is talking tough a crime? Marvelously,

Fitzgerald had already answered this question at his original media conference. When a Chicago reporter asked him, since when had merely "talking tough" become a crime, he directed her to the conspiracy statutes![36] The dirty little secret of the U.S. federal justice system is that if one does not have the evidence to convict a person of a crime, convict him of conspiracy. Everyone conspires with others on noncriminal matters—common conspiracy simply means working in secret for a common goal—so once it is allowed in a legal setting, it is shooting fish in a barrel to convict on "conspiracy" alone without an underlying crime. If U.S. prosecutors could convict a CEO like Lay or Kozlowski on a conspiracy charge without an underlying crime, surely they could get a scalawag like the Illinois governor without having to meet the higher standards of proof for committing an actual crime.

Until the nineteenth century conspiracy was not even considered a crime other than as an active conspiracy against the state, and it was not used generally until the twentieth century, when white-collar crime cases against the welfare state became so numerous. (Even today federal white-collar crimes are considered crimes against the U.S. government, not against the employer.) And it was not until very recent years that one could be convicted of conspiracy without being charged with an underlying crime once the act had been consummated.[37] Judge Learned Hand called conspiracy the "darling of the modern prosecutor's nursery." Conspiracy especially became the charge of choice for suppressing unions in the nineteenth century, prosecuting speech during World War I, and prosecuting drug crimes starting in the 1960s.[38]

Business executives and governors are one thing. What about the average person? He, too, is subject to prosecutorial excess. Most exonerations correcting legal abuse involved unsophisticated folks. Ninety percent of all criminal cases in this country are settled by plea agreement with prosecutors. In the modern-day United States the jury trial is almost extinct. This development reflects the fact that in a jury trial, the legal tools all favor the government.[39] The reason is that no one knows what the law is or how a jury even of one's peers will react to tough prosecutors and process-oriented judges. Today there are 4,500 federal crimes listed in 300,000 regulations that no one can possibly comprehend.[40] The defense lawyer Harvey Silverglate has estimated that ordinary Americans who think they are law-abiding are probably committing "three felonies a day" without knowing it.

The rate of prosecutions has doubled from 192 per one million in 1980 to 395 in 2009.[41] At a hearing on the matter, the chairman of the House Judiciary Committee, Republican James Sensenbrenner, decried the "erosion of the ideal of criminal intent" and referenced a case where a workingman was convicted of violating the Clean Water Act for trying to clean toilets when even the government had conceded it was inadvertent. The ranking committee Democrat, John Conyers, proposed "to get rid of the old myth that you are presumed to know the law" when there is more than any normal person could comprehend.[42]

Juries are easily confused by technicalities. Studies of forensic evidence from even simple procedures have shown significant errors. Hair analysis and polygraphing are especially well documented for defects; handwriting analysis is inconsistent; even fingerprinting and ballistic tests are subjective. Contrary evidence is routinely not given to defendants or defense lawyers, and internal Department of Justice studies are not made public, encouraging TV and Hollywood simplifications that mislead the public regarding their accuracy.[43]

Confusion is especially high when prosecutors invoke the hallowed word *science*. Science is complex stuff. DNA is now as widely used as fingerprinting to convict suspects of murder. Prosecutors use expert witnesses who claim 99.99 percent probability that the genetic markers found at a crime scene match those of the suspect. But as Northwestern University law professor Jay Koehler explains, "Unfortunately, and surprisingly to most people, the DNA test cannot identify the probability" of a positive match. DNA is too complex to match it all, so samples are used. Beyond the measurement error and inherent complexity, testing must match a DNA sample with some known source (such as a previous sample from the same person or from a close blood relative) and then extrapolate from there to come up with a probability of a positive identification. To do so, testers must rely on something known in statistics as "prior odds"—that is, the odds that the suspect is actually the person sought. These prior and coordinated estimates are not connected to the DNA evidence; they are inherently subjective and can override the empirical data. One study found dozens of partial matches of unrelated people in a database of 65,000 Arizona felons. As Koehler concluded, "The risk of human error far exceeds the risk of error due to coincidental match."[44]

The vagueness and multiplicity of federal laws make them impossible to know. Worse, ordinary citizens, even wealthy ones, often cannot match the aggressiveness of prosecutors and regulators working with basically unlimited resources at taxpayer expense, especially when courts have proved so willing to defer to so-called experts. At the same time, prosecutors are almost immune from punishment for their errors or misconduct. A Department of Justice investigation found that two federal prosecutors had engaged in "reckless professional misconduct" by hiding vital evidence favorable to

Senator Ted Stevens; Stevens was found guilty, which cost him his Senate seat and his party's ability to block objectionable legislation. Despite this "reckless professional misconduct," one prosecutor received only a forty-day suspension without pay and another a mere fifteen-day suspension. The supervisor found guilty of "poor judgment for failing to supervise" them received no punishment at all.[45]

Silverglate asked, If the enormously wealthy and popular financier Michael Milken—who pled guilty only when threatened that his younger brother would be prosecuted if he did not confess—is not immune from prosecutorial extortion, who is?[46]

What Went Wrong?

American Founder James Madison warned, "It will be of little avail to the people that the laws are made by men of their own choice if the laws be so voluminous that they cannot be read or so incoherent that they cannot be understood."[47] The sorry state of the law today demonstrates that America has turned its back on the traditional legal principles that built its civilization. Rather than basing its law on Lockean principles of a higher law translated into custom and popular understanding, America turned to progressive legal positivism to enable governing elites to enforce a welfare state that attempted to regulate all important aspects of social life.

First, beginning with progressives Woodrow Wilson and Franklin Roosevelt, Congress did "transfer the power of making laws" to professional bureaucracies, political executives, and judges to give them flexibility to control the complexities of managing welfare and regulating business. In doing so, it changed law from "established, settled" principles set under "common consent" to being made by experts who supposedly knew better. Second, such laws became so numerous and remote from public understanding and debate that they were no longer "promulgated" to or "known" by most people. Finally, as administrative discretion became more and more accepted, the law was "varied in particular cases" to advantage more sympathetic interests over less popular ones or to punish those who could not be found guilty of disobeying established laws but seemed deserving of punishment anyway.

As Madison, Locke, and Hayek argued, legal principles must be few in number, clear and simple enough to be understood, rooted deep in well-understood moral traditions, and equally and impartially applicable to all. Honesty, fair play, trust, lawfulness, respect for others' property, responsibility for oneself and others, and moderation in making demands on government all seem to be required for a traditional rule of law. Yet as early as the 1960s, Hayek found these traditions weakening, so that most American laws did not apply equally to all. There were special rules for all different classes of people: farmers, union members, the elderly, urban residents, favored businesses, minorities, the poor, the ill and disabled, and many others, all demanding special treatment under the law.[48]

Under the traditional Western sense of rule of law, officials must feel they are subject to it, not able to change law at whim to advantage some interest or another.[49] This requires a rule of law that binds morally rather than by simple coercion. Hayek argued that this type of rule of law, compatible with individual freedom, has historically arisen only from traditions that valued the family and private property.[50] Traditions associated with Judaic, Buddhist, Hindu, Islamic, and other traditions have supported the family, and this has allowed the major cultures of modern times to survive and prosper. But support for private property and the family together has been rare, basically confined to Greece and early Rome, transferred from them to Christianized Europe, and later transferred to their colonies in the new worlds of West and South. Respect for private property has more recently been transferred to Buddhist-influenced regimes in Asia such as Japan, Taiwan, Singapore, and Hong Kong. Still, support for both family and property together remains rather rare, and it is weakening even in the West.[51]

How did America and the West develop their peculiar sense of rule of law? Hayek traced a rule of law based on a binding morality that respected private property to the Middle Ages. Indeed, he said that a property-oriented society must "paradoxically" be based on traditional customs—against theft, for example—to legitimize privately held property and the freedom to hold, use, and transfer it.[52] The great Harvard legal historian Harold Berman argued that it was western Europe's unique beliefs and history that made its feudalism different from, say, Russia's or Japan's. During the late eleventh and early twelfth centuries, European church and business worked out arrangements for more modern commerce by creating guilds that jointly crafted moral guidelines allowing for freer economic behavior. This type of capitalism, mixing moral restraints and free means, developed only there.[53] Joseph Schumpeter even thought that this type of capitalism might be the final stage of feudalism rather than a separate stage of development prior to socialism. Capitalism, he argued, cannot exist without the feudal legal and moral structure supporting the necessary norms and division of power.[54] Even Karl Marx gave the "vigor" of feudalism credit for the rise of modern market capitalism.[55]

A 2008 book by economic historian Svetozar Pejovich, *Law, Informal Rules, and Economic Performance*, documents four essential but not planned contributions to this form of rule of law. A skeptical Pejovich basically views the early Christian church as relying on force to gain and maintain its authority and Russian Orthodoxy as a czarist invention of social control. Still, he gives credit to early Christian mores and institutions for creating a rule of law that encouraged modern economic prosperity by carefully identifying the specific acts that made freedom and prosperity possible.[56]

First, Christianity taught an individualist rather than a communal obligation from the beginning, something rare among world civilizations. At the very start, Paul convinced Peter that church membership was not to be restricted to a particular people or by a set of communal ritual practices. Earlier, Christ himself had made God's redemption individual, for each lost sheep or one prodigal son.

Second, Christianity transformed work from a slave's to a citizen's responsibility. Rome and most other ancient civilizations considered work and especially physical labor as beneath the dignity of a true citizen, whose obligation was military, governmental, cultic, or familial. The removal of the government from Rome to Constantinople—and with it much of the nobility and their slaves—eliminated two barriers to change. But the direct improvement in the status of work came in the sixth century at Monte Cassino from the monk Benedict's rule of "pray and work" as the ideal regimen of Christian social life. High-ranking men (and later women) were recruited into the order to perform holy labor. This emphasis on the value of work spread across Europe—as did the monasteries themselves—providing first efficient agriculture and then early manufacturing, in the process hallowing the work ethic so essential to capitalism.

Third, Christianity made the nuclear family the basis of society. It was the extended family that had dominated, and was the base of power for, Rome, Greece, and other early regimes. All social alliances in the ancient world were based on family ties and connections, which inhibited private trading between strangers. But in the sixth century, Pope Gregory I forbade four traditional practices: marriage to close kin, marriage to widows of close kin, the use of adoption to transfer children for family advantage, and concubinage. All these changes undermined the power of the patriarchal system, preparing the way for the modern nuclear family so necessary for the rise of bourgeois individualistic capitalism.

Finally, Christianity created the separation between church and state that led to constitutional separation of powers throughout Western civilization. When Jesus separated Caesar's reach from God's, he challenged the exclusive sovereignty over the individual that the state had claimed since time immemorial. The early church enforced this challenge through martyrdom. In the fourth century the bishop Ambrose refused an order from Emperor Valentinian that he believed adversely affected the church. By surviving the encounter, the Christian church became the first organization since the prophets to peacefully defy state power—and now such defiance took place on a more or less regular basis.[57] In the eleventh century Pope Gregory VII proclaimed church/state separation as an official church doctrine and created separate clerical courts. These actions encouraged other powers to demand separate mercantile laws and legal rights for parishes, cities, guilds, and other associations.[58]

Pejovich argues that all these moral and institutional changes were essential in creating the rule of law and constitutional separation that allowed capitalism and freedom to rise in Europe, especially in its common-law nations. He analyzes data from the 2007 *Index of Economic Freedom* to demonstrate that all seven nations rated most free and capitalistic were rooted in common law. In all cases, the common-law tradition had evolved from Christian roots in Europe; it expanded to include Hong Kong and Singapore, which received it indirectly from English colonialism, mixed with their favorable Buddhist roots. Most of the next most economically free nations were Christian-rooted too, including Japan, which also received its rule of law and consequent capitalism secondhand from the West.

Pejovich is not sanguine about extending a rule of law supporting freedom and modern markets to places where these roots do not exist. Few nations have become more private-property oriented in recent years, and some that did, as in eastern Europe, subsequently regressed, even when they had Christian roots. Commitment to a limited-government rule of law has declined markedly even in the home bases of Britain and the United States with the rise of the welfare state, given its communal rather than individual responsibility for welfare, work, and economic activity generally. Pejovich does not mention it, but the nuclear family has declined also, and the increase of national government power has threatened separation of powers.

As much as the libertarian Pejovich recoils from it, he comes to the conclusion that the type of rule of law that supports freedom and separation of powers is unique to the West. The state would have to impose it on non-Western populations, and even then sufficient rule of law would need to develop independent of state imposition. As economist Ljubomir Madzar noted, this would constitute a "massive engineering venture" inconsistent with the freedom element and as complicated as planning a market itself. Economist James Buchanan's hope that people would accept freedom and rule of law on rational grounds alone likewise seemed unrealistic, given the lack of progress on this front since Voltaire advanced the idea.[59] As even that French skeptic asked, allegedly referring to the grandiose visions of Rousseau, where does the necessary authoritative legitimacy for such a colossal undertaking come from? Did he propose to rise on the third day?[60]

Western Tradition Dead?

If freedom, capitalism, and prosperity depend on a vital Western moral tradition underlying a rule of law, it is not surprising that Europe and America are seen as declining. As early as the nineteenth century, Marx charged that Western capitalist freedom "piteously had torn asunder all the motley feudal ties" of tradition that had created it. Christian religion, common law, cultic morality, family, honored and courageous professions, small entrepreneurships, localities, and community associations all had been rationalized by the market, leaving only big business, "naked self-interest," and "callous cash payment." For a while these ties and especially religion as the "opium of the people" had protected capitalism, but as these protective strata wore away in the universal pursuit of money, its energizing and moral foundations were eroded. By his time, he pronounced, the whole western European rule of law tradition was dead.[61]

When the newly elected Benedict XVI took his first foreign excursion as pope to his supposedly Christian homeland in 2005, a massive media outpouring highlighted the secularized Europe he would confront. Germany's number-one newsmagazine, *Der Spiegel,* greeted the pontiff with a five-part series, backed by a massive public opinion poll, all under the title "When the German Pope Returns Home, He'll Find an Un-Christian Land."[62]

Only 10 percent of Germans attended church weekly. Each year 60,000 more Catholics were buried than were baptized, the latter totaling only 205,904 in 2003, 31 percent lower than in 1990. In the country of its founding, Protestantism was even more threatened: 180,000 left the church in 2003, and only 60,000 joined. East Germany boasted 15 million Christians when the communists took power but only 5.5 million after a half century of reeducation, with only 3.7 million left today. The *Der Spiegel*/TNS Infratest poll found that only 32 percent of Germans had great or very great confidence in the church, and even among the Christians, just two-thirds of Catholics and less than half of Protestants believed in the church's central tenet that there was a new life coming after death.

Germany was by no means alone. In fact, among European countries it was somewhere in the middle regarding religious adherence. Poland and Northern Ireland had the highest weekly participation, with 50 percent attending church weekly or more frequently—even higher than the United States at 40 percent. Italy and Portugal followed at about one-third attending per week. In Britain, as in Germany, 10 percent attended church weekly. Countries like Sweden, France, Belgium, the Netherlands, and the Czech Republic had the lowest participation at 5 percent or less. Belief in life after death ranged broadly too, but no European country had a rate as high as that of the United States, at 76 percent. In most of Europe belief in an afterlife ranged between one-third and one-half of the population, with Germany at 38 percent.

Actually, the sociologist Rodney Stark argued that Europe north of the old Roman Empire border of the Rhine never was very Christianized at the mass level. The lower level of religious identification in the north and east today reflects that pattern. Although Christianity originally spread to ordinary people through person-to-person social networks and conversions, after it became the dominant religion of the empire, it became so attractive to the new governing elites that control became more important than conversion. Even missionary activity beyond the old border was primarily aimed at elites; many adopted the new religion—and some very passionately, as the lists of saints confirm—but they did not necessarily spread it widely to their people. Consequently, in many areas old pagan ideas mixed with Christian ones that the masses considered Christian but the religious clergy did not.[63]

A similar pattern continues today. Although Europe is not orthodox, it is also not without the moral code that formed it. What seems strangest is how much Europeans say they pray. Most polls show that the overwhelming percentage of the population says it prays several times a day. Even according to the lowest estimates, almost all say they pray at least once a month, with only the French and Scandinavians saying only several times a year. Why would secularists pray at all? Why do majorities express belief in God and even life after death after years of secularization?[64]

The *Der Spiegel* poll even found two-thirds of young people saying it was cool to believe in something deeper than self. The magazine found that religious items like crosses and rosaries were "in." With little church attendance or religious education (although some countries teach religion in public schools) or support for many traditional beliefs, especially on sex and marriage, why would these attitudes and behaviors persist? Why would a million people, mainly youngsters, go to see the orthodox teacher Benedict in Cologne, where no rock star had attracted such a crowd?[65]

European beliefs are not orthodox, but when asked what they are, including choices of atheist, agnostic, or "no religion," people answer overwhelmingly "Christian": 97 percent in Ireland, 93 percent in Portugal and Spain—and even Norway, Finland, and Denmark—88 percent in Switzerland, 83 percent in Britain, 82 percent in Italy, 76 percent in Germany, 71 percent in France, and 68 percent in Sweden. Non-Christian religions range from a high of only 9 percent in France down to 6 percent in Britain. After all this time, those saying they have no religion represent only 18 percent in Sweden, 17 percent in Germany, 16 percent in France, and 12 percent in Britain, compared with 9 percent in the United States. When asked whether they believe in God, only Swedes report less than majority support (46 percent) for a supreme being, with most nations ranging around Germany at two-thirds support.[66]

It is clear that Christian beliefs and active participation in religious services and practices have attenuated. Yet some form of Christian identity and moral belief persists. Consider this: Sweden is the least religious nation in Europe. In 2000 it abolished its established church universal tax and created a "fee" to be collected only from those people who freely identified themselves as formal church members. As one might expect, membership in the Church of Sweden dropped dramatically in 2001. Almost all the rest of the population was expected to depart the church over the next few years. The now secularized population confirmed economic rationality and voted themselves free of the fee and the church, right?

Something curious happened. Now that there was a choice, a limited free market was created as a test. Church officials mounted a first-ever publicity drive urging church membership and support. Miraculously, membership stabilized, and the following year the church received $1.6 billion from 78 percent of the population freely identifying themselves with the church and paying the fee in a country where barely 3 percent attend church services other than weddings and funerals. In another odd situation, the largest Swedish hotel chain, Scandic, accommodated a complaint from an atheist and removed Bibles from its rooms—but later reversed course after a public outcry.[67]

European countries today still cling to their traditions, even to their Christian heritage in their prayer life, their major beliefs, and some central social activities like births, weddings, and deaths. They tend to have traditionalist attitudes on social mores too, contributing to low crime rates and societal harmony well beyond that existing in the United States.[68] As the Swedish example suggests, what survives may be more customary ways than orthodox religion, but Europe's historic traditions remain relatively strong.

Could this help account for the continuing higher scores on rule of law in those nations compared with the rest of the world and for the higher rankings in freedom and prosperity resulting from them?[69]

Western Synthesis

What makes Old Europe different is that both tradition and freedom values still seem embedded in its beliefs, laws, and institutions and to affect how its people live and govern themselves. These values seem more complementary than either/or, as Hayek suggests with his paradox that tradition is required to support law, which in turn allows for freedom. The idea of such a harmony comes from that tradition itself, from the Roman stoics, the Jewish prophets, and the early Christian fathers.[70] The idea that both tradition and freedom were required was formalized in the influential thirteenth-century *Summa Theologica* by the great Catholic philosopher Thomas Aquinas.[71] It was elaborated by the Protestant natural law thinkers Hugo Grotius and Samuel von Pufendorf, driven into the British social fabric by their pupil John Locke, and passed through him to America's Founders.[72] Historically, Western culture in its actual institutions and its functioning legal systems has been a synthesis of both tradition and freedom, no matter how paradoxical that may first appear.

Synthetic thinking is often criticized as illogical. The enormously influential French philosopher René Descartes argued that serious thought must reach back to one unquestionably true first principle and deduce everything else from it. Two first axioms violate the logical principle of noncontradiction.[73] The modern political philosopher Leo Strauss traced the necessity of choosing one valid first principle to Plato's Athenian school and was especially insistent that only one axiom can be correct, demanding it was either reason or tradition, philosophy or faith, human guidance or divine guidance, Athens or Jerusalem. "The dilemma cannot be evaded by any harmony or synthesis."[74] Any attempt is a "dualism" and logically invalid.[75]

Monist noncontradiction and plural synthesis, however, are both first principles with equivalent a priori status.[76] Both are axioms and cannot be displaced logically except by simple assertion. Whereas Professor Strauss could claim the heritage of Plato, Descartes, Rousseau, Hegel, Bentham, Kant, Leonard Hobhouse, A. J. Ayer, and many others, the "dualist" Hayek claimed Aristotle, Cicero, Aquinas, Montesquieu, Locke, Adam Smith, Edmund Burke, Tocqueville, Lord Acton, and Karl Popper among those on the pluralist side. And, as Hayek added, the latter group has the predominant legacy supporting freedom. Those who have supported freedom from the camp of monists such as Kant and Bentham were otherwise "tainted" by the unitary view, restricting rationality to ideals that had the unintended result of limiting the concreteness, spontaneity, and evolutionary nature of liberty.[77]

The critics of synthesis, of course, have a point. Certainly, Kublai Khan exceeded reasonableness by including Confucianism, Buddhism, Judaism, Christianity, and Islam within his own religion and culture. One should distinguish between syncretism—which includes everything helter-skelter, as did the Khan—and synthesis, which brings together the elements into a coherent argument. Aristotle considered the golden mean as the middle way between two extreme positions, resulting in the best possible position that is achievable. Popper and Hayek distinguished between inductive empiricism, critical rationalism, and axiomatic rationalism, with the balanced approach being the middle position.[78]

The American who most emphasized for popular audiences how essential synthesis has been to Western civilization was the modern political theorist Frank Meyer. What held the synthesis of freedom and tradition together was the "tension" between them, he argued. The dualism of both freedom and tradition in European culture was a historical fact even if it represented a rational dilemma. Meyer wrote:

> The dilemma is one which can only be solved by the classical logical device of grasping both horns. For the difficulty is that both its major premises are true; on the one hand freedom is essential to the nature of man and neutral to virtue and vice; on the other hand good ends are good ends, and it is the duty of man to pursue them. I deny only that in the real situations with which we are dealing these two premises are contradictory. Rather they are axioms true of different though interconnected realms of existence. How can true ends be established elsewhere than in the intellectual, the moral, the spiritual order? Where can the conditions of freedom be established but in the social order—which means since this is where force centers—in the political order?[79]

The synthesis was between a tradition mostly developed by trial and error over time that produced certain valued ends for social life and a political order of laws and institutions that allowed for freedom.[80] Tradition cannot be both means and end, because it cannot rightly be forced by political power and still be considered moral for those coerced. The point of both

Lord Acton's famous warning and J. R. R. Tolkien's Lord of the Rings tril-
ogy is that power inevitably corrupts. Of course, traditional and religious
identification was often spread by force and conquest, but no one considers
such use of power to achieve those ends to be moral. Freedom, then, must
be the first principle of the good political order. But freedom has no goal,
no ends, unless it is freedom itself, which cannot be guaranteed as the end
without forcing it—which undermines its legitimacy as a means.

Even within the political sphere, then, Meyer saw an essential role for
tradition:

> Freedom remains the criterion principle, the guide; but the application
> of principle to circumstances demands a prudential art. The intricate
> fibers of tradition and civilization, carried in the minds of men from
> generation to generation, always affect the realization of any general
> principle. Furthermore, no practical situation can be the realization
> of a single principle, however important. The compelling, if second-
> ary, claims of other principles, though not decisive to judgment in the
> political sphere in the way that freedom is, do nevertheless bear upon
> every concrete political problem.[81]

In other words, any attempt to achieve freedom requires tradition to
set the context within which a solution becomes concrete politically. Both
principles must be maintained, but they often compete and must be resolved
pragmatically before one takes any action.[82] Freedom and tradition were
synthesized not for political convenience but because both were essential.
The synthesis can be summarized as using the libertarian means of freedom
in a conservative society for traditional valued ends.[83] Meyer criticized his
associate Russell Kirk for making virtue the end of social life, but as these
considerations demonstrate, so did Meyer, as long as virtue respected freedom and was not forced. Although Kirk may have given less prominence to
freedom as a means, it is clear that he did not believe purely in tradition—
there are bad traditions, he argued, and good traditions cannot be applied
directly but must balance competing virtues. Most important, Kirk relied
not primarily on power but on community, church, the family, and other
nonpower means to achieve those ends.[84]

Of course, it is extremely difficult to maintain the tension, to steer a
course between liberty and individual rationality on the one hand and tradition and rule of law on the other, especially to preserve fragile freedom in the
balance. Few nations have been able to do so. In Meyer's words:

Freedom brings men rudely and directly face to face with their own personal responsibility for their own free actions. This is a shock. Remembrance of the fleshpots of enveloping security ever tugs insidiously at the souls of free men. But where mind and will have been clear and firm, the temptation has been rejected.[85]

So does it all depend on mind and will?

Seven

MORAL POWER AND
CREATIVE ENERGY

THE MOST FUNDAMENTAL FACT ABOUT human society is its population.
Nothing influences a nation's future more than increasing or declining
population, for supporting productivity, for maintaining armies, and even
as a source for the taxation government needs to pay the bills. Westerners
have preserved many aspects of their traditional beliefs, but there is one area
where they have not—and it may be the most important. No civilization or
nation can survive without people, and Europeans simply do not seem to
have the will to reproduce themselves.

Several years ago, Russian president Vladimir Putin read United
Nations data demonstrating that without some action to the contrary, Russia's population would decline from 146 million to 100 million by 2050—a
one-third loss of people. This roused him to make the problem the center
of his annual message to parliament. "We need to reduce mortality, have an
effective migration policy, and increase the birthrate," he declared. Since a
nation requires a "replacement rate" of 2.1 children per childbearing-aged
woman to maintain its level of population, Russia's woeful 1.4 fertility rate
guaranteed long-term decline. In presenting an ambitious and expensive
government program to increase births, Putin quoted Russia's Nobel Prize–
winning author Aleksandr Solzhenitsyn that solving this demographic problem was necessary for "saving the people," their nation, and its civilization.[1]

Russia was by no means alone. Most of Europe had similarly tepid fertility rates. The Czech Republic, Poland, and Ukraine were worse, at a 1.2
fertility rate, with Germany, Greece, Italy, and Spain not much higher, at 1.3.
Only Ireland was at a self-sustaining level, while France was close at 1.8. Britain, Denmark, and Sweden were also somewhat above average but, at 1.7, still

below replacement rate. In the rest of the world, countries most influenced by the West were also in decline, such as Japan, with a fertility rate of 1.4. The average rate for the whole developed world dropped from 4.4 in the 1970s to 1.8 by 2003. In the poorer developing world, rates dropped dramatically too, but from 5.9 to a still quite high 3.9.[2] More recent data show the same general patterns, with fertility declining somewhat further for most nations.[3]

The geopolitical implications of the European decline are enormous. Of the forty-three countries projected to decline in population over the next fifty years, 80 percent are European. Who would have believed in 1900—when Christian Europe and its North American offshoot held 30 percent of the world's total population and ruled much of the rest—that Europe's relative size would be cut almost in half by 2005, and that by 2050 European-based populations would be down to a mere 11 percent of the earth's population? The top countries in population will be India, China, and the United States. But they will not be as dominant, slipping from 42 percent of the world population to 37 percent in 2050. The Asian Islamic nations of Pakistan, Indonesia, and Bangladesh will be the next largest—together about the size of the United States. Latin America will grow substantially, to almost equal the population of Europe and the United States combined. Africa will be the biggest gainer, moving from 8 percent to 20 percent of the world population. And these trends are expected to continue over the next hundred years.

Even Christianity is not European any longer. In 1900, 82 percent of Christians were in Europe and North America, whereas only 39 percent are today, and by 2050 it will be only 28 percent. By 2050, none of the top ten largest countries on the planet will be in Europe, and only the United States and Brazil will be majority Christian with any sizable European population. For the first time not one European country will be in the top ten in terms of Christian population; surprisingly, China will be second (after the United States), Congo-Zaire will be fourth (after Brazil), and India will be fifth, followed by Mexico, Nigeria, the Philippines, Ethiopia, and Uganda.[4]

What can be done about population? Many countries preceded Russia in initiating expensive government programs to increase fertility, including France, Canada, Poland, and Sweden. The reputed success of these policies in France and Sweden led many socially conservative commentators in the United States to look with favor on them and on the "family friendly" policies of the early New Deal, proposing they be emulated and enhanced today. Substantial baby bonuses, family incentive programs, tax deductions, subsidized child care, discounts on services, and other government supports have all been proposed as solutions for the United States, whose fertility rate in 2003 was just at replacement level and dropped to 2.0 thereafter.[5]

The UN data, however, suggest the policies do not work. Only Sweden and France have had even temporary success. Sweden did increase its fertility rate from 1.7 in 1985 to 2.0 in 1990 after spending substantial funds during the 1970s and '80s—but the rate declined in 2001, to 1.6, below the starting point for its programs. The rate inched up again, to 1.7 in 2006, but that still was below its 1.9 rate in 1970, and over the past half century there has been a large net decline. France has been the model success story for fertility planning, praised for increasing its rate since the mid-1990s through aggressive government spending on family incentives. Although the UN data show an increase in fertility from 1.7 in 1994 to 1.8 in 2001 and 1.9 in 2006, the rate was 1.8 in 1975 before the government policy was adopted, and much of the increase has come from Muslim immigrants and illegals. No level of government spending that has been tried thus far has created a rate that would grow or even sustain a native European population.[6]

Government policies have actually assisted in the decline. The UN boasted in a news announcement accompanying its 2003 report, "Between the 1970s and the 1990s, the median level of contraceptive prevalence (any method) among all 192 countries increased from 38 per cent of women currently married or in union to 52 per cent. Among developing countries, median contraceptive prevalence rose from 27 per cent to 40 per cent. Government policies have played an important role in modifying reproductive behavior. By 2001, 92 per cent of all governments supported family-planning programmes and distributed contraceptives either directly (75 per cent) through government facilities, or indirectly (17 per cent), by supporting the activities of nongovernmental organizations, such as family-planning associations."[7]

There is always the possibility that future scientific gains or even the artificial creation of life might come to the rescue, although the twentieth-century eugenics movement has given that project a bad name. Some optimists believe rates can be raised naturally. They point out that the U.S. rate, though dropping in recent years, is up from a low of 1.8 in the 1990s. Yet even here the numbers are misleading. U.S. government data show that the European (non-Hispanic, nonblack) fertility rate in the United States has remained below replacement, essentially at 1.8 over this whole period. The causes of the U.S. increase included a stable African American replacement rate of 2.1, a strong Hispanic fertility rate of 2.7 (higher among Mexican Americans), and an increased proportion of Hispanics overall. The increase did not result from government policy—indeed, much of the immigration was illegal. Moreover, even these small increases could not make up for the dramatic decline that has occurred since 1950, when the U.S. fertility rate was 3.5. The United States is tracking the continental European decline.[8]

With Europe's fertility rate at 1.4 and still declining, depopulation or mass immigration is its future. The United States is better, but the rate for the European ancestor population is only 1.8 and Hispanic fertility has declined during the most recent recession.[9] Even with the estimated immigration, the United States will decline from 6.3 percent of the world population to 4.6 percent by 2050. So declining fertility will radically change even the powerful United States. As demographer Phillip Longman notes, "Ultimately, it is often the number of boots on the ground that changes history. Even with a fertility rate near replacement level, the United States lacks the amount of people necessary to sustain an imperial role in the world, just as Britain lost its ability to do so after its birthrates collapsed in the early 20th century."[10] Longman continues:

> Falling fertility is also responsible for many financial and economic problems that dominate today's headlines. The long-term financing of social security schemes, private pension plans, and healthcare systems has little to do with people living longer. Gains in life expectancy at older ages have actually been quite modest, and the rate of improvement in the United States has diminished for each of the last three decades. Instead, the falling ratio of workers to retirees is overwhelmingly caused by workers who were never born.[11]

There is little evidence the government can solve the "missing children problem" in the United States or elsewhere, as the data for Sweden and France demonstrate. The state seems to have neither the will nor the ability to convince people to bear children. It is often claimed that demography is destiny. What cannot be argued is that unless a country or a civilization has the will to produce children, it cannot endure. Countries need some energy source to generate a will to survive, procreate, and grow.

Why Children?

What could possibly generate such energy? One popular theory is that having children is all about nature, evolution, biology, and genes. Richard Dawkins put forward this view in his book *The Selfish Gene*, arguing that the instinct of genes is to maximize their fitness and reproduce better copies of themselves.[12] Having children, according to this theory, has nothing to do with traditional beliefs or religion, except as they distort nature. Indeed, the atheist Dawkins considers families' teaching religion to be "child abuse." He even wrote the script for a broadcast aired on British public television and in the United States titled *The Root of All Evil?* The evil root was religion.[13]

In the documentary, Dawkins says that religion's "irrational roots are nourishing intolerance and murder" around the world, especially from "the three Abrahamic religions," specifically targeting Jewish and Muslim "fundamentalists," "frightening" American evangelicals, and gullible traditional Christians, such as Catholics seeking cures at Lourdes. He characterizes Christianity's belief that Jesus had to be "hideously tortured and killed so that we might be redeemed" as a "nasty sadomasochistic doctrine." While these religions "preach morality, peace, and hope, in fact, they bring intolerance, violence, and destruction."[14]

That is why Dawkins decries the spread of religious doctrines by families, communities, and schools, both public and private. In a news release, the British TV network that aired Dawkins's documentary notes the professor's alarm at the fact that "the number of faith schools is increasing" in both Britain and the United States: "More than half the [British] Government's proposed City Academies will be run by religious organisations and there's a growing number of private evangelical Christian schools." Dawkins says that religious schools promote a "poisonous system of morals." He compares the teaching of religion to a virus that infects young people and spreads from generation to generation.[15]

It is interesting how Professor Dawkins, consciously or not, reaches back to Plato. The ancient Athenian philosopher expressed similar concern about children's being taught traditional religion. Without the intervention of the great philosopher's *Republic*, parents and the traditional community would teach myths rather than true morality. Unless the reformed state actually arranged and controlled marriages and separated children from parents, privileged families would accumulate power, money, brains, strength, beauty, and other qualities of birth and pass them down to future generations. If the guardians of the republic were not given control over families, private power would sustain injustice and inequality.[16]

But why this emphasis on teaching if it is all about genes? Based on a study he performed, Professor James Davison Hunter claimed that relatively few American children use explicitly religious reasoning anyway; most invoke more secular, psychological, emotional, and utilitarian terminology. Indeed, he argued that today the secular "vocabulary of psychology forms virtually all public discussion." That "behaviorally scientific" vocabulary replaced right and wrong with appropriate and inappropriate behavior that *felt* right to the individual, emotionally or psychologically. The problem for the behaviorist is that these "nonreligious" experts end up with a morality similar to the traditionalist ones. Their conclusions are subjective and on a "what we can all agree on" formulation, but the strange thing is that they mostly track traditional morality. The secular psychological priesthood, while claiming open-ended morality, concedes that telling people that they are free to do anything they desire is an invitation to chaos.[17]

Even the very strong genes-are-all atheist Dawkins has supported humans' "rising above nature." When questioned about his argument that sex outside marriage should not be considered wrong, he denied that he supported a "swinging lifestyle" but did not explain the contradiction. After saying that lying was not wrong, he added the curious exception against lying under oath: "Taking an oath is a sacred relic of our religious history which really does have some value. It retains a kind of sacredness which we respect, even though we no longer believe in the religiously sacred."[18] Is this not a bit of having it both ways, allowing historical but not "religious" sacredness? A serious atheist like Nietzsche would call this slipping traditional morality in by the back door.

The uneven replacement rates of different countries in similar environments make it clear that nature cannot explain all or even most procreation. Beliefs, cultures, and mores must matter too. Since time immemorial it seemed natural to have children. Even in primitive times, human children needed care for years, they often took the mother's life in childbirth, they frequently died early from disease, and they consumed scarce resources. With all of these biological costs, why would families or tribes regenerate themselves?

In early societies, male biological brute force could explain some reproduction, but traditional life, as anthropologist David Maybury-Lewis described it, operated more under social pressure and small-group consensus. These primitive peoples had a strong sense of "interconnectedness of things on this earth and beyond"—the extended family, informal groupings, the tribe, nature, and spirits beyond. They worked in a tradition-based "moral economy" that was "permeated by personal and moral considerations" based on gifts and social favors. Children were considered part of this bounty, and parents were expected and pressured to bear them as the proper moral choice. Moreover, children could contribute: the very young could feed livestock and gather nuts, berries, and kindling. If they were deformed or could not help, many societies accepted infanticide, especially of females. By a relatively early age, children—especially boys—contributed positively.[19] The economics of childbirth did not change even with the rise of agriculture, the larger settled communities it supported, and more formal institutions such as kingship and temple religions. Children remained social assets.

But capitalism and large-scale manufacturing changed everything.

Capitalism even provided a new rationale for judging the worth of children. As economic historian Joseph Schumpeter put it, under capitalism

> men and women learn the utilitarian lesson and refuse to take for granted the traditional arrangements that their social environment makes for them . . . and . . . as soon as they introduce into their private life a sort of inarticulate system of cost accounting—they cannot fail to become aware of the heavy personal sacrifices that family ties and especially parenthood entail under modern conditions and of the fact that . . . children cease to be economic assets.[20]

It did not take long to calculate the costs and have fewer children to enjoy the greater benefits and freedom. Contraception allowed pleasure without the costs. Working allowed women additional income and opportunities but delayed childbearing. Later marriages allowed further education that opened vistas but decreased fecundity. Cohabitation, single lifestyles, abortion, divorce, and adultery all increased choices but made childrearing appear more burdensome. All that stood against most of these were the Abrahamic religions.[21] At the same time, governments drastically increased taxation and made raising children more expensive, as did soaring demand for higher education. The modern welfare state offered to take over many burdens of child raising, sending the message to potential parents that children mainly represented a financial and social burden that must be alleviated, further reducing the incentive to bear children.[22]

It seems anything but "natural" to have children, especially in modern times. Indeed, why would any modern person freely chose to bear the burden of a household of children—more than one child anyway—after sitting down and calculating the cost? Biology cannot provide the motivation, rationality cannot, and patriotic nationalism (at least among Europeans) cannot. The decline of population in advanced industrial nations is not difficult to explain rationally. With modern choices and freedom, one might rather wonder, Why is there any childbearing at all?

Does Marriage Matter?

The Yearning for Zion Ranch community near Eldorado, Texas, had no difficulty bearing children—in fact, it freely produced several hundreds of them in just a few years from a small number of members. Yet on April 3, 2008, scores of police raided it and removed all 460 children from their parents because government officials opposed the "pervasive belief system" that produced so many offspring.

With all the freedom, openness, and tolerance of modern times, what was so wrong about this belief system that produced such a severe official reaction? The ranch was owned by the ten-thousand-member Fundamentalist Church of Jesus Christ of Latter-Day Saints, which had split with the central Mormon church when the latter abandoned polygamy in 1890. The local compound had come under official scrutiny when its fifty-two-year-old "prophet" of polygamous living was convicted of "accessory to rape" for performing an underage wedding in 2001. Its members openly practiced polygamy. The Texas Department of Family and Protective Services justified the raid by claiming that the children at the ranch compound were in danger of either participating in or becoming victims of sexual abuse or forced marriage. At follow-up hearings, however, the department admitted that at least fifteen of the twenty girls being investigated were probably over age eighteen. An appeals court ruled that there was not sufficient evidence of child abuse and returned the children to their parents; the Texas Supreme Court concurred.[23]

Clearly, opposition to polygamy was at the heart of the state decision to intervene. Plural marriage is illegal in every state and nationally. But why?

Polygamy, in fact, has been widely accepted across the world. The Jewish patriarchs practiced it and accepted concubinage. It was not until the eleventh century that an authoritative Ashkenazi interpretation banned the practice, and even then the ban applied only in Christian lands at first. Polygamy still survives among some smaller branches of Judaism.[24] The second largest religion, Islam, allows up to four wives to this day. Hinduism did not eliminate polygamy until forced to during British rule of India. Buddhism never forbade it, allowing consorts in addition to wives until various countries limited it, mostly in modern times and under pressure from Western interests.

Of the major belief systems, only Christianity has consistently declared polygamy immoral. A few errant emperors did allow it, and Martin Luther once said, as a means to explain the bigamist marriage of Philip of Hesse, that he could not "forbid a person to marry several wives, for it does not contradict Scripture." But Luther was in a very small minority even among Lutherans.[25] As long as Christianity greatly influenced Western society and governments, its views on monogamous male and female marriage prevailed. Only with the advance of secularism and multiculturalism did many begin to question conventional Christian marriage. The changes affected some Christian denominations, which allowed serial divorce and then marriage of same-sex couples.

The question then arose, If the moral exclusivity given to a permanent union between a man and a woman was not absolute, what was wrong with more than one partner? Why serial polygamy and not actual polygamy?

As a result, secularists have been forced to deal with polygamy. Beginning with a Utah child custody case in 1991, the American Civil Liberties Union (ACLU) has opposed laws forbidding polygamy, as has the Libertarian Party, under the logic that if people desire multiple spouses, they should be free to have them. Why? The left-libertarian *Nation* columnist Katha Pollitt explained that "every person I spoke to connected" allowing polygamy with supporting single-sex marriage. She quoted one famous ACLU director as describing support for polygamy as "the price" for obtaining gay marriage. Pollitt disagreed, calling polygamy "radically inegalitarian" because it means that several wives have only a part of one husband. But she concluded that monogamous marriage was unequal too and that "marriage itself has to go."[26]

Others have put forward a purely biological argument for monogamy. The Charles Darwin Professor of Anthropology at Rutgers University, Lionel Tiger, reasoned:

> One of the triumphs of Western arrangements is the institution of monogamy, which has in principle made it possible for each male and female to enjoy a plausible shot at the reproductive outcome which all the apparatus of nature demands. Even Karl Marx did not fully appreciate the immense radicalism of this form of equity. . . . The victims [of polygamy] are not only young women but young men too. They are reproductively and productively disenfranchised, and are in effect forced to leave the communities to become hopeless, ill-schooled misfits in the towns of normal life. No dignified lives as celibate monks with colorful costumes for them. Again, the issue is cross-cultural. Osama bin Laden has at least five wives, which means that four young men of his tribe have no date on Saturday night and forever. They may become willing jihadists, or desperate suicides eager to soothe their god by killing infidels and Americans.[27]

That is, society needs monogamy for reproductive peace. If men do not have dates, they will cause social unrest. "The fact is," Tiger continued, "despite all the blather about faith and freedom of religion, the men operating the various compounds in question are behaving in virtually the same manner as countless dominant males in countless primate troops observed over the years."

But if nature "demands" reproductive enfranchisement, how did so many human and animal social systems survive so long with polygamy? Indeed, how do some endure to this day? If all the apparatus of nature demands monogamous reproduction, why have serial polygamy and declining fertility evolved as characteristic of the modern West?

Without the Western moral tradition as a guide, secular rationality is left with one of three conclusions: marriage is demanded by nature to be monogamous; marriage is the free union of presumably any set or number of beings; or marriage should be eliminated. Secular hyperrationality provides no one solution. This is precisely why even rational agnostics like F. A. Hayek have argued that the freest society acts rationally in allowing its accumulated traditions to be its predominant social assumptions once rationality cannot solve the matter. The fundamental social paradox is that a free society must be based on tradition. If freedom has no base of assumptions on which to build, it will end in chaos or inert

Do Mothers Mat

Freedom and rationality would seem to re   tely
decide the matters of marriage and childrea   lity
rates indicate that cultural changes, most not   ave
given women the freedom to throw off long-standing traditions. As early as 1942, the pioneering feminist Virginia Woolf concluded that American women had achieved freedom and essential political equality with men. The only things holding women back from true equality, she said, were "phantoms" in their own minds. The most "oppressive" of these myths was the "angel in the house" ideal of the sacrificing mother and wife rather than the free and independent (and even somewhat selfish) woman preached favorably by this prophet of modern feminism.[29] Partly as a result of Woolf's persuasiveness, many American women today have left the home and its myths of sacrifice to join the worlds of power and competition.

Still, such phantoms have proved difficult to eradicate. A recent book and comprehensive study of procreation attitudes by professors Suzanne M. Bianchi, John Robinson, and Melissa Milkie, *Changing Rhythms of American Family Life*, was supported by the prestigious Russell Sage Foundation and the American Sociological Association and was based on an ongoing Census Bureau study Bianchi led for sixteen years. The headline announcing the book and study was intriguing: "Despite Mommy Guilt, Time with Kids Increasing." Why "guilt"?[30]

Given the liberation of modern women, "We might have expected mothers to curtail the time spent caring for their children but they seem not to have done so," reported Bianchi, the chair of the University of Maryland sociology department and former president of the Population Association of America. Women still performed twice as much child care and housework as men in two-parent families, and almost all of this in single-parent ones, even as they worked more outside the home. But the study reported that modern mothers had actually increased the amount of time directly spent with their children—for married women, from 10.6 hours per week in 1965 to 12.9 hours a week in 2000, and for single mothers, from 7.5 to 11.8 hours per week.[31]

The study added that "it seems reasonable to expect that parental investment in child-rearing would have declined" since the 1960s, when 60 percent of all children lived in families with a breadwinning father and stay-at-home mother, whereas today only 30 percent live in such families. Yet in 1965 all mothers spent 10.2 hours per week "tending primarily to their children—feeding them, reading with them or playing games, for example"; today, after dipping in the 1970s and 1980s, that number is "higher than ever at nearly 14.1 hours per week."[32]

How could this happen? As parents have fewer children, they feel "pressure to rear a perfect child," Bianchi explained. "It's almost like it doesn't matter how much they do, they feel they do not do enough."[33] The angel in the house was difficult to suppress. But there is just so much time to get things done. Something had to give. The authors admitted that the study measured only direct child care and did not measure the importance of what they called "availability," or just "being there" for children. The study did record something close to "being there" time but called it "housework," as if it were simple dusting and scrubbing; the amount of time mothers spent on that declined from 32 to 19 hours per week.[34]

As the study noted, in the 1950s mothers thought that too much time directly hovering over children was smothering them.[35] Much of housekeeping actually was "being available" time. Indeed, housekeeping was replaced in "almost a one-to-one trade," as Professor Bianchi phrased it, with paid work, which jumped from 8 hours per week in 1965 to 23 hours in 2000. But young American working mothers mainly chose part-time, part-year, and flexible and irregular hours so that direct time spent with children could increase.

Societal changes have made paid work and its accompanying rewards—money, status, and self-satisfaction—universally available to women. As a result, there are fewer two-parent families and fewer children per mother.

But somehow American mothers have limited paid work and transformed the workplace so they could spend more time with their children. They are not as available as their mothers were and have fewer children, but they may be even more adroit in using the time they are willing to be there with their children.

The emphasis women continue to place on childrearing, along with the fact that fathers still devote half as many hours to child care and housework as do mothers, suggests that after all this time, major sexual differences remain. Professor Steven E. Rhoads has documented these disparities in his book *Taking Sex Differences Seriously.* Whereas almost all men seem similar in valuing aggressiveness, competitiveness, and dominance, women seem to divide into two camps. The majority of women prefer marriage, nest building, and children to work and power, and only a minority favor power and position over family. Even most high-powered women in candid surveys reject role reversal and prefer a partner superior in earnings, status, and power. Most women believe that feminism has made it harder to combine jobs and family to have a successful marriage.[36] In short, traditional attitudes toward marriage and childbearing are still important, at least for those having children.

Most interesting, there is a traditionalist bias in the demographic differences, a self-selection that will greatly affect what the next generation will look like. As Phillip Longman, a self-professed progressive, observed:

> Single-child families are prone to extinction. A single child replaces one of his or her parents, but not both. Nor do single-child families contribute much to future population. The 17.4 percent of baby boomer women who had only one child account for a mere 7.8 percent of children born in the next generation. By contrast, nearly a quarter of the children of baby boomers descend from the mere 11 percent of baby boomer women who had four or more children. These circumstances are leading to the emergence of a new society whose members will disproportionately be descended from parents who rejected the social tendencies that once made childlessness and small families the norm. These values include an adherence to traditional, patriarchal religion, and a strong identification with one's own folk or nation. . . . Among states that voted for President George W. Bush in 2004, fertility rates are 12 percent higher than in states that voted for Sen. John Kerry.[37]

Those women having children are more religious and will produce a more religious future population, at least until aging and outside educational and cultural temptations intervene. The German magazine *Der Spiegel's* survey likewise found that religion was very important for deciding whether to have children. Of the two-thirds of German women who said they believed in God, almost three-fourths said having children was a "particularly important" duty of individuals. Only 46 percent of nonbelievers thought that having children was important.[38] Similarly, a study of fifty large countries found a positive relationship between religion and childbearing.[39]

The available social science data in the United States suggest that, contra Dawkins, religion is positively related to many helpful social behaviors, including higher levels of marital happiness and stability; stronger parent-child relationships; greater educational aspirations and attainment, especially among the poor; better work habits; greater longevity and physical health; higher levels of well-being and happiness; higher recovery rates from addictions to alcohol or drugs; higher levels of self-control, self-esteem, and coping skills; higher rates of charitable donations and volunteering; higher levels of community cohesion and social support for those in need; lower divorce rates; lower cohabitation rates; lower rates of out-of-wedlock births; lower levels of teen sexual activity; less abuse of alcohol and drugs; lower rates of suicide, depression, and suicide ideation; lower levels of many infectious diseases; less juvenile crime; less violent crime; and less domestic violence.[40]

Here at last is some attribute that seems to provide energy for positive social behavior and the will to produce future generations. The data make it clear that religious values—in the United States primarily Christian values but also other traditional religious values such as those of Orthodox Judaism[41]—are critical to the choice of childbearing. As much distress as that may cause Professor Dawkins and his friends, that source of energy might just make religion essential to the survival of civilizations.[42] It is curious that when the radical atheist and critic of Christianity Christopher Hitchens was asked whether the world would be better without religion, he simply replied, "No."[43]

Islam Has the Will

There is only one alternative cultural system that has the desire and perhaps the energy to challenge the United States and the West. China may rise to power, but it has no universal values to impose. In fact, Christianity is proliferating there in the face of a moral vacuum and declining official opposition.[44] India's Hindu culture is not imperial. The remaining world's cultural and religious systems are too small to have such ambitions, much less any prospect for success. But Islam is large enough, and the faithful are under moral obligation to generate the energy to procreate and to convert and reform the unfaithful world.

Osama bin Laden's ideology centered on the belief that Christianity was the engine that powered the West and especially the U.S. "Satan" to humiliate Islam and conquer its territory. But that engine, he argued, had become corrupt and lost its vitality, so that Islam would triumph over the West by God's right, will, power.[45] On its face, this seems a preposterous boast. There is simply no comparison between the military power of the Muslim world and that of the West. But insurgency can be effective, as the situations in Afghanistan and Iraq have shown.[46]

Moreover, Islam makes a moral challenge. Most of the world believes that simple morality, common respect, and everyday piety are more important than Western freedom.[47] The major worldwide indictment of the West and the United States in particular is that they are assaulting the rest of humanity with ubiquitous images of personal immorality and commercial avarice through Hollywood, television, the Internet, music, dress, and the rest.[48] Crime in the United States is high by world standards. The family is threatened there as well: marriage is less common, and in America, divorce shot up to more than ten times higher in a century, from 0.3 per 1,000 population in 1860 to 3.5 in 1960; it kept rising to 4.7, where it has remained pretty much ever since.[49] Can Western societies survive with such behavior so widespread?

Pro-family Islam is poised to triumph in the crucial area of population. Today, none of the top five countries in population, and only one of the top ten, is Muslim. But by 2050, two of the top five, and five of the top ten, will be Muslim—and two of the others will have large Islamic minorities. Only the United States and Brazil could be considered Western of these largest ten.[50]

Islam will become a major international force through weight of population. Over the next half century the Muslim fertility increase will be almost 100 percent, double that of Christianity, especially its more liberal forms. Christianity will have more adherents only because it starts at a much higher population level and is so fecund in Africa and South America. The five major Muslim powers will represent 17.5 percent of the world's people, about equal to India's share and almost four times that of the United States.[51]

Islam has taken His injunction to "increase and multiply" to heart, and the results will change the political dynamics of the planet. Bin Laden's goal to tame the Christian tension into a new cosmological sharia state continues after his death. Any such success would mean more worldwide polygamy;

more limitations on female work, travel, and clothing; less alcohol; more restrictions on non-Muslim religious expression; and more limitations on artistic, cultural, and moral freedoms. But this will also mean less pornography, divorce, and child and drug abuse.[52]

Interestingly, even Dawkins has expressed some regrets. Once, when interviewing Hitchens, he asked his fellow atheist, "Do you ever worry that if we win and, so to speak, destroy Christianity, that vacuum would be filled by Islam?"[53]

Moral Hazard

Western liberty, as we have seen, grew out of the tension Christianity created by dividing state and society and making the individual the arbitrator between them, with the resulting freedom spreading to secular institutions worldwide. So what happens if this moral code weakens? As Joseph Schumpeter warned, the real moral hazard for those already enjoying the economic and social benefits of freedom and capitalism in the West is that the decline of the moral code will spell the end of its law, its greater social freedoms, and ultimately its prosperity.[54] Given that it is the only possible moral system available for the great majority of Americans—as important as other moral systems are, Islam is not an option and the rest have too small a membership—is it possible that Christian belief might be necessary for the social survival of the United States?

Could American religion possibly be sufficiently motivating? The dominance of religious symbolism during the memorial services following the momentous September 11 terrorist attack was impossible to ignore in the United States, but even 9/11 services in Germany were highly religious in tone.[55] In crises, there seems no alternative to religious symbolism. As we have seen, religiosity is likewise important for more mundane activities such as marriage and having children, and for positive social attributes generally.

A 2009 survey by the Study of Secularism program at Connecticut's Trinity College seemed to challenge the assumption that U.S. religion remained vital. News stories on the report emphasized that the number of Americans identifying as Christian declined from 86 percent in 1990 to 76 percent in 2008, and that those identifying as religious declined from 90 percent to 80 percent. But internals of the report told a different story. Seventy percent expressed belief in a personal God, while an additional 12 percent said there was a "higher power," 5.7 percent were "not sure," and 6.1 percent refused to answer the question. In fact, only 2.3 percent actually gave the atheistic answer "there is no such thing" as God, and only 4.3 percent gave the agnostic response "there is no way to know" whether there is a God or not. Therefore, only 6.6 percent actually said they were truly nonreligious.[56]

In 2007 the Pew Forum on Religion and Public Life conducted a larger study on religious affiliation. The Pew study listed 16 percent as unaffiliated with any religion. But only 1.6 percent considered themselves atheists and 2.4 percent agnostics; 6.3 were secular unaffiliated and 5.8 percent were unaffiliated but religious. Therefore, contrary to the Trinity study headlines, only 10 percent of Americans should be considered nonreligious, while 80 percent should be considered Christian and the rest identify with other religions.[57]

In 2010 Robert Putnam and David Campbell released a major new study showing that Americans not identifying or participating in any organized religion rose from 6 percent to 17 percent since 1970. But, the researchers pointed out, "a large proportion of those who demur from indicating a formal affiliation believe religion is important, pray regularly, and even attend a given congregation on occasion." Moreover, one-third of those who when first questioned said they had no religious affiliation said they did have one just a year later. Others who said they had a religion switched to "None." Clearly there are many "unchurched believers" who are on the "edge" of religion but have religious beliefs. This is especially true for the young, who participate less but who mostly still believe.[58]

All such studies show that religion and specifically Christianity are much more important in the United States than Europe. The Pew Research Center concluded:

> Religion is much more important to Americans than to people living in other wealthy nations. Six-in-ten (59%) people in the U.S. say religion plays a very important role in their lives. This is roughly twice the percentage of self-avowed religious people in Canada (30%), and an even higher proportion when compared with Japan and Western Europe. Americans' views are closer to people in developing nations than to the publics of developed nations.[59]

A 2012 Pew Center study confirmed these findings in very similar language.[60]

Polls show large majority support not only for traditional beliefs but also for such actions as prayer, membership, and attendance.[61] Only 8 percent of Americans said they never prayed, while 73 percent said they prayed at least weekly.[62] Fifty-nine percent claimed religion could answer most of "today's problems," and 83 percent said God answers prayers. Sixty-three percent of Americans said they were an actual member of a church or synagogue, and 42 percent claimed they had been to a service within the preceding seven days, numbers that have not changed greatly since polls began in the 1930s.[63] While 48 percent of Americans watch the most popular annual secular sporting event, the Super Bowl, and 52 percent vote every four years for president, 62 percent of adults report that they went to church services at Christmas.[64]

Attendance at local congregation services is the most important aspect of religiosity in terms of predicting positive social behavior. Putnam and Campbell's most controversial conclusion was that it was religious attendance, not religious beliefs, that explained these positive behaviors. But the statistical models used to arrive at this claim cannot say objectively which comes first; beliefs and attendance are difficult to separate. Critically, social participation by secularists does not result in as high degrees of neighborliness.[65]

Lack of church attendance can also be attributed to attitudes about religious organizations and the nature of these groups as opposed to religious beliefs per se. Many so-called religious leaders do not even claim to be religious. In Sweden, the Ecclesiastical Department minister who ran its state church was a well-known atheist. A former archbishop of Canterbury was called "red" to symbolize his attraction to Marxism.[66] Churches run by Caesar with monopoly control have no incentive to work for membership, and mandatory religious taxes provoke resentment. U.S. sociologist Rodney Stark found that only 17 percent attended church in 1776 America, about the same as in Europe today. Most of the thirteen original U.S. states had established churches; those states eventually ended their monopolies and other denominations entered the religious "market," and by the 1900s, 50 percent of Americans were attending church.[67]

Stark has noted that in many primitive religions there is no connection between religiosity and acting morally. Greco-Roman gods were positively capricious. It was not until God was conceived as personal and concerned about humans—under Judaism, reformed Hinduism, Christianity, and Islam—that religiosity became associated with moral behavior.[68] What difference do these beliefs have on behavior? No ancient philosopher, for example, objected to slavery as immoral, but Judaism punished slave murder with death, and as early as the year AD 655 the Christian St. Bathilde of France, serving as regent after the death of her husband, King Clovis II, began the campaign to end a declining slavery.[69] By the thirteenth century, St. Thomas Aquinas condemned slavery as sinful, and popes formalized the condemnation beginning in 1430.[70] As Tocqueville noted, Europe was free of slavery for almost one thousand years, until the age of discovery.[71]

In a study of twenty-seven nations with Christian backgrounds, Stark found that "the greater the importance people placed on God, the less likely they were to approve of buying goods they knew to be stolen; of failure to report that one had accidentally damaged an auto in a parking lot; or of smoking marijuana. The correlations were as high in Protestant as Roman Catholic nations and whether average levels of church attendance were high or low."[72] In the United States, the more religious—primarily Christians— are happier and more satisfied with their lives. They are about twice as likely to volunteer to help the poor or elderly, to assist in school or youth activities, to help in neighborhood, civic, health-care or anti-disease programs, and to take leadership roles in such organizations. While 48 percent of the nonre-ligious say that people should "look after themselves and not overly worry about others," only 26 percent of religious people take this position about not helping the needy.[73]

In his book *Coming Apart* the political scientist Charles Murray finds four values most essential to economic success and happiness: industri-ousness, honesty, marriage, and religion. Surprisingly, although the upper classes were most attracted to the 1960s revolt against traditional values, their divorce rates are lower, marital happiness is higher, work rates are much higher, and out-of-wedlock births are a mere 5 percent. They have even "held the line" on religiosity. As Murray puts it, however, they do not "preach what they practice." The lower classes are the ones now most affected by the erosion of these values: more than 40 percent of white women with a high school education or less have children outside of marriage, lower levels of satisfaction with their lives, much lower levels of work participation, and lower levels of church attendance.[74]

Even prominent agnostics and atheists recognize the positive role reli-gious beliefs play.[75] Jürgen Habermas, who as leader of the prestigious Frank-furt School provided much of the intellectual firepower for the secular and revolutionary New Left movement in the 1960s, admitted in a 2004 meeting with Cardinal Joseph Ratzinger that secular modernism was "going off the rails." He praised religion for being a stabilizing force. Habermas continued:

> The theory that a religious structure with transcendental references is the only thing which can help a contrite modernism out of the dead-end it currently finds itself in, is becoming popular again. It is in the interests of the constitutional state to deal compassionately with all of the cultural sources which can be used to feed our citizens' awareness of norms and solidarity.[76]

Cardinal Ratzinger was more than accommodating in return. Recognizing that religion sometimes was too dogmatic and disrespectful of reason, Ratzinger conceded that "the divine light of reason" must be seen "as a sort of checking mechanism, through which religion must clean and tidy itself." But he added that a transcendental religion was necessary to provide a satisfactory motivation for human life because secular materialism simply offers no compelling inspiration for a virtuous or meaningful life. Commenting on the meeting, philosopher Rüdiger Safranski argued that there is a pragmatic reason for the "yearning for moral transcendence, because man himself does not trust himself to make his way on his own: What I have made up myself can't be as valuable."[77]

Author Tom Wolfe, a religiously unaffiliated skeptic, was characteristically blunt: "Anyone who thinks religion is bad for society is out of his mind."[78]

Justifying Morality?

Habermas was correct. Pure rationalism is a dead end. Primitive mysticism just has no consistency or staying power in modern times, but neither can rationalism fulfill its own promise to provide a single rational answer to moral questions.[79] As we saw in the case of polygamy, the enlightened cannot agree on what is morally rational or even whether there is such a thing as morality.[80]

Presumably a truly secular rationalism would reject all tradition and religion and moral truth itself. Nietzsche's logic is unrelenting. When all of the mystery and "truth" of tradition are rationalized away, the only thing left is the truth of power.[81] The allure of power can give energy, but it dissipates. As Max Weber noted, every new social movement is energized by a charismatic leader—whether it be Buddha, David, Alexander, Augustus, Constantine, Charlemagne, Napoleon, Hitler, or Stalin—but the energy is soon sapped in what he described as the "routinization of charisma."[82]

Manipulation, coercion, and fear find their energy and legitimacy in the glory of the state. Montesquieu identified the rewards from conquest and spoils as the basis for the long rule of the Roman Empire. But as Machiavelli complained, in the Middle Ages the Christian rules of war took away the legitimacy of sacking cities indiscriminately and dividing their spoils. Although these rules were often ignored, it became difficult for even the least religious to justify the ruthlessness necessary to make war profitable. Then, with the rise of divine right in the sixteenth century, war and conquest became profitable again. But Louis XIV's defeat at Blenheim caused Montesquieu to predict the end of royal right and the coming superiority of the commercial, capitalist state.[83]

With legitimacy transferred to the modern welfare state in the nineteenth and twentieth centuries, it looked like popular secular government could provide an alternative to monarchy, the market, and the church. But the taxes and regulations necessary to support the state fettered productivity, so that the state could not satisfy the insatiable demand for services. Then the babies stopped and so did the tax revenues. By the twenty-first century, Caesar was in trouble because he was so big and lacked the energy, funds, or legitimacy to refuse popular demands.

In addition, the mainline Protestant denominations that had provided the economic, cultural, and political vitality and legitimacy for America's rise seemed exhausted. In 1880 these denominations contributed 96 percent of the U.S. missionaries to foreign lands. When many changed their mission from teaching spiritual Jesus to "skepticism about supernaturalism,"[84] and providing secular social services to the poor instead, they shrank to only 27 percent of missionaries in 1948, and by 1996 that figure had dropped to 4 percent. Evangelicals teaching a religiously inspired Jesus filled the void and came to monopolize the Protestant mission field.[85]

The Catholic Mother Teresa was once praised for the social work her sisters performed for India's poorest that government was not providing. "We are not social workers," she replied. "We do this for Jesus."[86] Well-paid government social workers just do not have the same motivation.[87] Without some higher legitimizing notion, even the impetus to have children seems lacking, surely not the world's most distasteful obligation. Contrary to the secular plan, Caesar became impotent and incompetent and just about dead. God, on the other hand, looked like he might survive.

Why does this matter? The problem is that the legitimacy of the United States, unlike that of Europe or any other ancient nation, rests to a great degree on the claims it made on declaring its independence as a nation:

> We hold these truths to be self-evident, that all men are created equal, that they are endowed by their Creator with certain unalienable rights, that among these are life, liberty and the pursuit of happiness. That to secure these rights, governments are instituted among men, deriving their just powers from the consent of the governed. That whenever any form of government becomes destructive to these ends, it is the right of the people to alter or to abolish it, and to institute new government, laying its foundation on such principles and organizing its powers in

such form, as to them shall seem most likely to effect their safety and happiness.

Self-Evident Truths?

If there are no such self-evident truths, why is Nietzsche wrong? If God is dead, why is not everything allowed? Why must power not rule without limits other than competing force? Without some authoritative source, why are violence and fraud not acceptable, even the Holocaust? Machiavelli, who understood the importance of "unarmed power" as opposed to raw coercion, still thought unarmed prophets like Jesus must fail and was determined to prove it. Clearly, the primitive mystical faiths have been unable to withstand this logic of power. Yet the monotheistic faiths that rejected and displaced them seem mostly to have survived Weber's otherwise universal social law and somehow remain vital. Those teaching the reality of a Creator—Israel, Jesus, and Muhammad—all have had lasting effect and have not routinized, or at least not as yet anywhere near terminally.[88]

If there are self-evident truths for the United States, they—especially the idea of an endowing Creator—must come from the Judeo-Christian tradition, for most Americans in its Christian form. For all his worldwide importance, Muhammad has little relevance to the West. Christianity, however, rests on the claimed reality of a single event, the Incarnation, the assertion that God entered human existence to change it. As Meyer—of Jewish and secular background and then not a baptized Christian—argued, it is impossible to deny the energy and the resulting change that followed this event even if it might be difficult to credit the divine nature of the cause.

Whatever the explanation, freedom entered history in a dramatic way following this event, causing an enduring tension between liberty and order, state and church, love and power, and all the rest. It overcame the Roman Empire without a shot, then won Europe (not always peacefully) and has dominated the world economically and politically to the present. Time itself is measured in the modern world before and after the event.[89]

Richard Dawkins's "four horsemen" of atheism claimed that the result was evil rather than moral, simply producing wars and intolerance. The issue is, compared with what? A listing of history's death tolls from war, massacres, and atrocities does not include a major religious event until number seventeen, the Thirty Years' War. In fact, this was a dynastic struggle more than a religious war, but even if we attribute it to religion, the 7 million lives claimed fall far short of atheistic Hitler's and nationalist Japan's World

War II total of 55 million, or even nationalism's 15 million in World War I. The Crusades have been said to have killed 1 million, but that was over two centuries of separate engagements with different combatants.[90] And it is in killing one's own people that modern secular utopians really distinguish themselves from the religious cultures. The notorious Spanish Inquisition killed 44,701 by the most meticulous calculation;[91] the French internal dynastic "religious" wars killed some 3 million. But Lenin and Joseph Stalin's Soviet Union killed 55 million of its own, and Mao Tse-tung's People's Republic of China killed 35 million of its people.[92]

Even though the Christian church challenged the state, Caesar always remained in the dominant position. The king, after all, was rid of Becket. After Westphalia, religion had continuing influence, but it no longer had separate or dominant power. Cultic, nationalist, and utopian elements in the tradition were most influential in the seats of power.[93] Professor Stark deserves much praise for forcing a reluctant sociology profession into accepting that religious beliefs, as opposed to the mere practice of rituals, were and remain a significant motivator for social action. He is too good a social scientist, however, not to note government as the final arbitrator of power.[94] It was Emperor Frederick II who first made heresy punishable by fire.[95]

In Spain, as one secular critic conceded, "The Inquisition always was under the control of the crown" to promote state rather than church interests, and the king "would brook no interference by Rome in the Spanish church." Machiavelli himself congratulated King Ferdinand for using the "pretext of religion" in the Inquisition to advance governmental interests.[96]

Christianity, while having a checkered history like the rest,[97] can claim some major offsetting accomplishments. It is the most successful enterprise on earth, with perhaps 40 percent of the world's population, well ahead of any nation or other religion.[98] The great philosopher Alfred North Whitehead gave its belief in the rationality of its God and its support for universities credit for the rise of science.[99] As Svetozar Pejovich demonstrated, church decisions prepared the way for the market and its abundance. Stark's analysis suggests that Christianity's claim to a God who cared enough to die for humanity inspired the early church to assist its members during plagues. The simple administration of water and food (now confirmed by modern medicine) saved thousands as pagans left even close family members exposed to die. Caring for members, banning infanticide, and opening the first hospitals for ordinary people produced more early Christians, accounting for the rapid increase of Christianity.[100]

Christianity's accusers are its best public relations. Nietzsche hated Christianity for its mercy, Machiavelli for its emphasis on peace rather than power and war, Rousseau for its pluralism and divided power, Marx for its economic market, and bin Laden for its freedom.

A leading progressive scholar has argued that American legitimacy can rest merely on "morality tales" that do not claim truth or even profundity.[101] Yet the Declaration of Independence asserted that there were truths, that these truths were based on "the laws of Nature and of Nature's God," and that a Creator endowed Americans with the "unalienable rights" its people claim as theirs today. Can fairy tales substitute for truths, or must there be some reality to the claim? Are the skeptics correct that it is all myth and power? Or is the inconceivable conceivable, that there might be truth somewhere within that tradition, not merely that its beliefs might be necessary to support a decent social order?

Is there a rational basis for the Founders' belief in these self-evident principles? In his seminal 1950 article "Theology and Falsification," philosopher Antony Flew noted that belief in God is not scientifically falsifiable and therefore cannot be a scientific statement, while atheism was a scientific statement that could be disproved. His article was widely reprinted in anthologies during the following years as one of the definitive secular disproofs of theism. Yet in 2004 the unthinkable happened. Flew conceded that atheism was not falsifiable either. Indeed, he said that he "had to go where the evidence leads" and that was to theism, although to Deism rather than Christianity or Judaism.[102]

Flew's unavoidable concession was that both atheism and theism are equivalent presuppositions, similar to those for science itself. They are first premises, axioms, assumptions, neither more provable than the other. Alvin Plantinga makes an excellent case that naturalism itself as understood by Dawkins and company is less logical than theistic.[103] What then? To Blaise Pascal, arguably history's greatest mathematician, reason must then move to probabilistic logic. If the probability that God exists is as likely as the assumption that he does not, and if the rewards for belief are infinite (in an unending life after death) but the gains for nonbelief are merely finite (in this world ending with death), it becomes rational to believe in God. Even if the odds of God's existence are much lower, infinity still dominates the calculation and determines the decision.[104]

Pascal chose Christianity as the most reasonable basis for such beliefs. So did most of America's Founders and their inspiration John Locke.[105] So have most Americans since. This acceptance of the Judeo-Christian tradition is not definitive, but it is a fact. Meyer argued that there are only three possible reactions: One can deny any truth. One can try to impose one's own single traditional or utopian truth. Or one can accept there is a truth but not the right to impose it. That paradox can be accepted in humility and pride—humility before the majesty of transcendence and pride in the freedom of the human person. That acceptance requires willingness to live life on this earth at high tension, a tension of men conscious simultaneously of their imperfection and of their freedom and their duty to move towards perfection. The acceptance of this tension is the distinguishing characteristic of the Western civilization of which we are a part, a characteristic shared by no other civilization in the world's history.[106]

Whether finally true or not, this tension was what unleashed the energy for the rise of the West and especially of the United States. The idea of a Creator's caring transcendence is where Meyer and Hayek parted and is perhaps where faith enters into consideration,[107] although the secular Hayek was not without hope.[108] The closest he could come was to call these traditions "symbolic truths."[109] Meyer had faith that the energy generated by the tension between freedom and tradition is an actual truth that can cope with the deepest perils of modern times:

> The simultaneous understanding that there exists transcendent perfection and that human beings are free and responsible to move towards perfection, although incapable of perfection, no longer puts men in an intolerable dilemma: the dilemma either, on the one hand, of denying their freedom and their personhood and sinking back into cosmological annihilation within a pantheistic All, or on the other hand of trying by sheer force of will to rival God and, as Utopians, to impose a limited human design of perfection upon a world by its nature imperfect. The Incarnation, understood as the "flash of eternity into time," the existential unity of the perfect and the imperfect, has enabled men of the West to live both in the world of nature and in the transcendent world without confusing them. It has made it possible to live, albeit in a state of tension, accepting both transcendence and the human condition with its freedom and imperfection.[110]

This is a difficult balance to keep, as all Western history has demonstrated.

Eight

———✦———

THE CONSTITUTIONAL MIRACLE

RELIGION AND TRADITION APPEAR TO provide much of the energy necessary for a vibrant social life, but both can generate such passion that they can be dangerous to social order. Rousseau was correct to this extent. Freeing the individual from the cosmological consensus has made nations difficult to rule. Failure to accept the resulting tension has caused a great deal of mischief and bloodshed over the centuries. But as "Father of the Constitution" James Madison made quite clear, it is not only religion that causes social disruption:

> A zeal for different opinions concerning religion, concerning government, and many other points, as well of speculation as of practice; an attachment to different leaders ambitiously contending for pre-eminence and power; or to persons of other descriptions whose fortunes have been interesting to the human passions, have, in turn, divided mankind into parties, inflamed them with mutual animosity, and rendered them much more disposed to vex and oppress each other than to co-operate for their common good. So strong is this propensity of mankind to fall into mutual animosities, that where no substantial occasion presents itself, the most frivolous and fanciful distinctions have been sufficient to kindle their unfriendly passions and excite their most violent conflicts. But the most common and durable source of factions has been the various and unequal distribution of property. Those who hold and those who are without property have ever formed distinct interests in society. Those who are creditors, and those who are debtors, fall under a like discrimination. A landed interest,

a manufacturing interest, a mercantile interest, a moneyed interest, with many lesser interests, grow up of necessity in civilized nations, and divide them into different classes, actuated by different sentiments and views.[1]

Those social divisions necessitate some means to control them. In ancient Israel only judges were necessary; there was otherwise no administrative government. Judges basically rode a circuit, making decisions; it was up to the community freely to enforce their decisions or not. This nongovernment lasted perhaps several hundred years and was unique in history, although primitive tribal consensus rule had a similar lack of formal structure. The problem with judges' rule is that, as happened to the prophet and judge Samuel, "his sons walked not in his ways but turned aside after lucre, took bribes and perverted judgment." So the people demanded and received a king and formal government.[2]

Since then government power has been ubiquitous. Madison argued that there are only three possible solutions to the clash of interests. The first is to give government the power to suppress the divisions, "destroying the liberty that is essential to" allowing people to disagree. He argued that this is equivalent to the foolishness of destroying air to eliminate the danger of fire, which air allows to ignite. Freedom causes disorder, but it is also as essential to energetic social life as air is to natural life.

The second solution is to demand that all citizens have the same opinions—that all agree. This is the historical cosmological solution, the one advocated by Rousseau and the progressives. Madison dismissed this idea as "impractical" as long as people have different property, interests, and opinions and are allowed the freedom to express them.

The only solution to faction compatible with liberty is "controlling its effects" through the "proper structure" of a government in a constitution.[3] Madison wrote:

If men were angels, no government would be necessary. If angels were to govern men, neither internal nor external controls on government would be necessary. In framing a government which is to be administered by men over men the great difficulty lies in this: You must first allow the government to control the governed; and in the next place oblige it to control itself. A dependence on the people is, no doubt, the primary control on the government but experience has taught mankind the necessity of auxiliary precautions.[4]

This view of human nature—as not univocally bad or good but as a balance between angelic and troublesome tendencies—was set deep within the Western Magna Carta tradition.[5] The Founders saw differences, divisions, factions, and even conflict as innate to the tensions of social life, arising naturally even from minor disagreements.

Concern about conflict underlay the whole constitutional structure the American Founders created. They sought to form governmental institutions that would balance ambition against ambition, interest against interest, region against region, religion against religion, power against power. The Founders believed that without internal and external restraints, the people would abuse freedom. While they saw popular rule as the "primary" reliance, they also put great emphasis on, for example, courts isolated from popular pressures, mass jealousies, and political resentments. They were concerned that elected legislators or executives would seek popular favor against unpopular minorities and bias decisions in favor of the majority. Indeed, the fear that popular passion was bankrupting the states was the major reason they created a new Constitution to replace the old.[6]

The terrible 2010 Gulf of Mexico BP oil rig explosion was an occasion for a great wave of public resentment. It cost the lives of eleven platform employees and spread oil across several thousand acres, creating one of the largest man-made spills ever. President Barack Obama sought to appease the anger by famously saying he was consulting with the experts "so I know whose ass to kick." Interior Secretary Ken Salazar promised the public he would keep his "boot on the neck" of BP top executive Tony Hayward, recalling George Orwell's *Nineteen Eighty-Four*, which defined totalitarianism as "a boot stamping on a human face, forever." When poor Hayward testified before Congress, he was hit from both sides of the political aisle and was lucky to escape with his skin and any dignity at all.[7]

With the public still unappeased, President Obama followed words with action, insisting that BP create a $20 billion fund to pay for the negative effects of its spill. Did Obama have the legal authority to do so? "I doubt it," said University of Pennsylvania law professor David Zaring. "The Oil Pollution Act, which gives the government special powers in this area, caps economic damages for off-shore drilling at $75 million. The government can also require for the company to pay for clean up costs, and there's this interesting provision in section 2716 of the Act, which applies to offshore facilities in the event of catastrophe." But that provision would allow liability only up to $150 million in some cases, well short of the $20 billion the president demanded.[8]

When Congressman Joe Barton of Texas called the excessive amount the president demanded a "shakedown," he was forced by his own Republican

whip and leader to recant or lose his ranking position on the energy committee. The White House press secretary condemned Barton at his daily news
briefing, and the Democratic Party promised to run campaign ads against
all Republicans for supporting unpopular BP. The dean of the Washington
press corps justified this rebuke on the grounds that "almost everyone else"
cheered the president's action, making Barton's statement politically fool-
ish, which it undoubtedly was. The legality or lack thereof of the president's
action was irrelevant.[9]

The earlier popular uproar against Enron, the high-flying oil-trading
and financial company, spurred charges against its CEO, Jeffrey Skilling. He
was quickly convicted on several counts, including the crime of depriving
stakeholders of his "honest services" in failing to protect their investments.
He was sent to prison for twenty-four years. But four years later, the Supreme
Court overturned that part of his conviction because the term *honest services*
was so impossibly vague it did not allow a normal person to understand
beforehand that he might be engaging in criminal conduct. The same day,
similar convictions of celebrity publisher Conrad Black and powerful legis-
lator Bruce Weyhrauch were reversed, threatening convictions in at least a
half dozen other prominent cases.[10]

The Founders intended the courts to help keep the executive branch
from improperly yielding to popular pressure. More than two hundred years
later, the courts can still fulfill that role. After Enron executive Kenneth Lay
died of a heart attack brought on by the strain of his legal case, the IRS sued
his estate, saying he had failed to report as income payments he returned
to Enron as part of his effort to save the company. But Judge Joseph Goeke
found the transactions legitimate and dismissed the harassing government
attempt. After years of court cases and a lower court conviction against
AIG Insurance and General Reinsurance following the economic crash, the
Court of Appeals threw the case out as without merit. After the Department
of Justice maliciously prosecuted Senator Ted Stevens, U.S. District judge
Emmet G. Sullivan not only criticized the government but also appointed a
special investigator. The investigator's five-hundred-page report concluded
that the unfair prosecution was "permeated by the systematic concealment
of significant exculpatory evidence."[11]

In these days of ideologically divided and even partisan courts, what
was unique about these highly charged cases was that the judges agreed. It
is true that in the Skilling case the three most conservative justices wanted
to invalidate the honest services provisions entirely and the full majority
agreed only that Congress should make the concept more understandable.[12]
Yet the fact that the entire court overruled the convictions against popu-

lar anger was noteworthy. It was especially significant because the decision was written by progressive stalwart Justice Ruth Bader Ginsburg, who took great public criticism from leftist critics for supporting the "top dogs of business." A *Washington Post* op-ed called her decision "a free pass for the corrupt."[13]

The vague concept of depriving others of one's honest services actually had long been subject to judicial scrutiny and was overturned previously in 1987, after which Congress tried to tighten the definition. Still, according to Columbia University law professor John Coffee, executive branch prosecutors courting public opinion used "any kind of skullduggery" to keep broadening its application. "It's a technique used to go after the infamous as opposed to the criminal," added Washington attorney Paul Wareham, "and it's high time that it's over with." Negating such prosecutorial abuses was precisely what the Founders expected the courts to do when public opinion went against the rule of law.[14]

That was noteworthy, but where does this judicial power against public opinion stop, if anywhere?

The Constitution Is What Judges Say It Is

In law school, budding future judges do not read the Constitution. Lawyers rarely consult the whole document. Mostly they read only judges' opinions on specific cases, reading a few words from the Constitution or Bill of Rights at a time, followed by pages of legal opinions about what that phrase really means. One law book mentioned that a nonlawyer scholar had read its proof copy and suggested printing the entire Constitution at the end; the text's editor did so, reacting as if this were a novel idea.

The reason judges read other judges' and lawyers' opinions about the Constitution rather than the document itself is that the ruling judicial doctrine of legal positivism holds that the law and Constitution are simply what the judges say they are. That is what the "supremacy clause" says, correct? At least that is what the judges think; it must be so. As Democratic congressman Henry Waxman insisted, "When I went to law school they said the law's what a judge says it is."[15] Why bother taking the radical step of reading the Constitution when judges have the final say?

This view is a far cry from what the Founders thought. Although they put great emphasis on the courts to protect rights, they considered the judiciary as the "weakest" branch and thought there was much more to be said about what was supreme in the Constitution.[16]

The Constitution did not even mention the doctrine of "judicial review" of congressional and presidential actions. But very early on, Chief Justice John Marshall argued that the separation of powers itself made it essential for the judicial branch to protect its own rights and not allow the other branches to force it into acting unjustly. That is what the Supreme Court correctly did in *Marbury v. Madison*, and in the Skilling case, keeping the executive from improperly influencing a judicial decision. Not until the pre–Civil War *Dred Scott* case did the Supreme Court first declare that it could invalidate a law of Congress even if the law had nothing to do with the judiciary. It was perhaps inauspicious that the precedent for this more general judicial review power was a case ordering the return of a slave to his master.[17]

Once again Woodrow Wilson was in the forefront, saying that the courts were "the chief instrumentality by which the law of the Constitution has been extended" beyond its original narrow meaning. "If they had interpreted the Constitution in its strict letter," Wilson said, "it would have proved a straight jacket" to national development.[18] Today the power of the judiciary to override any act of Congress or president is taken for granted. Not long ago, in a judicial symposium covered by C-Span, a judge was asked what he would do in a specified legal circumstance concerning mandatory minimum sentencing. He replied, "I can do anything I want. I am a federal judge! [*Laughter*] I am only being a little dramatic. A federal judge has lifetime tenure and can do pretty much what he wants."[19]

Even the most conservative jurists are captured by the idea that judges for better or worse control the Constitution. In a major essay, the late appeals court judge Robert Bork—who was unfairly denied confirmation to the Supreme Court because his views of the Constitution differed from those of the Senate majority, basically on one issue, abortion—argued that the adoption of the Bill of Rights and the Fourteenth Amendment "ultimately led to a virtually omnipotent aristocracy" of judges, who had successfully "rewritten major features of the Constitution."[20] In no area has this been more true than in the critical realm of federalism. Bork observed that history has proved "a false hope" the original idea that the "structural features" of the Constitution would limit the power of the national government and that residual power would rest in the states or in its citizens. Bork wrote:

> The idea of confining Congress to the enumerated powers of Article I, Section 8 (an idea reinforced by the Tenth Amendment) is dead and cannot be revived. Contrary to some conservative fantasies, federalism was killed not by New Deal justices who perverted this aspect of the Constitution but by the American people and the realities of national

politics. The public wants a large and largely unrestrained national government, one capable of giving them what they want.[21]

Confirming Tocqueville's fears, Bork argued that if the people demand strong national government, the judges will interpret the Constitution to deliver it to them. The idea that the states or even the institutional structure as a whole can affect this is a fantasy. "Today, the vitality of federalism is reduced to the occasional limitation of some federal power that has absolutely no relation to an enumerated power. Such cases tend to be trivial." Notice that to the former judge it is "cases" that count. Especially in interpreting the Bill of Rights, it is "judicially enforced doctrine" that matters, not the structure of the Constitution, just as H. L. A. Hart taught.

Political scientists see the situation differently. They note that judges do not "enforce" anything. They need the executive to execute their decisions. President Andrew Jackson put it simply: "The Supreme Court has made its decision, now let it enforce it."[22] The high court had ruled that large tracts of land sold by the Cherokee Nation were not lawfully transferred even though the Cherokees had sound private property claims to sell the land.[23] Despite the judges' ruling, the executive never returned the land to its rightful owners.

Bork quoted a political scientist when he explained how the courts had taken power from the other branches through a political alliance with the "intellectual class" to change the meaning of the Bill of Rights. Although he considered it a political fantasy to challenge this view, in fact such political alliances can change, and new ones can alter the balance of power in interpreting the Bill of Rights. The president can nominate new judges or selectively enforce their decisions or delay or ignore them. Congress can consent to new judges or impeach old ones or even pass laws undermining or voiding decisions.

A 1957 study by the Yale political scientist Robert Dahl should be required reading for every judge and lawyer. He looked at major Supreme Court decisions over the nation's history and found that Congress—when it was very concerned about the subject matter—often "overrode" court decisions by passing laws that effectively nullified them.[24] Even today, Congress, the president, and the states can effectively overrule court decisions. In 1988, Congress passed the so-called Civil Rights Restoration Act with the specific intent of voiding a Supreme Court ruling that had limited the way antidiscrimination regulations could be applied to institutions receiving federal funds. In 1991, another congressional civil rights law overruled five court decisions made in 1989.[25] The second President Bush effectively delayed judicial review of the Guantánamo prisoner cases until well after he left office. Even the states have undercut Supreme Court decisions on separation of church and state, for example, as cases involving religious iconology at Christmas or prayer in schools keep coming to the courts decades after federal judges presumably settled the matter.

Bork concluded that the Bill of Rights has "far more viable relevance to individual liberties than do the structural safeguards stressed by Madison." In truth, the individual constitutional structures—the House, Senate, president, courts, and even the states—still all are active in its interpretation. The institutions endure, but the relationships are flexible, and they change. Judge Bork was correct that the court and the national government are the most powerful today. But political action can change this.

The Founders crafted enormously flexible structures, and they still pretty much operate how Madison envisioned it, with the institutions checking and balancing power but with no predetermined result. As strange as this unstable equilibrium seems, it has lasted longer than all of the more legalistic alternatives. It can adjust.

Federalism Alive

After the 2010 election, when the newly formed Tea Party movement had the effrontery to demand the restoration of the Constitution's Tenth Amendment, the *Washington Post*'s resident progressive fussbudget, Dana Milbank, appeared near to fainting. From his cozy summer vacation manse on North Carolina's Outer Banks seashore, he mused sardonically about "how different things will be here when the South secedes from the Union."[26]

Milbank was provoked by former congressman Zach Wamp's statement that he hoped voters would send a message on the Tenth in the upcoming election "so that the states are not forced to consider separation from this government." Somehow the highly paid journalist could not understand the word "not." Texas governor Rick Perry, former congressman Tom DeLay, Congressman Ron Paul, and Congressman Steve King likewise caused the timid soul to fall into vapors by mentioning the word *separation*, although none actually endorsed such a proposition.

After frightening his fellow D.C. high pooh-bah vacationers about secession's dangers, Milbank conceded that the actual agenda of the "Tenthers" was "secession's cousin, nullification." He was horrified that a Missouri ballot resolution had passed the previous week by a 71 percent margin; the resolution declared the Obamacare provision requiring all Americans to purchase government-approved health insurance to be constitutionally invalid and a threat to Missouri citizens' rights.[27] Milbank took hope in the fact that such nullification had been tried before and failed, when South Carolina was forced to retreat before the threatening President Andrew Jackson in 1832. One may note that given his views in the Cherokee case, Jackson is not quite the best source to say that the decision must be the courts'.

Milbank claimed that to nullify Obamacare was to void Article VI: "This Constitution and the laws of the United States which shall be made in pursuance thereof . . . shall be the supreme law of the land." If people think a law is unconstitutional, intoned the progressive scribbler, all they need to do "is challenge the law in court," by which he meant a federal not a state court. Otherwise, he said, if the Tea Party folks did not like the Obama mandate, they should elect a new president and Congress or pass a constitutional amendment.

The good *Post* journalist apparently did not notice that Article VI requires all laws—including Obamacare—to be made "in pursuance" of the Constitution. If not, they are not the law of the land. If Obamacare or another law is, in fact, not a legitimate power of the federal government, the Tenth Amendment says, "The powers not delegated to the United States by the Constitution nor prohibited by it to the States are reserved to the States respectively, or to the people." Although the Tenth may be "dead" to the judiciary, that is what the amendment says. Who or what decides which provision is dead or not?

The correct answer is that the Constitution decides. But what is the Constitution? Madison summed up how the new government would act:

> In the compound republic of America, the power surrendered by the people is first divided between two distinct governments, and then the portion allotted to each subdivided among distinct and separate departments. Hence a double security arises to the rights of the people. The different governments will control each other at the same time that each will be controlled by itself. . . . Whilst all authority in it will be derived from and dependent on the society, the society itself will be broken into so many parts, interests, and classes of citizens, that the rights of individuals, or of the minority, will be in little danger from interested combinations of the majority. In a free government the security for civil rights must be the same as that for religious rights. It consists in the one case in the multiplicity of interests, and in the other in the multiplicity of sects. The degree of security in both cases will depend on the number of interests and sects; and this may be

presumed to depend on the extent of country and number of people comprehended under the same government. This view of the subject must particularly recommend a proper federal system to all the sincere and considerate friends of republican government.[28]

The Constitution is all about separation of powers, between branches and between national and state spheres. The Constitution separates powers, but the boundaries are flexible so that each can check the others. Rights are balanced, not determined on abstract principles by an all-powerful court. Indeed, Article III gives Congress the power to exclude certain rights from the appellate jurisdiction of the federal courts, which it has done in some cases. Presidents can and do decline to enforce laws they consider unconstitutional; most early presidents did so with laws about returning slaves, and most modern ones do with anti-racial-preference decisions. As Professor Dahl proved, Congress has in effect overridden Supreme Court decisions throughout history.

The states are likewise part of the constitutional separation, no matter how much progressives dislike that fact. Most federal programs are administered by the states. The enforcement of these laws differs greatly by state, depending on how important or constitutional the local officials think they are. Similarly, most federal court orders on state decisions are referred back to state courts to enforce, and the locals have great discretion in how they respond. Sometimes they delay until things become moot; sometimes nullification—a better term is *interposition*, when states interpose their power between their citizens and the national government—is more subtle. Wise state officials do not directly confront presidents or courts, any more than Congress does, but what they do with regard to their own laws and federal laws is often decisive.[29]

Interestingly, to pass the Obamacare bill, Congress needed to add four sections allowing states to escape the intent of the law: in providing state waivers from the individual mandate, in specifying means to avoid the new business taxes, in determining the allocation of subsidies to the new state "exchanges," and in waiving the federal standards for minimum benefits. In fact, more than a thousand state waivers were granted within the first six months of the bill's passage. Relying on the states to demand such waivers became the main opposition strategy—a way to delay implementation of Obamacare.[30]

It is often assumed that federalism failed African Americans. It is true that the national Supreme Court took the critical step of declaring state segregation unconstitutional in *Brown v. Board of Education* in 1954, but that decision overruled an earlier Supreme Court decision—*Plessy v. Ferguson* (1896)—which held that segregation was constitutional. If the United States had been organized as a central state, slavery probably would have been protected in all states. As it happened, because the regime was federal, sixteen states outlawed slavery before the Civil War. Many states passed civil rights laws before the federal government did, and even today many states enforce civil rights laws more vigorously than do national agencies.[31] Moreover, it was the national Congress that passed the Fugitive Slave Act of 1850 and the Supreme Court that issued *Dred Scott.*

In recent years, state attorneys general have increasingly been suing the feds for ignoring the Tenth Amendment. The states are far from dead. More than half the states challenged Obamacare, and the Virginia and Florida cases were approved by lower federal courts and partially accepted by the Supreme Court.[32] There was a movement to repeal the Seventeenth Amendment, which provides for the direct election of U.S. senators. A Firearms Freedom Act to void federal gun restrictions passed seven states and was under consideration in twenty more. Legislatures in at least four states passed outright nullification acts against the Real ID Act. Obamacare provoked seven state sovereignty resolutions. Medical marijuana laws to preempt federal laws passed in fourteen states. In the 2005 case *Gonzales v. Raich*, the U.S. Supreme Court ruled that the federal government could ban possession of marijuana even in those states that had legalized medical marijuana. But the Bush administration did not enforce those federal drug laws, and the Obama administration de facto nullified them.[33]

The truth is that state nullification and interposition are as American as apple pie—from the Virginia and Kentucky resolutions offered by Madison and Thomas Jefferson in 1798, to the New England revolt against the Embargo Act of 1807, to the de facto nullification of the Fugitive Slave Act by Wisconsin, Ohio, Kentucky, Massachusetts, and other states, to the Obama administration's nullification of *Gonzales v. Raich*, to the rise of the Tea Party and Tenthers.

Please do pass the smelling salts to poor Mr. Milbank.

Who Is in Charge?

It took a self-professed nonintellectual, President George W. Bush, to teach the professors, lawyers, politicians, journalists, and judges something about how the Constitution actually operates when he asserted absolute presidential control over the firing of U.S. attorneys in 2006.

The Democratic-led Congress immediately began challenging the president's right to fire the attorneys. At the time, it was widely assumed that Congress could file such a challenge and that, of course, the Supreme Court would then decide who was right. Even if the president ultimately prevailed, Bush would be hobbled for the rest of his term, fighting in court, begging the ultimate power to tell him what he was allowed to do. Almost no one understood how the U.S. Constitution really worked.

The legalist myth is that the courts are not political and are immune to political pressure. In 1895 William Howard Taft, then a federal circuit judge and later president and chief justice of the United States, pointed out:

> The opportunity freely and publicly to criticize judicial action is of vastly more importance to the body politic than the immunity of courts and judges from unjust aspersions and attack. Nothing tends more to render judges careful in their decisions and anxiously solicitous to do exact justice than the consciousness that every act of theirs is to be submitted to the intelligent scrutiny and candid criticism of their fellow men. In the case of judges having a life tenure, indeed, their very independence makes the right freely to comment on their decisions of greater importance, because it is the only practicable and available instrument in the hands of a free people to keep such judges alive to the reasonable demands of those they serve.[34]

When the Bush White House announced that it would refuse to allow U.S. attorneys to enforce a judicial contempt proceeding threatened against Chief of Staff Joshua Bolten for his role in the firings, congressional opponents were outraged. Senate Democratic Leader Harry Reid called it "an outrageous abuse of executive privilege"; Senator Charles Schumer said Bush was "hastening a constitutional crisis"; and Congressman Henry Waxman claimed that it "made a mockery of the ideal that no one is above the law."[35]

Did these hyperaggressive legislative attack hounds think the constitutional framers would leave the president defenseless against harassment by Congress? Did they think the president reported to the Supreme Court? Professor Mark Rozell of George Mason University apparently did, saying President Bush's decision would mean "the president's claim of executive privilege trumps all."[36] Well, no, it does not. The Constitution has a solution. While no court can touch the president, Congress can impeach him. That is how the Constitution is supposed to work.

One cannot really blame the progressive intellectuals. The Constitution goes against every conception about how government and society should work. Historically, almost everyone has believed that someone must be in charge. As the professors put it, sovereignty must be vested somewhere. Otherwise an organization has no center and supposedly cannot work. But the U.S. Constitution is based on separation of powers, where no one power rules but where the different institutions check and balance one another's power. The absence of a center place to resolve differences is the reason intellectuals of the Founding era (and every era since) predicted that the Constitution would fail.[37] The drama of the Constitution is that such an "illogical" arrangement is in fact the world's longest lasting.

Congress, as the more direct representative of the people and the creator of all law, might seem the center of power under the Constitution. But to dilute this great grant of power, the Constitution created two houses, a House where state representation was based on population and a Senate where each state had equal representation. Further, a president was granted a veto power over every action, and that veto could be overridden only by a two-thirds majority in each house, a very difficult consensus to achieve in a representative legislative body. With this internal division of power and an external veto, Congress is limited in what it can accomplish.

So is the president supreme? The veto is certainly a powerful weapon. Yet it is a negative rather than a positive power. The president cannot pass a law or act without congressional authorization or at least forbearance. Although presidents have acted on their own in what they proclaimed to be emergency situations, the Constitution balanced this executive discretion by giving Congress the power to impeach them or withhold the funds for everything they want to do. Courts can overrule their decisions.

Well, then, are judges—made so independent with life terms and the ability to interpret laws and the Constitution—supreme? No, courts need the executive to enforce every ruling they issue, which presidents such as Jackson and Abraham Lincoln have sometimes refused to do. Meanwhile, Congress must grant appropriations for courts to be able to hold trials and punish those convicted, and it has the power to set courts' appellate jurisdiction, the vast majority of the judiciary's current authority. At the end of the day, the Bill of Rights is too important to be left to any one institution.

All of this is balanced by independent states. The Founders thought the states had the real democratic power of the people behind them because they were closer to them and were trusted more. Even as the new Constitution granted more powers to the federal government, states were left significant independent power, whose limit is debated up to the present day. It is important that only the states can amend the whole Constitution: three-fourths of the states must vote to ratify proposals. While two-thirds of both houses of

Congress may propose amendments, two-thirds of the states by themselves (with merely procedural intervention by Congress) can also propose amendments and change the whole nature of the system without any participation at all from the president.

The lead-up to the Civil War dramatically illustrates how constitutionally divided power works. In the 1857 *Dred Scott* case, the Supreme Court declared the Missouri Compromise over slavery unconstitutional. With the only agreed-upon solution voided by Congress as well, the Senate, House, and president then checked one another so successfully that they could not agree on any alternative. But this judicial supremacy did not last. Frustration with the court's ruling led to the election of Abraham Lincoln and a more Republican Congress to break the logjam. The Southern states, in turn, refused to accept this and exercised their claimed right to secession, which led to war among the states. To execute that war, Lincoln exercised unprecedented powers, even abolishing appeals to the courts, holding 13,535 prisoners without habeas corpus protection—including 31 Maryland state legislators. When the Supreme Court ruled that he had acted unconstitutionally in exercising that power, Lincoln refused to allow enforcement of the judicial order.[38]

So did Lincoln's power to suspend even habeas corpus prove that the executive is the real power? Well, the strongest American president was assassinated and followed by the weakest, Andrew Johnson. Significantly, Congress came within one vote of removing Johnson from office for merely exercising the essential executive power of removing appointed officials (which was why Bush acted quickly). Although Johnson survived impeachment, his presidency was powerless. Congress overrode the constitutional separation of House and Senate—to which the Supreme Court deferred—by creating a joint Reconstruction Committee of party leaders from each house that made all decisions; subsequently both houses adopted those decisions overwhelmingly by party-line vote, assuring that the veto became a nullity.

That is how the constitutional checks and balances really work. In fact, no one is in charge.[39] In different circumstances, one institution is more powerful and other times another is, sometimes overwhelmingly powerful. The Supreme Court took hold of the whole pre–Civil War policy process but was ignored a few years later. The states dominated in the early years and caused civil war but then declined in power. President Lincoln was almost a dictator but was followed by an almost helpless Johnson. Lincoln dominated the House and Senate, but the Reconstruction Congress simply ignored the president. At any given time, one institution dominates—as the Supreme Court and national government tend to do today—but the instrument the

Founders created always allows for another day and a different balance of constitutional forces.

 Even most Americans would not recognize the reality of the Constitution as the Founders created it. In each era, the people are convinced that the existing balance of power is the constitutionally correct one. Most would probably dismiss the idea that there is no single, ultimate source for power. The Founders' idea was so radical that *The Federalist Papers* called it a "new science of politics"—the idea that a people could disperse power over a large expanse of territory, into a divided legislature, an independent court, a restricted executive, and sovereign states and still have a successful government. To work, the House, the Senate, the president, the Supreme Court and subordinate courts, the "sovereign" states, and an amendment process that can change all the rest—all of these need to agree or defer, or one or more institutions will block action.

 Senators, congressmen, presidents, judges, and all state and local officials take a solemn oath to defend the Constitution. But the Constitution necessarily means what those who swear the oaths interpret it to mean, not what someone else tells them it means. As President Jackson said in vetoing a bank bill:

> The Congress, the Executive, and the Court must each for itself be guided by its own opinion of the Constitution. Each public officer who takes an oath to support the Constitution swears that he will support it as he understands it, and not as it is understood by others. It is as much the duty of the House of Representatives, of the Senate, and of the President to decide upon the constitutionality of any bill or resolution which may be presented to them for passage or approval as it is of the supreme judges when it may be brought before them for judicial decision.[40]

 That is not how things usually play out today. George W. Bush famously signed the McCain-Feingold campaign finance bill, even though he said he had "serious constitutional concerns" about its validity, rather than vetoing the bill, as he was constitutionally empowered to do. He said he would leave it to the Supreme Court to decide its constitutionality.[41]

 President Jackson had a better understanding of constitutional structures and separation of powers. When one branch pushes too hard, the others can strike back. True, the Founders recognized that if each branch pushed its powers to the limit, the system would break—and that was precisely what happened in 1860. But no one would divide power into so many parts if the idea were for the central government to be the major decision

maker on all important social matters. This frustration of the original plan
is responsible for the current political deadlock.

The Constitution, however, is totally overshadowed by the much better understood Declaration of Independence, with its universally celebrated
holiday on the Fourth of July. Who even knows when Constitution Day is?
July 17 would be the most meaningful date. That was the day the Constitutional Convention defeated the proposal to make all state laws reviewable by
the national government. Even James Madison thought this proposal was
"essential," for he believed that rationality demanded a single central source
for settling matters. He was devastated at the defeat, but as the Constitution
evolved through the deliberations of many different people with conflicting
interests, he began to understand the federalism they had created. There was
a central government, but it was divided and therefore able to do only a few
things well. Madison even came to credit "providence" for bringing together
a group of leaders whose joint thinking produced a "double security" federal
system that was beyond any one mind's rationality beforehand.[42]

No One in Charge?

Adoption of the Constitution did not change the historical fact that most
peoples and cultures want agreement, with someone in charge. The Founders' Constitution requires the ability to live with Frank Meyer's "state of
tension," which keeps things from being pushed to the breaking point. If
support for the tension weakens, so does support for the old open-ended
Constitution. The desire to have someone in charge is overwhelming to the
more progressive-minded, who have no tradition that would tolerate such
ambiguity. That helps explain why so many Americans today think that the
Supreme Court will set everything right, resolving differences when Congress and the president disagree.

Given world history, the more interesting question is why would anyone
agree to a Constitution that separates power and leaves no one in charge?

Iran, for example, tolerates no such ambiguity. Its Guardian Council of
the Constitution is composed of twelve members; Iran's constitution specifically grants the council the power to veto all laws passed by the legislature, including on elections and who is eligible to participate in them. Only
half the members of the council are approved by the legislature. Unlike the
U.S. Supreme Court, which claims that its decisions are final, the Guardian
Council must refer vetoed laws back to the legislature—which is popularly
elected—for revision. If the legislature and council cannot agree, an Expedi-

ency Council—whose membership largely overlaps that of the council (both of which are dominated by appointees of the supreme president)—becomes the ultimate arbitrator. Someone is in charge.

What accounts for the historic shift in the United States from a belief in constitutional separation and balance of powers to a professed judicial supremacy more like that of Iran—that is, more like almost all the rest of the world, which vests ultimate power somewhere in pursuit of a common goal? Why is it so difficult for modern Americans to agree with or even understand the Founders, who held that ultimate power resided only in the structure of the Constitution and that no one branch had the final power to interpret or enforce it, including the "supreme" court?

The man most responsible for this change in attitude was America's "great world revolutionary," Woodrow Wilson.[43] Back in 1885, Wilson was blunt about why someone must be in charge. He had just returned from observing European governments and came away enormously impressed with how they concentrated government power to do good for society. The rising power Prussia made a particularly strong impression, for it had created the first welfare state. The problem with the United States, Wilson said, was specifically that its "federal government lacks strength because its powers are divided." This is the constitutional "defect which interprets all the rest," he argued. The American Founders simply "shrank from placing sovereign powers anywhere." The problem was the Constitution itself: "It is therefore manifestly a radical defect of our federal system that it parcels out power and confuses responsibility."[44]

The Founders were so obsessed with dividing power, Wilson claimed, because they believed it would inevitably lead to abuse. But power could be harnessed to do positive good, he insisted. The United States must at least follow Britain and combine the legislative and executive branches. Unified power and the accountability that resulted from having one institution responsible for all decisions, he concluded, were the "essential constituents of good government." As early as 1900, Wilson could applaud the shift of authority from Congress to the president, a concentration of power that had helped initiate the Spanish-American War. He advanced that centralization mightily when he became president a few years later.[45] Except for his immediate successors, Warren Harding and Calvin Coolidge, and later Ronald Reagan, the presidents who followed him more or less accepted Wilson's progressive vision rather than the Founders' view of the national government as being limited in its positive powers.

Nothing seemed strange to America's Founders about a triune central government and a federal Constitution of multiple regional governments.

Their culture had placed diversity of power in its very godhead, proclaiming a triune but also single rational God. Although other cultures had plural elements in their religious belief systems, Christianity went the furthest both to unify and to diversify its fountainhead through fusion and synthesis.[46]

Two major developments have weakened this tradition over time. First, a strong unitarian movement developed within U.S. Christianity that questioned a trinitarian God as irrational. This view came to dominate established mainline Protestant denominations through their principal theology schools, headed by Harvard, as early as the 1830s.[47] Second, the secular idea that there must be a single rational and scientific solution to all problems came to dominate the universities, the schools, the arts, the media, and the culture generally. As this view became popular, the older trinitarian view became less credible for government too.[48] When the "science of administration" appeared as the single crowning resolution of all difficulties, the old constitutional balance seemed an anachronism.

The inability to comprehend the idea of unity in diversity of power makes it impossible for progressives to see the world as the Founders did. At the heart of Western tradition is paradox, tension, ambiguity, subtlety, balance. There is a single Constitution but separate legislative, executive, and judicial branches; a national but also separate state and local governments; a single society but also churches and synagogues of many denominations and an infinite variety of private and public social entities that can be accommodated only by a vast social market allowing separate free choices. Once the subtlety of that synthesis cannot be comprehended, the Constitution as the Founders understood it cannot stand. It must be controlled.

Traditionalist Constitutionalism?

Progressivism was by no means alone in its desire to suppress the tension. As Frank Meyer argued, the desire to assert control can come from traditionalists or utopians of many stripes. Traditionalists may try to recover some "pantheistic All" to recreate a virtuous order supervised by a reconstituted cosmological state. Or there can be a rush to something entirely new, "to impose a limited human design of perfection upon a world by its nature imperfect," to use government power to establish a utopian version of freedom or justice as the end for society. Either way, the goal is to force a unitary vision in place of an open-ended Constitution.

According to Meyer, pure traditionalism and pure libertarianism are "both distortions of the same fundamental tradition" that undergirds the

Constitution.[49] Both have attempted to suppress the constitutional tension. Meyer was particularly critical of those traditionalists he called the New Conservatives—as opposed to the old conservatism of the Founders—who were inspired by professors Clinton Rossiter and Peter Viereck. In the name of tradition, they blamed Western individualism and freedom for weakening the ability of the state to inculcate virtue in modern times. Meyer especially targeted Rossiter's demand to reject the "indecent anti-statism of laissez faire individualism," which the professor claimed had undermined support for both traditional virtues and a compassionate welfare state.[50]

These so-called New Conservatives in fact adopted the same solution that two early twentieth-century philosophers of modern progressivism had proposed. T. H. Green and Leonard Hobhouse argued that the necessary reform of classical liberalism was to make a distinction between positive and negative freedom.[51] As Rossiter stated the required change in the New Conservatives' worldview: "The conservative should give us a definition of liberty that is positive and all-embracing, not negative and narrow. In the new conservative dictionary, *liberty* will be defined with the help of words like *opportunity, creativity, productivity,* and *security.*"[52]

Progressives offered different words to define "positive" liberty—terms like *equality, welfare, compassion,* and *fairness.* In either case, though, the result was the same: their ideology transformed liberty from a means to an end. The old meaning of liberty—as "freedom from" rather than "freedom to"—allowed individuals to set their own goals as long as they obeyed a few, understandable, general "negative" rules restricting one person's liberty from infringing upon another's. Changing that meaning gives government a positive role of deciding what "freedom to" entails. Conflating positive and negative liberty especially confounds the constitutional principle that the national government is limited in what it may properly do.[53]

Rossiter could legitimately claim the term *conservative* because he argued, properly, that conservatism implied realism. From that he concluded, not necessarily correctly, that conservatism must accommodate itself to the reality of the existing state. Rossiter argued that the New Deal had become so successful under Franklin Roosevelt and his successors that the only option was to conserve the basically unlimited government of the welfare state. He claimed that the Constitution's commerce, general welfare, and necessary and proper clauses essentially allowed the national government to undertake any type of social activity it wished, overruling the constraints of Article I, Section 8, and the Tenth Amendment. This New Conservative realism demanded only that the welfare state be administered with prudence, frugality, and respect for personal opportunity. Its more expansive view of the

Constitution proved so attractive that it became the theme of Republican presidents Richard Nixon, Gerald Ford, the two George Bushes, and to some degree Dwight Eisenhower.

Other social conservatives sought to resolve the tension by having the United States become an official "Christian nation," unifying power to translate Christian civic morality into public law.[54] Yet as early as AD 180 there already were a dozen Christian sects. By 431 the Assyrian Church had split; in 1054 the eastern and western churches separated; and in 1517 the great Protestant division began. In the United States, where eight in ten people accept the Christian designation, there are many denominations, with 26 percent of Christians considering themselves Evangelicals, 24 percent Catholics, 18 percent mainline Protestant, and 11 percent "other." Since this diversity exists as a result of disagreements over the very meaning of Christianity itself, with denominations differing on key issues such as abortion, the family, and morality, it is difficult to see how a Christian label could provide something as precise as unity on specific policies.

The opposite position is articulated by Professor James Davison Hunter. His view is not quite Anabaptist in requiring no contact with the state, but it does propose rejecting both coercion and quietism. It argues that Christians should not use power to force good. A proper religious stance "disentangles the life of the Church from the life of America" and "decouples the public from the private" to freely work out Christian peace and love among those around us locally. Christians should not worry about changing the world, which is considered impossible for man and simply up to God.[55] Indeed, forcing unification through government has been rejected by all but a few small groups within Christianity and is not really an option.[56]

One need not go as far as Hunter to recognize that the use of government power to impose either morality or welfare has not been successful. Christian conservatives have not been able to impose a loving, caring charity that humanizes the bureaucratic coldness of the welfare state; nor has a Rossiterian secular pragmatism been able to create a financially prudent welfare state. A Constitution unlimited in its power as supported by these pure traditionalists has only added to the red tape, insensitivity, and bankruptcy of the welfare state. More important, a tradition that allows the state to define its virtue has no objective standard at all. If it allows government to say what is virtuous or not based simply on the distribution of existing political forces at the moment, it is setting morality on the basis of power rather than of what is right.[57]

Libertarian Constitutionalism?

Certainly libertarianism should not have an argument against a freewheeling, open-ended Constitution that has no principle other than separating power as its operative principle? In theory, pure libertarianism defines freedom as without any tradition, contentless. But freedom with no content restrictions has no goal, no objective toward which human beings could or should move, unless the purpose or goal is contentlessness itself, in which case freedom incongruously becomes an end rather than a means.[58] Most self-described libertarians would be shocked to be linked to Rossiter and Viereck, but they have attempted to resolve the tension in the same manner, by defining "freedom" in a positive way that forces their own desired ends.

This was well illustrated in a 2005 debate under the topic "Conservatives and Libertarians: Can This Marriage Be Saved?" America's Future Foundation held a roundtable forum on the question of whether Meyer's philosophical "marriage" of libertarian means and traditionalist ends should be dissolved. Nick Gillespie of the libertarian magazine *Reason* made the case for divorce. Gillespie criticized conservatives for too much government spending and regulation when Republicans were in power, especially under the Bushes. But the conservatives agreed with him on this. The real issue was that the conservatives supported what Gillespie considered repressive institutions such as family and church, whose "authoritarian" obligations undermined modern free lifestyles, while a true libertarian must support freedom absolutely.[59]

When asked what his position would be if freedom led to the free choice of authoritarian institutions like the family, community, and religion, Gillespie responded: "That is a good question, but history shows no such tendency. Freedom leads to freedom." Not only did this avoid the question, but F. A. Hayek—whom Gillespie had quoted in support of his libertarian position—was clear that such institutions were what countered the state historically and allowed freedom to develop.[60] When asked specifically whether freedom must be defined as a means rather than an end, Gillespie was forced to agree, but again he denied that free means could lead to traditional ends. In fact, if Hayek was correct, history proved the opposite, that these "authoritarian" institutions were the sources of freedom, not the obstacle.

Gillespie was asked about the power of the progressive national courts in thwarting freedom. Interestingly, Gillespie denied that the courts were restrictive; he argued that they had generally played a pro-freedom role. Pure libertarianism defines positive freedom in a manner that requires a particular societal end: free lifestyles. This is the difficulty for the pure libertarian.

He requires the power of the state, through a Supreme Court isolated from public opinion, to enforce his type of freedom. Unless the national courts intervened to overcome private, local, state, and national "prejudices," "libertarian" free lifestyles would be frustrated by social pressures from traditional local social institutions, as the pure libertarian Emerson warned.

Pure libertarians require that the state define marriage to include the single-sex lifestyle. But it was the state following the French Revolution that usurped the power of churches to issue what were then their own private marriage contracts. Why would a means libertarian not favor reprivatizing the marriage contract, respecting the church's copyright defining it as between one man and one woman, and support civil unions as another private alternative? In the debate, Gillespie objected to a questioner's use of the term *sodomy* in reference to the Supreme Court's overruling a Texas statute on the matter; the *Reason* editor called it disrespectful, since this was now a protected constitutional right. It seems strange for a pure libertarian to interdict words because they are sanctified by the state.

Actually, freedom does not necessarily lead to freedom when defined as "free lifestyles." Freedom is unpredictable. What actually takes place under the means of America's hyperlibertarian Constitution cannot be set beforehand. In fact, Americans freely choose "authoritarian" institutions like family, church, and local community associations precisely to restrict their "free lifestyles." These individuals freely choose a traditionalist lifestyle instead. A contentless "freedom" is not appealing to them. Government courts in fact force "free" lifestyles against popular beliefs. The Constitution's freedom is not an end to Americans but a means toward a safe, free, moral, devout, loving, and ordered life. Should government deny them this freedom because under its newspeak only "free lifestyles" are labeled and enforced as freedom?

Agreement or Nonconformity?

Progressivism, pure traditionalism, and ends libertarianism are united in rejecting the Constitution's only end as being the balancing of power to leave state, local, and private sources to positively define the good ends of social life. Instead these three ideologies maintain that there is one right end for social life called positive freedom, which the state exists to promote. All three derive their positions from the philosophers of positive freedom. All three progressive doctrines reject the truly authoritarian solution of eliminating freedom as the means, but each assumes that everyone will agree that its version of positive freedom is the one right end if only all understood it correctly.

Although these three doctrines differ on goals—one favors scientific administration; another, traditional morality; the third, free lifestyles—they agree that people should pursue the same goal, *their* goal. That is, all three share the cosmological assumption that there should be a natural consensus on the proper end of society, an agreement that government officials and judges must enforce. Madison responded that expecting people to hold the same opinion on such matters was "impractical" and that the "propensity of mankind" was to have different beliefs and arrive at different conclusions.

The progressive position is that this agreement can come about through democratic participation.[61] But a widely reprinted analysis of the citizenship necessary for the modern welfare state calls this view into question. In the study, former Harvard University president Derek Bok conceded that while some public participation was important in a democracy, popular involvement in referenda and local activism did not necessarily lead to sound results as understood by those with the best understanding of the problem, the policy experts. Public opinion polls demonstrated that people did not want to give more time to active citizenship to understand the issues. Only half the people even bothered to vote. Consequently, Bok concluded, citizenship could not be active in a national welfare state. The public could be involved only through indirect means such as citizen education, support for public interest group surrogates, and voting to sustain the expert decision makers.[62]

Right at the beginning, the major theorists of the progressive welfare state recognized the paradox. As Gunnar Myrdal noted, for the experts to improve social welfare they must be free to plan more comprehensively. But progressivism also taught that democracy required people to participate in the government to give it the necessary legitimacy. That very participation could create pressures against the best expert-designed programs. In the progressive view, for the welfare state to be successful, power must be centralized in the hands of expert planners and popular participation must be limited to symbolic rather than active citizenship.[63]

The Constitution's Founders understood that national participation was necessarily symbolic for average citizens. That is why they devised a system where active citizenship was local and national responsibilities were limited. Tocqueville found that the early Constitution freely produced active citizen participation locally. This made the new nation work better than any other; greater participation at the levels closest to citizens even led to greater love of country.[64] The welfare state, by contrast, required a complacent, common national citizenship where citizens deferred to government experts, as Bok and Myrdal frankly admitted.

A modern study reported in the *Journal of Social Studies Research* asked eighth- and twelfth-grade students what citizenship meant to them. First of all, almost all the students had an answer. They were not uninterested, as the progressives assume, but they were not focused on national symbols either. As in Tocqueville's early America, national government was missing from their thoughts. The spontaneous response of the majority was that citizenship involved helping people in their communities and through their churches. Another one-fifth of the respondents said that citizenship meant obeying the rules of the community, religion, and school. The remaining one-third said: patriotism (undefined), loyalty, respect for others, and doing good work and being employed.[65]

In other words, local community is still alive, at least at this early age. From the progressive viewpoint, it is the responsibility of those who understand to liberate the people from these parochial but free ways of home, community, church, and school. Instead people must move into a nationalized scientific and/or free-lifestyle culture—delivered through a progressively inspired moral intelligentsia and mass media, starting in infancy with children's television, through teen music, art, and entertainment, and finally to an adult culture supported by government and establishment art.[66]

To a great degree, the progressive project has succeeded in both concentrating power and inculcating alternative lifestyles. In the face of this divorce of a significant part of the culture from its underlying tradition, what can the traditional constitutionalist do? The pure traditionalist must accept the changes as the new tradition or absolutely oppose them. What about those who support the old constitutional citizenship based on both traditional morality and individual freedom? The only solution would seem to be loyalty to the Constitution and to local participation but a peaceful yet resolute nonconformity toward the accepted progressive values and the outcomes to which they lead.

When progressive intellectual E. J. Dionne Jr. interviewed Cardinal Joseph Ratzinger in the 1980s, he could not comprehend how this seemingly intelligent man could insist on moral positions that conflicted with the views of a majority of Americans of his own tradition. Why could he just not compromise with those people, who mostly took libertarian views on social issues, especially on sexual matters? Ratzinger replied: "If it is true that a Christian faith taken seriously means nonconformity with a not inconsiderable number of contemporary social standards, then a more or less negative image is unavoidable." Ratzinger concluded that in a confused world, the obligation of a moral tradition, Christian or otherwise, is to recover the capacity for nonconformity rather than seeking either elite or mass approval.[67]

Ratzinger argued that traditionalists needed to develop an "adult faith" that did not depend on "the trends of fashion and the latest novelty" but was rooted in "a criterion by which to distinguish the true from the false." For traditionalists, this must be in God; for Christians, in Jesus Christ, who created in love the "only thing that lasts," the "human person." The traditionalist should not fear that "having a clear faith based on the creed of the church is often labeled as fundamentalism," not when the widely accepted alternative, relativism, really means "letting oneself be 'tossed here and there, carried about by every wind of doctrine.'" In truth, Ratzinger concluded, the only alternative to tradition is "a dictatorship of relativism that does not recognize anything as definitive and whose ultimate goal consists solely of one's own ego and desires."[68]

This nonconformity was very different from Emerson's following his own heart, for Ratzinger's view was "conformed and united" within a broad Judeo-Christian tradition. Yet freedom was part of that tradition too, as a consequence of the human person's being the "only thing that lasts." Once the cosmological veil is torn, the individual is freed from every restraining bond of clan, tribe, people, nation, and even family. As Jesus phrased it, "From now on there will be five in one family divided against one another, three against two and two against three."[69] Released from every social group restriction, each individual must freely accept or reject the truth by him- or herself, guided by tradition or not. This individual free choice creates the tension that made Western civilization so dynamic, a dynamism that can be resolved only through something equally powerful—what Ratzinger identified as love.

This freedom does not require rebellion from or even disloyalty to the social order or the government, but it does require a certain peaceful nonconformity toward them. Love of nation still may be high, but it cannot be blind. There must be tolerance and even love for all other individuals, traditions, and religions, since traditional values cannot rightly be imposed on other individuals. Such a tolerance can even accept that relativism is dominant and that it must be confronted in free and rational debate rather than through power.[70] Freedom is essential to human nature, Ratzinger argued, but it must be in the context of the Magna Carta tradition that identifies "constitutional democracy as being the only system realistically ensuring freedom."[71]

Progressivism has successfully overridden much of the old Constitution and tradition, consolidating significant power for and public conformity to its transformational vision. But Jürgen Habermas was correct that the whole progressive, enlightenment, rationalistic experiment is at a dead end.

Its rational tool for reform is under attack even in its university redoubt by a relativism and postmodernism whose adherents teach against rationality itself.[72] Progressive modernism requires a quiescent, conformist citizenry, but the resulting decline in energy and creativity weakens its welfare state socially, morally, and financially. The insurmountable obstacle is that concentrated power and uniformity cannot work in a complex world freed from cosmological unity and racked by tension. Freedom, tradition, and Constitution require nonconformity toward power, and progressivism demands submission to it.

One or the other must yield.

Nine

———◆◆———

A CONSTITUTIONAL WAY FORWARD

H ALFWAY THROUGH HIS FIRST TERM, President Barack Obama received
good news when the economists who officially decide such matters
announced that the Great Recession had ended the year before. The bad news
was that the government still reported an unemployment rate of 9.6 percent.
Worse, even after he poured massive stimulus dollars into increasing local
government employment, after the initial increase those jobs had declined by
77,000; this was the largest one-month drop in city jobs in thirty years. State
governments lost jobs too.[1] If total civilian labor force participation were as
high as before the recession, unemployment would actually be 11.5 percent.[2]

The problem for the president was that since the recession had ended in
June 2009, his stimulus could not possibly have had time to deliver whatever
recovery took place. In fact, it was the so-called recovery that concerned
Americans. The "recovery" felt more and more like long-term stagnation,
as Japan had been experiencing for two decades.[3] The Obama economy hit
bottom at a 1.6 percent annualized growth rate in the third quarter of 2009;
although it rebounded nicely to 5.0 percent the next quarter, it declined to
3.7 percent and then only to 1.7 percent and 2.3 percent in 2010.[4] Nor would
things get much better: the *best* quarter in 2011 saw a growth rate of only
2.8 percent; in 2012 the top mark was 2.7 percent, and the average was only
2.2 percent.[5] It was beginning to look more like stagnation forever.[6]

There had been thirteen recessions since 1929, and the experts in the
Treasury and the Federal Reserve neither predicted them nor controlled
them very well.[7] In 1975, President Gerald Ford enacted a stimulus, and
another was passed over his veto in 1976; neither worked enough to save his
presidency. His successor, Jimmy Carter, adopted a stimulus his first month

in office, and another was passed in 1977; neither avoided the recession in 1980 that led to his defeat. Only when Ronald Reagan rejected a temporary stimulus did recovery follow. George W. Bush tried a stimulus, and it cost his party the presidency in the following election. Barack Obama doubled down with a much greater stimulus and it did not seem to work economically either.[8] Even the Federal Reserve, after investigating its own record, conceded that its "historical forecast errors are large in economic terms."[9]

The Obama administration had increased total government spending to 24 percent of gross domestic product (GDP), the highest rate since World War II. But with growth still sluggish and joblessness remaining stubbornly high, there was little to show for the government's extensive and expensive interventions. *Washington Post* columnist Robert Samuelson noted in 2011 that America had accepted the "fundamental principles of contemporary economics" that the government knows how to prevent another Great Depression and to promote strong recoveries. But this "pretense of knowledge" had proved wrong, Samuelson said, and "the public is now disbelieving."[10]

President Obama managed reelection, but the International Monetary Fund predicted that U.S. growth for 2013 would be merely 2 percent.[11] The experts had failed and the public was skeptical. But that does not mean there is no other way forward.

The Fusionist Alternative

There seems only one major political movement in the United States that directly challenges the progressive premises and has any possibility to replace it. Before the 1950s, there were pure traditionalists and libertarians who opposed the dominant progressive ideology, and there were Republicans who were "do it slower than the Democrats" moderates. But there was no alternative that questioned the ruling progressive axioms on principle and presented a real challenge to its power. There was none, that is, until *National Review* magazine came along in 1955.[12]

The magazine's editors differed on many points, but they united in opposing the dominant progressive welfare state. One editor, Frank S. Meyer, expressed the hopes of the new movement:

> Power has only the next to last word in the affairs of men—not the last word. Power is wielded by men, controlled by men, divided by men, limited by men, as they are guided and inspired by their intellectual and spiritual understanding. There may be a gap of years, of decades,

between the onset of the impotence of a false world-view and the decay and defeat of the power structure which has arisen on the foundations of that world-view. But its defeat is, given time, the necessary result of the reemergence of truth in the consciousness of those who are concerned with matters of the intellect, with matters of the spirit, of those who—though they may have little control over material power at the moment—determine the foundations of the future.[13]

To *National Review*'s founding editor, William F. Buckley Jr., the alternative foundations that needed defending were "freedom, individuality, the sense of community, the sanctity of the family, the supremacy of the conscience, the spiritual view of life." Constitutionally, that meant freedom was meaningful only "in proportion as political power is decentralized." These traditional "verities" were threatened by the welfare state and required a principled response.[14] At first the new doctrine was inchoate but grew from the interactions of its creative but divided staff, which needed some common ground from which to publish a coherent enterprise. It became known as conservatism or "fusionist" conservatism, a synthesis of traditional Western values and the need for individual human freedom to achieve them.[15]

The movement's most recognizable and most popular leader was a longtime reader of that magazine and personal friend of the editors, Ronald Reagan. To a great extent, the success of this fusionist conservative movement in readdressing constitutional values through decentralized freedom must be judged by what he did or did not accomplish in its name.

As he assumed the presidency in 1981, Reagan reminded an audience of conservative allies in Washington of their roots. After listing "intellectual leaders like Russell Kirk, Friedrich Hayek, Henry Hazlitt, Milton Friedman, James Burnham, [and] Ludwig von Mises" as the ones who "shaped so much of our thoughts," he discussed only one of these influences at length:

It's especially hard to believe that it was only a decade ago, on a cold April day on a small hill in upstate New York, that another of these great thinkers, Frank Meyer, was buried. He'd made the awful journey that so many others had: He pulled himself from the clutches of "The [communist] God That Failed," and then in his writing fashioned a vigorous new synthesis of traditional and libertarian thought—a synthesis that is today recognized by many as modern conservatism.[16]

The new president outlined the ideas Meyer synthesized as the principles for this new conservative movement:

It was Frank Meyer who reminded us that the robust individualism of the American experience was part of the deeper current of Western learning and culture. He pointed out that a respect for law, an appreciation for tradition, and regard for the social consensus that gives stability to our public and private institutions, these civilized ideas must still motivate us even as we seek a new economic prosperity based on reducing government interference in the marketplace.

Our goals complement each other. We're not cutting the budget simply for the sake of sounder financial management. This is only a first step toward returning power to the states and communities, only a first step toward reordering the relationship between citizen and government. We can make government again responsive to the people by cutting its size and scope and thereby ensuring that its legitimate functions are performed efficiently and justly.

Because ours is a consistent philosophy of government, we can be very clear: We do not have a separate social agenda, separate economic agenda, and a separate foreign agenda. We have one agenda. Just as surely as we seek to put our financial house in order and rebuild our nation's defenses, so too we seek to protect the unborn, to end the manipulation of schoolchildren by utopian planners, and permit the acknowledgement of a Supreme Being in our classrooms just as we allow such acknowledgements in other public institutions.[17]

The essence of this fusionist synthesis was "cutting the size and scope" of the national government and "returning power to the states and communities" to allow the traditional "social consensus," "robust individualism," and the free market to restore prosperity and civic vitality. In sum, the goal was to restore the limited government the Constitution set up in Article I, Section 8, and the Tenth Amendment.

Ronald Reagan could claim some success in translating these ideas into action. Although he increased defense spending to contest the Cold War, he decreased nondefense discretionary government spending—which, after all, was all he promised—by 9.5 percent absolutely, the only modern president to achieve a net reduction over his terms of office.[18] His 23 percent tax cut drove down total spending from a projected 23.8 percent of GDP to 19.3 percent.[19] Reagan even reduced total domestic spending, including entitlements, from 17.4 percent of GDP in fiscal 1982 to 15.6 percent in fiscal 1989,[20] shifting more responsibilities to states, communities, and private institutions. Allowing a freed market to seek its own level led to a prosperity enjoyed for two decades, right up until the latest economic collapse. Fifty-five countries followed with tax and regulatory reductions of their own; trade was increased, and world income rose too. Indeed, during the most recent economic crisis many nations that had learned from Reagan weathered the storm better than America did.[21]

Reagan's attempt to restore the old Constitution has come under scrutiny from many directions but perhaps most provocatively from historian John Patrick Diggins. Even the esteemed conservative columnist George Will was wooed by Diggins's book *Ronald Reagan: Fate, Freedom, and the Making of History*. Will concluded from it that Reagan ultimately failed in his restoration because he told "people comforting and flattering things they want to hear," promising them that all their desires could and should be met. This pandering led to the unconstitutionally large and bad government that followed Reagan's terms in office, Will concluded.[22]

The worst charge to level at a democratic politician is that he cannot say no to things people should not have. Because such leaders depend on popular votes, the easiest thing is to say yes to every desire. More than two thousand years ago, Aristotle argued that this is why democracies do not last.[23]

Only a brilliant academic like Professor Diggins could make a convincing argument that Ronald Reagan was actually the cause of our present discontents, including big government. Diggins maintained that the 1980s were America's "Emersonian moment" because Reagan sometimes quoted optimistic phrases from the radical individualist Ralph Waldo Emerson. Even more, he said, it was Reagan's mother who was the real culprit, since her simple Christian religious faith pushed him into utopianism. Diggins caught Reagan writing in a 1951 letter that "God couldn't create evil so the desires he planted in us are good."[24]

It is this meager gruel that proved to the good professor that Reagan had adopted the "Emersonian faith" that "we please God by pleasing ourselves." Supposedly, Reagan believed with Emerson that people act on their own passions only and that these passions have no evil side, so leaders should say yes to all expressions of them. The determining proof was that Reagan's "theory of government has little reference to the principles of the American founding," when "the wisest of [the Founders], James Madison," insisted that "government's principal function is to resist, modulate and even frustrate the public's unruly passions." The Founders had created a separation-of-powers Constitution "to check the demands of the people," in Diggins's words, whereas Reagan blamed government for what was "inherent in democracy itself," supposedly giving in to people's rash desires.[25]

Diggins described himself as being somewhere "to the right of the Left and to the left of the Right." But he was an expert on the Left,[26] and he

suffered the leftist assumption that anyone who believed in individualism and optimism must be an Emersonian. To the wise men of the Left (as
opposed to Leninist apparatchiks) it must be either Emerson or Rousseau
(or Marx, properly understood)—the free, optimistic, selfish individualist,
or the rational, caring communalist.[27] There is nothing in between, no synthesis. Diggins was not a typical leftist, but he had the same rationalistic
belief that the Enlightenment made traditional thinking obsolete. He reasoned that because the Founders were serious people, their principles must
be Enlightenment rationalist, not silly Emersonian optimism sprinkled with
a bit of idealistic religion.

In Diggins's view, Reagan and other "fundamentalists" rejoiced at the
sight of "the word 'God' in the Declaration and other documents," but they
failed to recognize that "the founding is not the Declaration but the Constitution," which does not mention God or tradition.[28] To make the charge
that Reagan was a simplistic theological optimist and the Founders were not,
Diggins had to ignore that Emerson rejected Christianity and that Christianity did recognize evil. Even more, he had to exclude the Declaration of
Independence as an American founding document! This is the opposite
extreme from the Declaration "creedalists" who would exclude the Constitution.[29] Obviously, both documents are essential to the founding principles.

In a presidential speech that apparently escaped Diggins's scholarship,
Reagan synthesized the Constitution and the Declaration. Here the president referred specifically to the man he supposedly forgot, James Madison,
and to the constitutional limitations on democracy he supposedly did not
understand:

> Madison knew and we should always remember that no government is
> perfect, not even a democracy. Rights given to government were taken
> from the people, and so he believed that government's touch in our
> lives should be light, that powers entrusted to it be administered by
> temporary guardians. He wrote that "government was the greatest of
> all reflections on human nature." He wrote that "if men were angels, no
> government would be necessary. If angels were to govern men, neither
> external nor internal controls on government would be necessary. In
> framing a government," he said, "which is to be administered by men
> over men, the great difficulty lies in this: you must first enable the gov-
> ernment to control the governed, and next oblige it to control itself."

Led by Madison and Jefferson and others, the authors of the Constitution established a fragile balance between the branches and levels
of government. That concept was their genius and the secret of our

success—that idea of federalism. The balance of power intended in the Constitution is the guarantor of the greatest measure of individual freedom any people have ever known. Our task today, this year, this decade, must be to reaffirm those ideas. Our Founding Fathers designed a system of government that was unique in all the world—a federation of sovereign states with as much law and decision-making authority as possible kept at the local level. They knew that man's very need for government meant no government should function unchecked.

We the people—and that is still the most powerful phrase—created government for our own convenience. It can have no power except that voluntarily granted to it by the people. We founded our society on the belief that the rights of men were ours by grace of God. That vision of our Founding Fathers revolutionized the world.[30]

Is this a utopian optimist who overlooked the founding principles and the Constitution? Is this a man who believed in unchecked satisfaction of the desires of the governed, that democracy was perfect, or that individuals were not subject to higher authority? Yes, he recognized the power of the people, but he specifically quoted from *The Federalist Papers* to emphasize that men were not angels and that the people needed external controls.

In these comments, and in his statement on Frank Meyer, the fusionist Ronald Reagan answered Diggins's charges. His remarks on Meyer clearly stated the nature of the synthesis between libertarianism and traditionalism that was the basis of his philosophy. His remarks on Madison clearly demonstrated his understanding of the Constitution. Was this president who successfully brought many of these philosophical principles to fruition driven only by emotion? Was the man who called the Soviet Union an "evil empire" oblivious to evil in the world? Was the man who faced down that empire and changed the world's view of government and the economy simplistic? Was the only modern president to reduce nondefense discretionary spending absolutely and total domestic spending relatively unable to say no to popular desires? Who are these people talking about?

Libertarian Manqué?

Despite Reagan's successes, he and his limited-government constitutionalism came under fire immediately afterward from his own vice president and direct successor, George H. W. Bush. In accepting his party's nomination at the 1988 Republican National Convention, Bush called for a "kinder, gentler" country. As protective wife Nancy Reagan was reported to have whispered under her breath at the time, kinder and gentler than whom? No one missed the point that he was making a significant break from his predecessor.

The basic argument against Reagan's constitutional fusionism was that it was simply libertarianism with traditionalist camouflage—what the libertarian economist Murray Rothbard called the ideas of "a libertarian manqué."[31] Meyer, according to this view, was a clever libertarian out to hoodwink traditionalists.[32] Yet Meyer's fusionism was clear that freedom was not enough and that tradition was essential in interpreting freedom itself.[33] No political decisions even on coercion, fraud, or property could be made without using tradition to settle between different free means: "Freedom remains the criterion, the principle, the guide; but the application of principle to circumstance demands a prudential act." Meyer added that "no practical situation can be the direct reflection of a general principle," even that of freedom. "The intricate fibers of tradition" are always required to "affect the realization of any general principle."[34] Still, his words were often dismissed as merely part of the disguise.

Later, George W. Bush confronted Reagan's limited-government constitutionalism more directly with the idea of "compassionate conservatism," where the national government would not be limited but would respond whenever someone hurt. In a *Washington Post* column and later in a book, *Heroic Conservatism*, Michael Gerson, Bush's top speechwriter and a close presidential adviser, laid out the most comprehensive argument against Meyer-like "anti-government conservatism," saying it was not traditionalist, not "morally driven," and not dedicated to "economic and social justice" at all. Gerson claimed that any truly moral program must be based on "the social teachings of the Jewish and Christian traditions," especially on formal Catholic social thought as systematically outlined in its magisterium, even though Gerson himself was proudly an Evangelical Protestant. He insisted:

> The difference between these visions is considerable. Various forms of libertarianism and anti-government conservatism share a belief that justice is defined by the imposition of impartial rules—free markets and the rule of law. If everyone is treated fairly and equally, the state has done its job. But Catholic social thought takes a large step beyond that view. While it affirms the principle of limited government—asserting the existence of a world of families, congregations and community institutions where government should rarely tread—it also asserts that the justice of society is measured by its treatment of the helpless and poor. And this creates a positive obligation to order society in a way that protects and benefits the powerless and suffering.[35]

What were Gerson's more moral "creative proposals"? He called for a national health-care system, "affordable" college education, programs to encourage "savings, ownership and financial literacy," and a way to address "the largest economic challenge of our moment—the recovery of economic mobility." He chided libertarians for opposing the Bush administration's massive interventions to help the poor, failing to acknowledge even the possibility that limited-government conservatives thought such big-government interventions were neither authorized by the Constitution nor supported by good sense.

Gerson called the Bush Medicare prescription drug bill a "good example" of a "contribution to the justice and fairness of American society." Regardless of its constitutionality, he ignored the possible inequities involved: that seniors were the wealthiest age class in the United States and that poorer younger citizens were forced to subsidize them in that bill. Nor did he say anything about the fact that the program added an estimated unfunded liability larger than Social Security's, to be paid for by far fewer of these less wealthy young citizens. Moreover, Gerson did not emphasize that most of the actual successes he mentioned (such as lifting the oil drilling ban and allowing religious groups to participate equally with nonreligious groups for federal contracts) merely repealed the national government's bureaucratic intrusions.

The essence of the "compassionate conservative" program was to use national government to solve virtually all of society's problems. In Gerson's words, "the bold use of government to serve human rights and dignity is not only a good thing, but a necessary thing." Gerson did not acknowledge that this "bold use of government" could lead to worsening conditions and override the rights of private institutions. He did not accept that becoming "the party of idealism, action and risk" and "eager purity" was precisely the hubris that led to the decline of the welfare state, stagflation in the 1970s, and the crisis of entitlement spending today.

Gerson also ignored Professor James Davison Hunter's concern that it is immoral to use power to force such moral values. Hunter called Christians' use of such power "Constantinian," referring to how Emperor Constantine recognized and supported the church but then controlled and politicized it. The politicization of moral impulses, Hunter argued, led the Religious Right to demand much from national government and compromise too much to get what little it did. That, in turn, led to a decline in the Religious Right's political power. He recommended that Christian moralists "be silent for a season" and instead be active helping their neighbors in their communities. In Meyer-like language, Hunter suggested that until God restores Jerusalem, "there are tensions that the church must not only live with but deliberately and actively cultivate."[36]

Although Gerson recognized the law of unintended consequences that made traditional conservatives reluctant to give too much power to national government, in the end he considered this concern an excuse not to act. Only a response using national laws and regulations counted as a moral action. In other words, Gerson was a modern welfare state progressive following in the path of the New Conservatives like Clinton Rossiter. The only difference between Gerson and a Gunnar Myrdal was that the Bush speechwriter gave a religious rationale. In that sense Gerson was more like Woodrow Wilson, who used similar religious symbolism. Indeed, Gerson's description of compassionate conservatism as "restless reform and idealism and moral conviction" could come right from Wilson, whom Gerson cited favorably in his book.[37]

But the most serious charge against Gerson was that his own prescriptions for a moral conservatism did not take seriously the very Catholic social thought he said a true conservatism must follow. All of his proposals involved the national government, meaning that Gerson disregarded his own requirement of relying on "families, congregations and community institutions"— the institutions the Founders expected to solve social problems better than big government, and the area of civil society where, in Gerson's own words, "government should rarely tread." The Catholic social thought Gerson cited so approvingly was actually quite clear on the matter. Way back in 1931, Pope Pius XI wrote:

> It is wrong to withdraw from the individual and commit to the community at large what private enterprise and industry can accomplish; so too, it is an injustice, a grave evil and a disturbance of right order for a larger and higher organization to arrogate to itself functions which can be performed efficiently by smaller and lower bodies. This is a fundamental principle of social philosophy, unshaken and unchangeable.[38]

In 1991 Pope John Paul II strengthened this doctrine of decentralized "subsidiarity" with a direct condemnation of the abuses of bureaucratic welfare state intervention. Tracing his logic back to Pope Leo XIII in 1891, John Paul II argued:

> In recent years the range of such intervention has vastly expanded, to the point of creating a new type of State, the so-called "Welfare State." This has happened in some countries in order to respond better to

many needs and demands, by remedying forms of poverty and deprivation unworthy of the human person. However, excesses and abuses, especially in recent years, have provoked very harsh criticisms of the Welfare State, dubbed the "Social Assistance State." Malfunctions and defects in the Social Assistance State are the result of an inadequate understanding of the tasks proper to the State. Here again *the principle of subsidiarity* must be respected: a community of a higher order should not interfere in the internal life of a community of a lower order, depriving the latter of its functions, but rather should support it in case of need and help to coordinate its activity with the activities of the rest of society, always with a view to the common good.

By intervening directly and depriving society of its responsibility, the Social Assistance State leads to a loss of human energies and an inordinate increase of public agencies, which are dominated more by bureaucratic ways of thinking than by concern for serving their clients, and which are accompanied by an enormous increase in spending. In fact, it would appear that needs are best understood and satisfied by people who are closest to them and who act as neighbors to those in need. It should be added that certain kinds of demands often call for a response which is not simply material but which is capable of perceiving the deeper human need.[39]

While invoking subsidiarity, Gerson's compassionate conservatism looked to the national government first, last, and seemingly always.[40] There was no test whether programs were constitutional. There was hardly a mention of local government in Gerson's magnum opus. He overlooked the fact that his big-government conservatism undermined a "fundamental principle of social philosophy" and thus was not moral at all under the very standard he offered by which to judge his old New Conservative philosophy as superior to Reagan's fusionist vision.

Moral Markets?

Is it in fact possible for a fusionist, limited-government constitutionalism to solve the enormous social and welfare problems that beset society in the modern world while still meeting Gerson's moral test that the "justice of society is measured by its treatment of the helpless and the poor"? Constitutional government as understood through the Tenth Amendment expects most social life to be local and private. Gerson's "compassionate" welfare state does not meet his own criteria, but how would limited government's first solution, the private market, be rated under such a moral standard?

Progressivism in its roots was socialist in the sense of using national government to solve social problems. But it was also capitalist in another respect, embracing the idea of "economies of scale." Progressivism believed that the success of mass production for household goods, automobiles, and manufacturing generally "proved" that larger production units run by "scientific managers" produced goods more efficiently, as Woodrow Wilson made clear in his pathbreaking article on administration.[41] Scientifically breaking a manufacturing or assembly process down to smaller, more routine tasks and then combining them in ever larger, continuous process organizations to create efficiencies of scale would result in greater production, wealth, welfare, and prosperity for all.[42]

This idea of rationalizing large-scale bureaucratic ways captured the imagination of all—progressives, socialists, communists, fascists, and capitalists. Everyone went into bigness as business corporations led a whole new degree of prosperity by the late nineteenth century. Capitalists were the first to regret the blind pursuit of bigness. It turned out that larger was not necessarily more efficient in the private sector. Large corporations began a massive internal decentralization movement in the mid-twentieth century, which waxed in the 1980s and has not abated to this day. To some extent, the change came as a result of the shift from manufacturing to a service economy, but even manufacturing switched to smaller internal units with more localized autonomy.[43]

The size of the firm mattered too.[44] It turned out that by century's end, private firms of more than 500 employees posted a net loss of 645,000 jobs, while smaller firms produced the 11.8 million net new jobs that represented prosperity for the twentieth-century United States.[45] One of the reasons that Europe lagged was its much greater dependence on large, more bureaucratic firms. In a more competitive environment, smaller firms were forced to produce or fail.[46] Government took longer to learn the limits to large size, but the collapse of the Soviet Union convinced most that there were huge costs to government centralization and bureaucracy. The assumption that government bureaucracy provided the scientific solution gave way to the idea that the market was more efficient than government.

Even the Great Recession did not substantially change the dynamics, although many more people justified increased government intervention to contain the crisis. Even at its lowest point, President Obama was still singing the merits of private business.[47] Schumpeter's view—that the essence of capitalism and its success was its creative destruction—had largely won the intellectual debate.[48] The good news was that market freedom had no peer in creating new products and wealth. The bad news was that it destroyed old forms and institutions in the process. Thomas Friedman's incredibly influential book *The Lexus and the Olive Tree* (1999) told the story most effectively. Being a columnist for the progressive *New York Times* and a two-time Pulitzer Prize winner, he was credible making both cases.

Friedman concluded that the market and even creative destruction were essential if most of the world was to rise from crippling poverty. He even gave Ronald Reagan some credit for "one of the key turning points in American history": when the president fired the air-traffic controllers and proved that managers did not have to be cowed by market-inhibiting labor unions in critical industries. Friedman's conclusion was rather remarkable, given that intellectuals tend to lean left and be suspicious of the market.[49] When a prominent figure like Friedman said there was no choice—that there is a world market and a nation must either join it or suffer from poverty—who could gainsay it?[50]

At the same time, Friedman found that this market efficiency was accompanied by a sense of loss of local values, of community, of the "olive tree"—the land, people, and setting that make this place familiar and comfortable to my family and my neighbors. The very efficiency of the market threatened old ways and beloved institutions around the world. That was an unavoidable feature of a global economy: nations could not control the market, not even the powerful United States. No one was in control of the destruction, which left everyone in fear that "markets are determined by foreigners"—that is, by international markets. How can we trust our sense of self, our livelihoods, and even our lives to those we do not know?[51] The sense of loss permeated not only the developing countries but also wealthy ones like the United States. The largest antiglobalism protest, after all, was organized in Seattle.

The reaction in the United States, with its great prosperity, was not comprehensible to Friedman. The market was so obviously needed for mutual growth that he could not understand why a progressive Congress at the time refused to extend free trade, except that "the AFL-CIO labor union federation had become probably the most powerful political force against globalization" and defeated it.[52] Friedman did look to national and international governmental bodies to control the negative effects—he called Republicans "mean-spirited" for not believing that the International Monetary Fund or national governments could mitigate many of the resulting social problems. But Friedman's bottom line was that struggling workers in emerging nations must participate in markets or perish. The fact that free markets are essential for the poorest to rise is, one would assume, sufficient for most reasonable people to concede that this primary tool of a free constitutional order is moral as well as efficient.

Moral Libertarianism

Progressive economics professor and Nobel winner Robert M. Solow has gone so far as to claim: "Everyone has known for a long time that a complicated industrial economy is either a market economy or a mess. The real issues are pragmatic."[53] Although the market provides growing wealth, improved sanitation, better health, and other benefits, are Friedman and progressives generally correct to be concerned that something important is missing? Is pure libertarianism simply incompatible with traditionalist moral concerns for the poor, freedom being unable to handle what slips through the cracks of the market?

Here the two presidents Bush differed. The father sounded optimistic that his "thousand points of light" of free voluntary activity could significantly ameliorate market failures for the poor. But his son declared that "government would never be replaced by charities and community groups."[54] How naïve to believe that pure libertarianism could care about, much less solve, traditionalist concerns about the helpless and the poor.

Actually, it is not naïve, according to Edward Feser. Professor Feser, whom *National Review* has called "one of the best contemporary writers on philosophy," stated that there are only five justifications for libertarianism and that "none of these arguments plausibly supports the idea that libertarianism is incompatible with a strongly traditionalist outlook."[55] At bottom, he claimed, traditionalist Edmund Burke and libertarian F. A. Hayek agreed that tradition was the foundation of both society and freedom. They shared the view that "a human being is not a mere animal, but a rational being with the power of free moral choice, a *person*—a creature made, as religious conservatives would put it, in the image of God." Both came together in supporting the dignity of the individual person, concluding that individuals cannot be considered mere objects by any institution, including the state.[56]

Frank Meyer, though suspicious of the idea of communal obligation, also agreed that supporters of freedom must accept the validity of voluntary associations freely formed and their resulting obligations, as well as the "necessary and inescapable associations without which civilized life is impossible"—the family and the state.[57]

Polls demonstrate that the great majority of more libertarian economic conservatives are also social traditionalists and tend to participate more in religious and associational life.[58] Tocqueville actually saw free associational and religious life as the very corollary of free individualism. Americans of his day did not wait for orders from national experts to help their neighbors; they organized associations, schools, churches, enterprises, and local governments, acting freely in accordance with the religiously derived public morality that surrounded their everyday lives.[59]

Robert Putnam's widely praised article (and later book) *Bowling Alone* questioned whether volunteerism was still vital in the United States. He reported more social isolation in every part of daily life than in the recent past, reversing the Tocqueville uniqueness. From its peak in the 1960s to 1997, total voluntary association membership had declined by almost half. Informal social activities, from having friends to dinner to talking on the phone, had declined too. Social dining went from an annual average of twelve to fourteen occurrences in the 1970s to only eight by the late 1990s. These declines in communal ties were related to the pressure on people's time, especially on full-time working women; to lower support for family and other socializing values among younger generations; and especially to television, which substituted being a spectator for face-to-face social involvement. And Putnam wrote before social media and other online activities had taken off.[60]

Putnam noted that all of the major modern voluntary institutions—the Boy and Girl Scouts, the Salvation Army, B'nai B'rith, the churches, March of Dimes, Hull House, the United Way, Rotary, Big Brothers, the Red Cross, and so on—predated the New Deal.[61] But he did not draw any conclusion about why. Had the welfare state actually retarded the growth of voluntary associations, as Pope John Paul II suggested? It seems no coincidence that the great voluntary institutions were created before progressivism had great effect. Why make the effort and sacrifice necessary to form and support a voluntary group when welfare statism offered the easier solution of simply asking government experts to handle the problem? Putnam's data provide support for a displacement hypothesis. Civic participation increased during the early years of the welfare state but clearly leveled off after the state began to displace more functions.[62]

The voluntary sector is a shadow of what it could have been had the state not arrogated and regulated so many of its functions. In one little example, several years ago the state of Nebraska required all private schools to meet new demanding administrative requirements for students who were to be expelled for disciplinary purposes, forcing Boys Town into closing Father Flanagan High School for lack of staff to fulfill the requirements. Never mind that the school was among the first to provide probation supervision for youth offenders and supervised nurseries for teenaged mothers; it did not do things the state's way and was forced out of operation.[63] To compensate for millions and millions of such displacements, it is not unreasonable to argue that more libertarianism and less welfare statism might in fact increase total welfare. Charles Murray proposed more resources for voluntary institutions and less for the welfare state as a way out of its languor—to encourage individual responsibility, including the responsibility and joy of children, which he saw as a natural response to more freedom and less government "help."[64]

To compensate for decades of such displacement, it might even be appropriate to establish a transitional charitable tax credit that would give the choice of contributing welfare funds to a private charity or to an existing government charitable program—that is, a private free choice would be at the expense of a government alternative, and vice versa. The taxpayer could direct whatever share of his or her tax payment that was allocated for government-directed charitable and welfare purposes to the Department of Health and Human Services, say, or to the Salvation Army. If citizens preferred government, so be it. But if they preferred free means, they would have the choice to support a renewed charitable community with the resources necessary to combat any negative effects of the market while still allowing it to provide its great wealth and efficiency.[65]

The evidence indicates that Americans do not prefer government. When asked which organizations played "an important role in solving social problems in your community," respondents overwhelmingly chose local and voluntary institutions as the most essential. The local police led the way, being named in 58 percent of responses; churches and other houses of worship were named by 56 percent; nonprofits like the Salvation Army were named by 53 percent; "friends and neighbors," 51 percent; local PTAs, 47 percent; local government, 43 percent. The national government hardly drew a mention, ranking fourteenth out of fifteen institutions, barely edging out labor unions. State government was twelfth.[66]

Even with all the disincentives, the independent sector remains a major U.S. resource to ameliorate market effects.[67] Compared with other nations, the United States has had high and stable levels of joining, volunteering for, and giving money to civic associations.[68] Today the United States ranks second worldwide, with 15 percent of its population volunteering for charity—close behind Australia, which stands at 18 percent, and well ahead of the next highest, the Netherlands, at 8 percent.[69] In recent years, charitable giving has exceeded $300 billion per year,[70] with individuals in the

United States giving more than twice as much as a percentage of total wealth to charity as the next most generous nation, the United Kingdom.[71] Even more fundamentally, most benevolent activity is directed by family, church, and community charity without formal membership—with family remaining the most valued and most important welfare institution. There has been little decline in attachment to these "little platoons" over time.[72]

Libertarian Governance?

Did Ronald Reagan's fusionism or even pure libertarianism really propose that government should be "replaced by charities and community groups"? As important as voluntary associations are in providing for a constitutional general welfare, libertarians are not anarchists. Even the purest libertarian must accept a government to control coercion and fraud, enforce property rights, and handle foreign policy. But is any further governance compatible with individual freedom and a limited constitutionalism?

Governance can be fully voluntary. Sixty million Americans rely on purely private covenants for their housing and community governance. These covenants are enforceable through the courts, but property owners mostly govern themselves through homeowners associations, which can modify provisions when a consensus for change exists. Before zoning laws, property owners successfully used covenants to protect residential land use, and still today areas under zoning, especially in high-density urban areas, could be allowed to petition to come under covenant and associational governance, assuming racial abuses have been outlawed.[73]

Still, some problems are difficult to solve with pure freedom. Most libertarians believe that certain "neighborhood effects" may require some government involvement. These effects occur when freely acting neighbors come into involuntary contact with one another in transactions with unintended negative results.[74] Examples range from cigarette smoke wafting into a neighbor's window to noise disturbances to something as serious as pollution. Neighborhood effects do not fit easily in the libertarian coercion-versus-free-activities paradigm, by which the state is supposed to control coercion and otherwise let freedom reign. Private contracts and covenants can reduce these effects significantly but not eliminate them entirely.[75] That is why even Adam Smith, John Locke, and F. A. Hayek allowed governments to perform certain social functions beyond limiting coercion—functions they thought could not be performed privately.

In his final statement, his magisterial *Law, Legislation, and Liberty*, Hayek proposed that local government perform these necessary social functions, being the least statist—indeed, semivoluntary—and most effective alternative.[76] Local governments are attractive to libertarians because they compete in a market of governments like a business; they must offer acceptable services to attract and retain taxpaying citizens and corporations.[77] Local governments are closest to the individual facts of the situation, decreasing complexity and communication problems, keeping costs and benefits closer to the individuals who gain or lose from the transactions.[78] Local governments tend to be less abusive, since they are less powerful, bureaucratic, and monopolistic than national or even state governments. Most important, nations and even states are too large to offer most citizens easy access to alternative governments, so people have limited ability to leave unattractive situations. With local government, by contrast, one can exit relatively easily if one dislikes what is taking place there.[79]

Local government, then, is more like a voluntary association than a sovereign state.[80] Its similarities to a purely private association are most clearly expressed in the premier local government, the municipal corporation. In the United States the typical settlement pattern was for informal communities to become formal organizations. Even the term *corporation* is private, and municipalities hold contract-like charters. In most places, local government functions were in operation before they received any coercive functions or recognition from state authorities. Even afterward they were just loosely overseen by limited-function counties except to control crime. For a period, they were in fact voluntary associations and still are in many ways. Indeed, as Hayek noted, Western freedom developed from the charters granted to the urban corporations of Europe in the Middle Ages, both in giving rights to citizens and in fostering ideas of freedom, contract, property, and competition.[81]

Legally, local governments are subject to state control and even elimination, and they have circumscribed powers and responsibilities. Most often, they are given little control over matters of coercion; what control they do have usually falls under the tight supervision of the state government. With state and national governments enforcing civic and property-rights restrictions over them, abuses are generally easily controlled.

It is telling that progressivism was as opposed to "parochial" local government institutions as it was favorable to expert national control of the private sector. Woodrow Wilson wanted to make "town, city, county, state and federal government live with a like strength," to make them "all interdependent and cooperative" as one national community.[82] Progressivism not only wanted to consolidate national power; it also wished to move local governments into larger, "more efficient" units. Economies of scale suppos-edly worked for private activity, so they should be applied to governmental activity too. Larger representational areas for legislators, consolidated school districts, unified municipalities, and consolidated county governments were as important to progressive centralization as state preemption and national regulation of private entities.[83]

The progressive reforms smothered the creation of new local entities. Such reforms included using the multiservice county to substitute for the founding of new municipalities; consolidating municipalities by, for exam-ple, creating massive cities from scores of towns; encouraging municipali-ties to annex nearby unincorporated areas; and simply making it difficult to create new municipalities.[84] There are no more municipalities, townships, and towns today than there were in 1900, despite the enormous population growth over this period.[85] There were 217,000 independent school districts in 1927 and 127,000 as late as the New Deal; there are only 14,000 today.[86] The result of consolidation was gargantuan, red-tape-infested, inefficient counties and school districts, mirroring the overbureaucratization of their national counterparts.

The first centralization was city consolidation in the nineteenth cen-tury. New York City was created from scores of local governments and cities in the name of efficiency, resulting in a bureaucratization that deterio-rated services and eventually led to bankruptcy and loss of vitality.[87] These "reforms" were pushed at the state level to limit immigrant power. Under the New Deal, the emphasis shifted to national planning, trying to design ideal city types. But the bureaucrats and experts failed in building greenbelt towns and became dissatisfied with "slum creation" public housing. In the 1950s and 1960s the new fashion became "urban renewal" of central cities. By the late 1960s the great critic of city planning Jane Jacobs had so success-fully undermined government experts—for destroying four times as many homes as they built and evicting a million people, 90 percent of whom paid higher rents in substandard housing—that some new direction was required.[88] Rather than letting city social life build spontaneously, as Jacobs desired, the next set of planners tried to force her high-density vibrancy on the suburbs, allowing development only along "smart growth" transit lines. The only problem was that people did not want to give up their cars and would not live or shop there.[89] Finally, planners decided that subsidized single-family mortgages were the answer, but that led to the housing bubble and the Great Recession.[90]

If progressivism was wrong about the centrality of economies of scale for the private sector, the federal government itself acknowledged that it was equally wrong about government. In a unique admission from a government agency, the U.S. Advisory Commission on Intergovernmental Relations concluded in the late 1980s that it had been wrong to believe that small governments could not attain economies of scale. It had not considered that they could use private contracting or joint municipal operations to gain efficiencies.[91] There is even evidence that these arrangements can be more efficient.[92] Today hundreds of thousands of free contracts exist between local governments.[93] Unlike voluntary associations, local governments can even confront and check national or state bureaucracies with their own officials. As government administrators, they are experts in contesting over power, and often legal protections give them some immunity not available to others, thus increasing the incentive to protect local interests against uniformity.

Most U.S. cities are too big.[94] Small governments can involve average people in leadership, whereas large ones require experts in bureaucratic politics.[95] To serve average people rather than organized interests, large ones must be subdivided. While mayor of Indianapolis in the 1990s and later as deputy mayor of New York, Stephen Goldsmith supported a "municipal federalism" that would empower smaller community entities to perform tasks that government civil service unions would or could not. During the same period, Philadelphia created business districts to get "difficult" jobs such as garbage collection and neighborhood cleanup done by smaller entities not restricted by union rules and their much greater costs. The most popular idea in local government is transferring functions to private sources to save money and better accomplish the mission, although public employee unions often frustrate these plans.[96]

Small local governments provide a free libertarian means to build a true traditionalist community, which should be communal rather than coercive.[97] They can revive a "community spirit which has been largely suffocated by centralization," as Hayek put it.[98] An incredible variety of smaller governments can be and have been created. Businesses can form independent districts and even private "cities." Indeed, two-thirds of U.S. office space is within "unincorporated census-designated places" such as Tysons Corner, Virginia, and malls like Houston Galleria in Texas.[99] Cities have innumerable alternatives to create community: community associations, street governance, amenity cooperatives, neighborhood councils, street-closing regimes, block readjusting, community schooling, and many others.[100] These are small enough to protect the olive tree but are too limited in scope to frustrate freedom and markets. Because small governments must compete, they must be responsible, since people can easily move elsewhere. Since a city must raise its own funds, it faces limits to its profligacy, unlike some Santa Claus in Washington printing magical money. Under competition, priorities must be established and rational decision making is encouraged.[101]

Traditionalism and libertarianism come together on decentralization as a solution, as Ronald Reagan did in often praising Main Street, local government, and neighborhood communities.[102] The United States today is divided on most important values questions, so centralized decisions are either forced on dissenting minorities or compromised into irrationality. How much more efficient and compassionate it would be to decentralize the hapless bureaucratic welfare state though these libertarian means. This step would allow more freedom and vitality as well as more traditionalist community, welfare, and public order. From the most traditional Amish or Hassidic, to the conventional suburbs, to the free lifestyle of San Francisco or even "sin city" Las Vegas, why not let communities compete and let diversity prevail?

The results of such competition will be mixed for libertarians. When the president of the largest and most important libertarian think tank in the nation heard the argument that local government was more like a voluntary association than a government, he retorted that local governments could be very oppressive. He said they could even tell a person what color to paint his door or how to arrange her lawn! "Indeed, I hate that about where I live." When asked where he lived, he admitted that he actually dwelled within a homeowners association. When told that he must have freely chosen to live there and that since it was not a government but a private association he must have freely agreed, at least implicitly, to those restrictive rules, he sheepishly admitted that this was the case and that he could have no legitimate philosophical objection.

Residential community associations or homeowners associations are purely private and voluntary organizations, but they can perform most local government functions. They are in fact the fastest growing type of community in the United States, with many more people living under this governance than in the nation's large central cities.[103] They are freely chosen for their traditionalism. Their success suggests that the free means of markets, voluntary associations, and local governments can, perhaps with some assistance from state governments, solve any conceivable traditionalist social, health, or welfare problem now handled by the national government—and can do so more freely, more efficiently, and more humanely. How do we know? The citizen customers tell us. In virtually every poll since the 1930s, Americans have preferred their local government to state government and even more strongly to national government for trust, efficiency, community, and satisfaction with its services.[104]

Routinization of Conservative Charisma

With all of President Reagan's accomplishments and his allies' attractive proposals to extend them, how did the fusionist conservative movement lose power? What could be more appropriate than that William F. Buckley Jr.—the man who contributed the most energy and charisma to the rise of the modern conservative movement—should be the one to explain why, and upon his eightieth birthday at that?

Age had not dulled his civility, wit, or readiness to tell the truth even if it hurt. "I think conservatism has become a little bit slothful," he conceded in 2005. "In the absence of [its earlier] challenges, there were attenuations . . . [which] at this point haven't been resolved very persuasively."[105]

His pessimism about the state of the movement he founded extended to what he agreed was his "greatest accomplishment," the founding of *National Review* magazine in 1955. He modestly took credit only for harmonizing its content—"I brokered it"—among "an extraordinary mix" of contributors in an "open laboratory of unhampered thought." The by-product of publishing this magazine—what Meyer called its "hard-fought dialectic"—was fusionist conservatism. As Buckley noted: "At its finest, *National Review* seethed with controversy and creative energies, its pages largely given over to analyses of competing philosophies and politics, balanced by critical introspection."

No one could accuse *National Review* of seething with controversy today.[106] For a man so dedicated to the proper word, *slothful* fits perfectly. "Conservatism," said Buckley, "except when it is expressed as pure idealism, takes into account reality." While his magazine praised President George W. Bush as a conservative icon, Buckley bluntly countered, "Bush is conservative, but he is not a conservative," a profound difference. Bush was not elected "as a vessel of the conservative faith." To the extent Bush was conservative, it was as a traditionalist. He did try to reform Social Security, but he also nominated Harriet Miers to the Supreme Court and his Medicare prescription drug benefit added an enormous unfunded liability. He even signed a campaign finance act he said was unconstitutional, hoping that the Supreme Court would perform his constitutional duty for him. Although *National Review* criticized some of these activities, the criticisms were muted, and the magazine downplayed libertarian concerns that Bush's domestic discretionary spending dwarfed Bill Clinton's.[107]

The closest the latter-day *National Review* came to passion was in its support for the war in Iraq—what it called Bush's "twilight struggle" against terrorism—and the need to bring democracy to the world.[108] In the interview, Buckley said that the war on terrorism was "detached from national dimensions" and required new solutions. More important, Buckley declared that the war in Iraq was "anything but conservative. The reality of the situation is that missions abroad to effect regime change in countries without a bill of rights or democratic tradition are terribly arduous." He was careful to add: "This isn't to say that the [Iraq] war is wrong, or that history will judge it to be wrong. But it is absolutely to say that conservatism implies a certain submission to reality; and this war has an unrealistic frank and is being conscripted by events."[109]

The point was that the first Bush presidency had seriously compromised the principles of the fusionist conservative revival. The movement had already begun dissipating by the waning Reagan years and it clearly fell back further under the administration of his successors. Yet the ideas remained strong enough to overturn the Democratic Party's forty-year control of the House of Representatives a few years later. They even forced President Clinton to declare, "The era of big government is over," no matter his lack of seriousness in uttering the phrase. But under Presidents George W. Bush and Obama, who expanded government dramatically, the conservative movement suffered severe "attenuations," as Buckley put it.

Still, Buckley did not rule out all hope. When asked whether the conservative movement could undergo a revival as it had under his leadership, he replied, "I don't think there is any way to avoid it." For fusionist conservatism to be reinvigorated, however, its fundamental principles must be restored.

The rise and decline of the conservative movement followed the natural path for power formulated by the great sociologist Max Weber, his "routinization of charisma." All new broad social movements begin with a leader or leaders whose personal qualities or insights or accomplishments inspire others to join the cause and perhaps reach power. If the leader is discredited or dies, the movement normally expires. But some with special charisma have so inspired followers that the movement survives. Even in those cases, however, the original spirit cannot be long sustained. The movement either withers or merges into the existing power authority (perhaps modifying it) and becomes bureaucratized.[110]

The Buckley movement survives today merely as a political coalition rather than as a coherent intellectual synthesis. Political scientist Aaron Wildavsky identified four broad political cultures: individualist, deferential, egalitarian, and fatalist.[111] No single culture constituted a majority in the United States: individualism (which corresponds to libertarianism) represented about one-third of the U.S. population; deferentialism (traditionalism) equaled about one-fifth; egalitarianism (progressivism), almost one-third; and fatalism (with no coherent philosophy but with some nationalistic elements), another one-fifth.[112] Pure libertarians view nature as benign and encourage individualism, experimentation, and entrepreneurship, believing that Smith's "hidden hand" will make everything turn out right. Pure traditionalists are not so optimistic, but they do think nature can be at least tolerable for human social life if institutions like the family, church, and community are vibrant. Both limit government in favor of private institutions. Egalitarians, meanwhile, view nature as ephemeral, and fatalists view it as capricious—and both views require the strong hand of government to control harmful nature.[113]

From a strictly empirical perspective, Wildavsky claimed that the normal ruling coalition was the libertarian-traditionalist one. The two cultures can cohere because they both basically hold a positive enough view of human nature so as not to require an all-powerful government, which gives a sociological as well as a philosophical basis for some sort of libertarian-traditionalist connection. In the United States, however, the political success of the coalition came at a cost to the philosophical synthesis. While the intellectual core of the new movement was fusionist, many traditionalists remained traditionalists and many libertarians remained libertarian. Each of the separate social tendencies sought political advantage and tended to increase the tension.[114] To a great degree all started to call themselves "conservative." That allowed easier political organization but also suggested more unity than actually existed, causing more disenchantment with the confused results.

The conservative power formula continued to work politically through the 2004 election, but it had expired philosophically and energetically well beforehand. Fusionist constitutional conservatism was created under the charisma of Buckley, Meyer, Hayek, and others, took organizational form under their activist disciples, and won power under Reagan. But it ended up mostly being merged into the Republican Party and bureaucratized to the point that its founder conceded it was dormant and needed revival if it was to survive at all.

Ten

HISTORY'S MOST EXCITING ADVENTURE

The contrast between President Barack Obama's first and second inaugurations could not have been more dramatic. Gone were the hope and promise. The expectation of a program "for the ages" had dissipated.

A *Washington Post* editorial expressed disappointment that Obama in his second inaugural address "sounded like he was still running against Mitt Romney."[1] A few weeks earlier, an end-of-year editorial had asked, "Why is the nation's leader not embracing and then explaining the balanced reforms the nation needs?"[2] Around the same time, influential progressive journalist David Ignatius remarked, "It's depressing that after four years of gridlock, a president who won what was supposed to be a decisive election is back once again to the politics of gridlock."[3]

What had happened? The ambitious president had achieved much of his transformational agenda. He passed an unprecedentedly large $830 billion stimulus program, pumped an additional $2 trillion into the economy through Federal Reserve bond purchasing, allocated billions of dollars to multiple mortgage-protection plans, instituted major Dodd-Frank financial reforms, bailed out two automobile firms, instituted a $1.7 trillion health-care program, and ran $5 trillion in deficits. His predecessor had passed his own $700 billion bank asset support program, a $125 billion insurance firm bailout, a $600-per-person tax rebate, and a multitrillion-dollar prescription drug program. Together the two had spent a greater percentage of national wealth on domestic prosperity than in any previous period of American history.[4]

What was the result of all this activity to fix the economy? Unemployment went from 5 percent or less in the years before the Great Recession to almost double, at 9.9 percent. It remained above 9 percent for nearly two years, and only weeks before Election Day 2012 did it finally fall below 8 percent—at which point it was still higher than before Obama took office.[5] Of the 7.4 million jobs lost during the recession, fewer than half, only 3.5 million, had been added back. Since the 2009 recovery, growth had averaged 2 percent annually; the historical average was 4.6 percent. Many potential workers had stopped looking for employment, so that the labor force participation rate had fallen to a thirty-year low of 63.6 percent and remained flat. Since the end of the recession, household income had decreased 4.8 percent.[6] This was the most tepid economy since the decade-long Great Depression.

What more could the federal government do about the related area of welfare and social policy? In the United States there already were 70 bureaus in six different agencies to help feed hungry children. There were 105 programs in nine agencies to encourage math, reading, and science. There were 75 work-training programs. But a comprehensive General Accountability Office study reported, "Little is known about the effectiveness of most programs."[7] In health care, the Congressional Budget Office studied all thirty-four programs to reduce hospital admissions over the preceding ten years and concluded that all "had little or no effect."[8] As Brookings Institution expert Paul Light had concluded, this vast array of national programs drowns in layers of conflicting bureaucracy. Regulation micromanages every human activity in a manner Lilliputians would envy, and the uncertainty it creates may be more damaging than its actual policies.[9]

The whole welfare state apparatus fails the basic rule-of-law requirement to be understandable and applied equally. Hundreds of thousands of regulations must be consulted to avoid thousands of possible criminal activities. Annual business compliance costs reach $16 billion, according to the Obama administration; the Heritage Foundation puts the figure at $40 billion.[10] The Dodd-Frank financial reforms alone added 259 new rules and 188 "suggestions" that led one bank to announce it was cutting thirty thousand jobs as one means to comply.[11] The Sarbanes-Oxley Act so finely regulated public stock offerings that it forced many U.S. firms to register overseas, leading the London Stock Exchange to feature photos of Senator Paul Sarbanes and Congressman Mike Oxley to thank them for the additional American business.[12]

How confident are government officials that all this regulation will cure the economic crisis and spur growth? Federal Reserve chairman Ben Bernanke conceded that assessing risk is subjective. The TARP inspector general was more blunt, concluding in his report that in defining "systemic failure," the government makes decisions "as much on gut instinct and fear of the unknown as on objective criteria."[13] The naïve belief of early progressivism that what the experts do is really scientific has been shattered.

The $16 trillion Social Security long-term deficit is enormous, but at 1.2 percent of GDP it is minuscule compared with Medicare's shortfall, which government actuaries estimate to be 10.7 percent of GDP. This alone might require massive income tax increases. Almost all experts concede that these massive obligations are enough to sink the economy.[14]

On top of the spending shortfall, the Federal Reserve has actually planned to increase inflation. With Bernanke claiming that inflation was too low, in late 2010 the Fed decided to purchase an additional $600 billion in Treasuries on top of $2 trillion in credit already on the books.[15] The idea was that if investors believed that inflation would increase in the future, they would perceive the Fed discount rate, already near zero, to be lower than zero and would invest more in the current economy to avoid a longer-term decline in value. But as economist Alan Reynolds correctly predicted beforehand, investors simply demanded higher yields to offset the inflation expectation and shifted to commodities, negating any positive effects and leaving potentially ruinous inflation for the future.[16]

President Obama supported Bernanke, saying that the move was necessary to prevent "being stuck with no or very limited growth, and I think that's the Fed's concern." But the Fed experts were no longer speaking with a single authoritative voice. Dallas Federal Reserve president Richard Fischer was so impolitic as to respond, "The remedy for what ails the economy is, in my view, in the hands of the fiscal and regulatory authorities, not the Fed." Kansas City Fed president Thomas Hoenig took the unusual step of publicly opposing the proposal. Even a supporter, Fed governor Kevin Walsh, was concerned. "There are significant risks that bear careful monitoring," he warned, specifically mentioning the dangers of runaway inflation, a steep drop in the dollar, and disruptions in the Treasury bond market.[17] Carnegie Mellon economist Allan Meltzer concluded that the Fed simply had no plan to deleverage without a resultant massive inflation.[18] The cautious Bank for International Settlements also expressed doubts, saying, "Once the time comes to tighten monetary policy, the sheer size and scale of [the Fed's] unconventional measures will prevent a timely exit from monetary stimulus, thereby jeopardizing price stability."[19] Reflecting world opinion, German finance minister Wolfgang Schaeuble called the Bernanke pro-inflation policy "clueless."[20]

But America's political leaders did little to change the failed thinking. As the *Washington Post*'s Robert Samuelson later noted, even the Obama debt-reduction commission—which at least recognized the seriousness of the government's budget problems—did not give a compelling reason *why* spending must be reduced. Instead, the Simpson-Bowles commission simply "performed an accounting exercise to shrink the deficit"; it "ducked" the larger political challenge of explaining why the notion of so-called entitlements needed to be rethought completely. The reality that could not be spoken was that it was irresponsible to allow the elderly to retire for twenty-five years or more and have the younger generations pay for it with substantial reductions in their future standard of living.[21]

The overheated reaction even to the panel's modest proposals underscored just how big a political challenge it will be to confront reality. When the commission chairmen released their report, Nancy Pelosi, then Speaker of the House, declared it "simply unacceptable." Speaking for a powerful progressive constituency, AFL-CIO president Richard Trumka said that the commission "just told working Americans to drop dead." The plan couldn't even get past the commission itself: the proposal failed to achieve the required supermajority of votes, with seven of the eighteen panel members voting against the plan.[22]

These two problems—a Fed-weakened dollar and an entitlement explosion—are poised to come together to produce what could be the defining crisis of the modern welfare state. The government actuaries have presented unassailable data showing that the entitlement explosion will begin hitting hard somewhere around 2016. Even if President Obama was willing and courageous enough to present entitlement reductions and was successful in adopting them—all of which is highly doubtful, given that the problems cannot even be seriously discussed politically—the coming crisis has been ignored for so long and the latent inflation so deeply embedded that it is unlikely he could act in time. The conditions are ripe for low growth and high inflation, the sort of crippling "stagflation" we experienced in the 1970s, only much more severe.

In this scenario, doing more of the same old Keynesianism would be suicidal. The only force holding off the day of reckoning is that the rest of the world is doing worse. But some totally unpredictable foreign economic or political crisis could become so acute that worried foreigners would stop buying U.S. notes and the whole edifice would crumble.[23]

The regulatory state devised for a Great Depression eighty years ago has failed. Progressives' only response is that they were not given sufficient power or money. Who could be more convincing in response than the most successful social democrat of the twenty-first century thus far, former British prime minister Tony Blair? In discussing the 2008 recession in his autobiography, he argued, "First, 'the market' did not fail, one part of one sector did." Blair continued:

Second, government also failed. Regulations failed. Monetary policy failed. Debt became way too cheap. But that wasn't a conspiracy of the banks; it was a consequence of the apparently benign confluence of loose money policy and low inflation. . . . Third, the failure was one of understanding. We didn't spot it. You can argue we should have, but we didn't. . . . It wasn't a failure of regulation in the sense that we lacked the power to intervene. Had regulators said to the leaders that a huge crisis was about to break, we wouldn't have said: There's nothing we can do about it until we get more regulation through. We would have acted.[24]

In other words, all the power and expertise of the two most competent welfare states could not determine that a problem was developing or how to fix it once it occurred.

As Samuelson put it, this simple fact proved conclusively that progressive Keynesian economics was bankrupt and did not know how to successfully regulate the economy.[25] In his most important insight, Nobel economist F. A. Hayek had predicted that central regulatory authorities simply cannot have enough information about what is happening in trillions of complex transactions taking place within a modern national economy and around an interdependent world to control them effectively.[26]

The Constitutional Way Back

As the *Wall Street Journal*'s Holman Jenkins insisted, even if an immediate crisis is avoided, the long-term consequences of not taking drastic action now are almost as severe. Middle-class taxes must increase by half again even to cover current Washington spending. State and local taxes would have to increase $1,385 per household just to cover pensions for their workers, to be paid either by higher state taxes or bankruptcy. Inflation alone will reduce the real value of entitlement payouts and savings. Physician waiting lists will become longer; the rich will escape these but the poor will stand in line. Growth will inevitably slow.[27] And everyone will protest.

Even if the less severe crisis is the most likely, the most relevant historical guide still might be democratic Weimar Germany, ravaged by inflation and debt following World War I. Unfortunately for the world, Germany's constitution was new and it broke under the strain. The greatest asset for the United States in such a crisis is that its Constitution is the longest-surviving in the world and already has broad support. The Constitution would be the only possible rallying point for those hoping to survive the calamity with a government that continued to support individual freedom. More important, its "double security" federal system provides an outlet for relieving the central problem of the modern welfare state, its rigidity.

As we have seen, the Federalist vision was based on dividing power into an unheard-of variety of institutions: a divided legislature, a veto-wielding executive, a jealous court, numerous semi-independent states, innumerable local governments, and a private sector larger and more varied than the rest combined. Society was made stable not through the primitive idea that a bridge must be made increasingly solid to prove strong but according to the insight that it should be made of intertwining and even loosely connecting cables and materials that provide flexibility to survive the most powerful winds of change. But progressivism demanded control, in effect cementing the modern bridge in the hope of solidifying it but in fact eliminating the essential flexibility. The only alternative to holding markets and governments too tightly is to loosen the grip on both.

The Weimar case also underscores the dangers of inflation, which finally drove Germany into despotic hands. This is why the Federal Reserve's weakening of the dollar is so dangerous. But the negative world reaction to the Fed's maneuvers provides some hope for an alternative. Then World Bank president Robert Zoellick, a former top U.S. official, even mentioned the formerly taboo solution: gold. Besides urging a mix of world currencies to reduce pressure on the dollar alone as a single standard, he added, "The system should also consider employing gold as an alternative monetary asset today." Having a real money market of alternatives set value would avoid the problem of relying on central bankers' guesses and manipulations.[28]

Restoring a free market must be the center of any constitutionalist plan to unleash a prosperous and expanding economy. In 1920, 1981, and 1987, severe economic crises were met and solved by loosening the economy to let it hit bottom, allowing the market to adjust. Each time it was freed, it snapped back quickly and recovered vigorously. Markets likewise require regulations that are based on generally understood broad rules (rather than micromanaging), reasonably low taxation, and limited debt and spending. Indeed, the taxes people are willing to pay should set spending; the opposite is conventional government policy today.[29] In the 1980s President Reagan proved that with sufficient commitment, the rigidities of overregulation, high taxation, and exploding government spending can be loosened to some degree.

As for government, the crisis in modern public administration requires a fundamental recasting of how administration is understood. Political scientist Vincent Ostrom made this point persuasively. The progressive view is that administration means tight management, which necessitates a national center of power to effectuate it. But Ostrom noted that even Max Weber recognized a fourth, if "marginal," type of administration that he called democratic administration.[30] This actually was the type Alexis de Tocqueville described as dominating in the early United States. Its central concept was federalism, the idea that administration was not top-down management but polycentric association based on free compact.[31] Opening government administration to constituent preferences and local requirements explicitly rejects the Wilsonian insistence on a single scientifically correct solution.

Federalist administration operates, in Ostrom's words, through "cooperation, competition, conflict, and conflict resolution rather than through command and control by an overarching hierarchy of officials." Governments, especially local governments, can produce public goods by "hiring employees to accomplish the task, by contracting with other producers, or by some combination of these methods." Ostrom noted that "these options can give rise to quasi-market arrangements within a public economy," which can be more efficient than command and control.[32] The most important aspect of decentralization is that it allows a substantial number of average citizens and local officials to exercise control over their lives and forces them to accept responsibility rather than relying on and blaming someone else far away.

In many ways, even state governments are almost as rigidly centralized and bureaucratic as the national government. The same can be said about large urban counties and cities that can be reduced to human size only by further decentralizing their functions. If there were as many local governments per population as in the early twentieth century, there would be twice as many as there are today, all available to perform welfare duties more humanely and efficiently.[33]

Bureaucratic government schools can be chartered, districts can be based on one school, and scholarships can be given for private schools to make them more open, competitive, and effective, as they generally were before the progressive consolidations.[34] Of course, equality before the law must be protected, but free covenanting can be decentralized within those bounds. Businesses can form independent districts and private cities. Voluntary associations, churches, families, community associations, and neighborhood entities can assume formerly governmental functions with closer attention to individual differences, thereby encouraging free communities of interest and reinforcing commonalities and moralities. Flexibility works better. As the federal government conceded in the wake of Hurricane Katrina, the effective work in emergencies is overwhelmingly local. Even in the largest bureaucracy, military counterinsurgency policy is more effective when executed locally.[35]

There are few government functions other than national defense, security, and protection of a national market that states or local institutions cannot perform better than the federal government. Being closer to both the problems and the individuals affected, locals can act more efficiently and humanely.[36] With fewer responsibilities, the national government can focus on the remaining ones, which provides some hope for surviving the welfare-state crisis and starting to build a freer and more humane society. As Medicare, Social Security, Medicaid, and federal employee benefits begin consuming the national budget, there is an opportunity to restore constitutional federalism by returning the other programs not authorized by Article I, Section 8, to the states, where the Founders intended them to be. A grand compromise might accept the inevitable and add a reformed Social Security and Medicare amendment to the Section 8 powers and return the other programs to the states and localities.

Is such a polycentric, federalist constitutional revival possible? Ronald Reagan's favorite story was about a very optimistic child whose parents were worried that his overly positive view of life would not prepare him for its troubles. The father had an idea: when Joey came down on Christmas morning, his father told him he would receive no presents and pointed to a room piled high with manure, saying, "That's all you're going to get."

Joey thought for a moment and ran excitedly outside, returning with a shovel. "What's the matter with you?" pleaded the father. "There's nothing more." Joey began shoveling and breathlessly replied: "With all this manure, there must be a pony in here somewhere."

There is, in fact, a better Constitution buried somewhere beneath the present confusion.

Ideological Framework?

The first step in clarification is to reject rigid ideological and utopian thinking. Ideologies use reason to deduce detailed conclusions that follow directly from their monist assumptions. Simply apply the formula and the results follow. This axiomatic approach failed miserably for the modern secular ideologies and has led to deadlock under progressivism. By contrast, the historic Western synthesis, based on two first premises in tension, provided the formula for the West's successes. This type of probabilistic rationality offers a predisposition to action rather than an ideological machine processing solutions.

Those who most influenced the modern American revival of this synthesis,[37] including Hayek, Buckley, Meyer, and Reagan, all rejected rigid ideological thinking.[38] Their fusionist synthesis asks which free means can best accomplish good ends. As Meyer argued, tradition provides the energy and the goals; individual freedom and its rationality are the means. Freedom is the "criterion principle" that guides all else, but by itself it has no ends, no answers about where to aim. Applying the principle requires a "prudential art" refined by the "intricate fibers of tradition." Tradition sets the ends for action, including allowing choice. The basic formula is simple: search the tradition to determine the good end to be accomplished, and use freedom to adjudge the means in a hierarchy—first leaving it to the individual to act, then to the family, then to the community, local government, regional government, and only to the national state when there is no other way.[39] Yet applying this to complex reality is anything but axiomatic.

Some have argued that the fusionist conservatism of Reagan, Buckley, and Meyer was not in fact a synthesis of freedom and tradition but an ideology of anticommunist nationalism.[40] Nationalism certainly has been a powerful force, perhaps the most powerful force in modern times.[41] But in the United States, even though love of country has been a central part of the American tradition, ideological nationalism has not had a real advocate other than perhaps President James Polk, who added California, Texas, New Mexico, Arizona, and more to U.S. territory but is mostly forgotten today.[42] Teddy Roosevelt has a following among so-called neoconservatives; Bill Kristol and David Brooks even wrote a manifesto on "national greatness conservatism" promoting Roosevelt's ideas, but in it they conceded that this viewpoint did not have a large popular following.[43] The great success of the "national greatness" vision was in helping convince President George W. Bush to adopt the Wilsonian ideology of promoting democracy worldwide and playing a more active role in achieving it.[44]

The esteemed modern political thinker Irving Kristol, in his definitive article "The Neoconservative Persuasion," argued that America's real "identity is ideological" and should be. The criteria for taking foreign policy action, he said, must extend beyond the traditional question of whether the action must be taken "to preserve our national sovereignty." Large nations like the United States

> inevitably have ideological interests in addition to more material concerns. Barring extraordinary events, the United States will always feel obliged to defend, if possible, a democratic nation under attack from nondemocratic forces, external or internal. . . . No complicated

geopolitical calculations of national interest are necessary. Behind all this is a fact: the incredible military superiority of the United States vis-à-vis the nations of the rest of the world, in any imaginable combination. . . . And it is a fact that if you have the kind of power we now have, either you will find opportunities to use it, or the world will discover them for you.[45]

Finding opportunities to use power internationally because one has the power to do so is properly labeled ideological, and it is a radical departure from the traditional U.S. focus on national interest. Secretary of State (and later President) John Quincy Adams famously declared that America "does not go abroad in search of monsters to destroy." The United States "might become the dictatress of the world," but then "she would no longer be the ruler of her own spirit." This modest view remained dominant until Woodrow Wilson in the early twentieth century and was not fully displaced until the global meliorism of President Lyndon Johnson in the Vietnam War era.[46]

Although his name is often invoked by those supporting a nationalist ideological approach to foreign policy, Ronald Reagan held the more traditional view. Reagan was second to none in his love of country, but in his first speech to the United Nations he declared: "The record of history is clear: citizens of the United States resort to force reluctantly and only when they must. Our foreign policy, as President Eisenhower once said, 'is not difficult to state. We are for peace first, last, and always.'"[47] As his close associates Martin and Annelise Anderson demonstrated conclusively in their book *Reagan's Secret War*, peace was his driving passion as citizen and chief executive. He did not look for opportunities to demonstrate U.S. power; in fact, he sought to control American power.[48]

For America's friends, President Reagan had a very simple promise: "We will not use our friendship to impose on their sovereignty, for our own sovereignty is not for sale."

As for the enemies of freedom, those who are potential adversaries, they will be reminded that peace is the highest aspiration of the American people. We will negotiate for it, sacrifice for it; we will not surrender for it, now or ever. Our forbearance should never be misunderstood. Our reluctance for conflict should not be misjudged as a failure of will. When action is required to preserve our national security, we will act. We will maintain sufficient strength to prevail if need be, knowing that if we do so we have the best chance of never having to use that strength.[49]

Even America's enemies were reminded that peace was the goal—but also that if U.S. national security was threatened, America would act to preserve it. It was a balance. Force was sometimes necessary. But the United States should act only when "action is required to preserve our national security"—our nationalism, not anyone else's. When action was required, the United States must have the strength to prevail—but the goal was not to use that strength. To avoid using force even for national security, to keep the peace, we will "negotiate for it, sacrifice for it."[50] President Reagan did tell the British Parliament in 1982 that America had an obligation to promote freedom and democracy in the world, predicting that Marxism would end on the "ash heap of history." But in that very speech he also said—referencing Winston Churchill—that war with Marxism, including the "evil empire," was not inevitable or even imminent. He promised that the competition "can be conducted on a peaceful and reciprocal basis."[51]

Five years later he signed a nuclear forces reduction treaty with the Soviet Union's Mikhail Gorbachev, producing the most significant movement toward disarmament in modern times. By the treaty's deadline of June 1, 1991, a total of 2,692 nuclear and conventional ground-launched ballistic and cruise missiles had been destroyed, 846 by the United States and 1,846 by the Soviet Union (which had more to begin with). This mutual reduction of power was both "peaceful and reciprocal."

National interest always requires prudential calculation. Irving Kristol himself conceded this point by using the terms *extraordinary* and *if possible*. Ronald Reagan understood this fundamental truth. Rather than looking for "opportunities" to demonstrate power, he hoped "never [to have] to use that strength." When President Reagan calculated that a military operation was not worth the cost, he withdrew. Indeed, George W. Bush's first FBI director and one of Bush's White House staffers criticized Reagan for his "timidity" in withdrawing ground forces from Lebanon in 1983 after U.S. Marines were killed in a massive bombing there.[52]

The proof of President Reagan's nonideological approach was that he actively committed fewer U.S. ground forces on foreign soil than any modern chief executive other than Jimmy Carter.[53] He likewise accepted a large constitutional role for Congress in foreign policy.[54] When he first reached out to communist chief Gorbachev, a prominent conservative leader called Reagan a "useful idiot for Kremlin propagandists" for undermining ideological anticommunism.[55] But Reagan's practical fusionism, based on its traditions and values, proved the critics wrong. As Margaret Thatcher said, he made his case by his winning the Cold War "without firing a shot."[56]

President Reagan's strength was his belief in the power of his tradition.

As he explained in his final major speech to the world at the historic London Guildhall in 1988, his search for freedom and democracy

> would be not so much a struggle of armed might, not so much a test of bombs and rockets, as a test of faith and will. . . . Here, then, is our formula for completing our crusade for freedom. Here is the strength of our civilization and our belief in the rights of humanity. Our faith is in a higher law. Yes, we believe in prayer and its power.[57]

Reagan's fusionist conservatism has been disparaged as being ideological in ignoring freedom by pursuing traditionalist social goals such as opposing abortion. But even the purest libertarianism requires government to secure life and property against coercion. When government performs these legitimate libertarian functions, this does limit freedom, but necessarily so. The default position in the fusionist tension is to use free means rather than forbid choice, but, as Meyer also noted, freedom needs a context that considers facts. Both require consulting tradition. As far as abortion, libertarianism actually requires government to protect innocent individual life against coercion, which abortion clearly is.[58] Science does not help, since the fetus is clearly life. The issue is whether the fetus is human life.

Freedom provides no solution here. The fact that abortion also affects the potential mother merely adds a second person to the matter, as in any two-party personal or property dispute. If there were two adults, neither would have the right to take the life of the other. The issue still is whether the fetus is an individual person. Freedom must use tradition to decide such specific cases. But even tradition is not dispositive here. Although the traditional Christian and Jewish positions declared that the unborn were individual persons with rights and forbade abortion, some of their denominations allow it today. For those with clear traditional views, the decision can be made on the basis of their individual beliefs that human life begins at conception and, therefore, that abortion is coercion and thus properly controlled by government. Without a clear traditional or convincing rational conviction, however, one can resolve the matter only as best as one can by consulting the common sense of one's tradition.

Ronald Reagan's solution was typically practical but based on tradition and freedom too. He initially supported a woman's right to decide whether to have an abortion as the free choice of the potential mother, since it was not clear that the fetus was a person. But he was not sure. He finally resolved the matter with an analogy. When one is hunting in dense woods and the object that is to be shot is unclear, tradition requires the huntsman not to fire his weapon. In case of doubt, he is to assume that human life is present and not take the risk, however small, to harm individual human life. Reagan reasoned that it was the same for abortion. Since it is impossible to know precisely when a fetus becomes a person, prudence requires doubt to be resolved in favor of life and that the potential infant be protected by the states, if necessary through a constitutional amendment.[59]

Ideology provides automatic, uncalculated conclusions, but a sophisticated Hayekian probabilistic rationality requires prudential resolution of values in tension based on some tradition, in Reagan's case the Judeo-Christian Western tradition underlying American society and its constitutional order.[60]

Protective Strata

Is it possible to restore the tension between freedom and tradition, to restore the Constitution's polycentric federalism, for modern times? To have any chance of success, such a project must first take a cold, hard look at what democratic politics is really all about. As with almost anything, America's preeminent Founder, James Madison, is a good place to begin: "Democracies have ever been spectacles of turbulence and contention; have ever been found incompatible with personal security or the rights of property; and have in general been as short in their lives as they have been violent in their deaths."[61]

The Founders favored popular rule, but they opposed what Madison called "pure democracy"—where the people rule directly—and indeed opposed the whole underlying rationale for ideological democracy itself. Those supporting this democracy, Madison continued, "have erroneously supposed that by reducing mankind to perfect equality in their political rights, they would at the same time be perfectly equalized and assimilated in their possessions, their opinions and their passions." This cannot happen without also taking away their freedom. So the "great object" of the Constitution was to prevent both minority and majority assaults on freedom and "at the same time preserve the spirit and the form of popular government." The rights of the people could be protected only by "a proper federal system" that balanced diverse powers, leaving people free to act under the law as individuals and with their neighbors to create a good society.[62]

To a great degree the constitutional checks on pure democracy have endured. Even the clumsy but effective-for-federalism Electoral College has been preserved, as many found to their amazement in 2000 when

George W. Bush lost the national popular vote but won the election state by state. What is missing today is a sense of popular control. Tocqueville explained what happens when government expands to fulfill the "principle of equality":

> It covers the surface of society with a network of small complicated rules, minute and uniform, through which the most original minds and the most energetic characters cannot penetrate, to rise above the crowd. The will of man is not shattered, but softened, bent, and guided; men are seldom forced by it to act, but they are constantly restrained from acting. Such a power does not destroy, but it prevents existence; it does not tyrannize, but it compresses, enervates, extinguishes, and stupefies a people, till each nation is reduced to nothing better than a flock of timid and industrious animals, of which the government is the shepherd.[63]

Joseph Schumpeter taught a generation of political scientists that modern national democracies are actually contests between ambitious elites representing strata of different national interests and ideals; the people's vote can decide only which elite shall staff the institutions of power. As the great mathematician the Marquis de Condorcet demonstrated conclusively as early as 1785 (costing him his life in the French Revolution), as issues become more complex, the relationship between what people want and voting results becomes tenuous.[64] Only a small percentage of people can grasp the high-level abstractions necessary for national policymaking. "The masses are short term" and local, Schumpeter wrote, so to be successful electorally in a large nation, leaders cannot conduct academic seminars but instead must radiate a "mystic glow" that appeals widely to ordinary people's imaginations and to various strata of interests.[65]

The English aristocracy, for example, preserved limited government and private property well after the rise of democracy and the decline of its feudal role. With its bravery, stiff-upper-lip courage, loyalty, and overall prestige, the aristocracy represented perhaps better than any other protective stratum in history a heroic mystical ideal that successfully won mass support. It had an emotional appeal that more mundane backgrounds lacked. As Schumpeter put it, businessmen have "no trace" of the mystical, for the "stock market is a poor substitute for the Holy Grail." The aristocrats' military- and rural-based social stratum had contempt for the dry rationalism and soft living of the bourgeoisie, but the bourgeoisie were better coalitional allies than the socialist Left, which was directly out to destroy the aristocrats' feudal culture. The tories in both parties provided a "protective framework" that supported limited government and capitalism, whose erosion the ungrateful bourgeoisie precipitated themselves by rationalizing away the feudal glamour of their protectors.[66]

In a modern democracy the issue is who or what ideal can provide legitimacy for the leadership strata. Who has the charisma, as Weber called it, the sacred appeal, the aura, the magic of leadership, and the ability and power to motivate and inspire? A protective stratum is not a conspiracy but a vision. Yet none lasts forever. As Marx predicted, when rising bourgeois competition weakened the English aristocracy, workers organized into powerful labor unions and were joined by a "small section" of discerning capitalists (such as Engels) and socialist intellectuals (such as himself) that became a powerful enough stratum to prevail.[67] In the United States, progressivism consciously set out to displace its ruling White Anglo-Saxon Protestant protective stratum by deriding noblesse oblige and limited government, promoting democratic ideology in their place, and adopting government policies to replace WASP capitalism with a welfare state.

The movement was inspired by the great twentieth-century educator and philosopher John Dewey.[68] The John Dewey Project on Progressive Education at the University of Vermont explained the larger goal of the philosopher and his disciples:

> Led by Dewey . . . during the 1920s, when education turned increasingly to "scientific" techniques such as intelligence testing and cost-benefit management, progressive educators insisted on the importance of the emotional, artistic, and creative aspects of human development—"the most living and essential parts of our natures," as Margaret Naumburg put it in *The Child and the World*. After the Depression began, a group of politically oriented progressive educators, led by George Counts, dared schools to "build a new social order" and published a provocative journal called *The Social Frontier* to advance their "reconstructionist" critique of *laissez faire* capitalism.[69]

That is, progressive education's goal was to "build a new social order" by turning U.S. schooling from teaching traditional academic knowledge, with its goal of maximizing individual rationality, responsibility, and leadership, toward the more progressive ideal of preparing children for equality, "socially engaged" citizenship, and high self-esteem. The means was to emphasize emotion over intelligence, standardized over targeted curricula, and a communal over an individualist ethic. It sought to promote a common

curriculum, focusing on emotional rather than abstract intellectual learning, and promoting social rather than individually competitive interrela-
tionships—all aimed at replacing capitalist freedom, provincialism, traditionalism, and entrepreneurship with a national democratic welfare state.[70]

This movement has had great effect on abstract intellectual learning.
With all its wealth, internationally the United States ranks only sixth in reading (behind Hong Kong, Russia, Finland, Singapore, and Northern Ireland),
eleventh in math (behind those same countries, plus South Korea, Taiwan,
Japan, Belgium, and England), and seventh in science (behind South Korea,
Singapore, Finland, Japan, Russia, and Taiwan).[71] The national No Child
Left Behind Act, passed in 2001, promised that all children would become
proficient in math and reading by 2014. But for all the federal money and
bureaucrats thrown at the problem, improvement has been modest at best.
The 2011 National Assessment of Educational Progress, often called "the
nation's report card," showed that nearly a decade of effort had produced an
insignificant increase in reading scores for fourth-graders and only a small
increase in math scores.[72] As the first products of No Child were graduating
high school, the ACT test of 1.6 million secondary students found that only
24 percent scored high enough on math, reading, English, and science to
ensure they could enter college; meanwhile, 28 percent could not score high
enough on even *one* of these sections to be eligible for a college program. The
composite score in 2007 was 21.2 on a 36-point scale and actually declined a
bit to 21.0 in 2010.[73] In 2012 the SAT reading score dropped to a four-decade
low.[74] In 2006, 35 percent of all PhDs, including 43 percent in science and
engineering and 70 percent in electrical, civil, and industrial/mechanical
engineering, were awarded to foreign-born students.[75]

Although U.S. students have made little gain in math, science, and reading, they have done well at achieving Dewey's goal of collective self-esteem.[76]
Teaching nonbourgeois morals is now a staple of the American educational
system—from prioritizing self-esteem, to proscribing trans fats, to teaching
pantheistic environmentalism. In responding to an admirer who argued that
demographics favored conservatives since only religious parents were having
children, Judge Robert Bork noted that this advantage was soon reversed as
conservatives sent their children to schools and universities that then accul-
turated them into progressivism.[77]

Over time, progressivism has moved closer to Dewey's emphasis on creative leadership and away from Wilson's stress on scientific administration.
The failure of the progressive "best and brightest" to manage the Vietnam
War and of Keynesian economists to resolve the stagflation of the 1970s
undermined the mystical illusion that these experts could control events.

Although this vision was still powerful enough to inspire Obama's transformational agenda, Judge Jones–type court decisions, and Richard Dawkins–style cultural critiques, progressives came to emphasize their deeper understanding and greater emotional sensitivity to provide the mystic glow necessary for leadership. Leading lights such as Princeton professor Richard Rorty, specifically referencing Dewey, emphasized the experts more than the expertise of progressivism. Rorty stressed the obligation of the "liberal ironist" intellectual to downplay scientific planning and to instead sensitize people into supporting progressive social welfare goals.[78]

Whether successful by other standards, progressives have been enormously resourceful in changing traditional attitudes and achieving power. Progressives have built an impressive stratum consisting of industrial, service, and especially teacher and government employee unions (the top contributors to political elections); civil service expert managers; and university, media, cultural, foundation, and public interest intellectuals and donors who shape policy through supporting studies, lobbying, litigation, popular entertainment, and public relations.

Developing support for an alternative protective stratum has proved difficult. Institutions on the right have been divided on the major issues and value questions. Religion and business are two natural components of an alternative stratum, but libertarians often stress their anticlericalism and traditionalists their anticapitalism. No ideal or interest can survive without a protective political framework to support it.

A Happy Band

Building a competing protective framework to reestablish the essential role of the Western synthesis can start with Thomas Jefferson and John Adams.[79] Both came to agreement in their later correspondence that a freely self-selected and localized "natural aristocracy" is the likely and proper leadership for a limited constitutional government like the one they established. The only alternative was a national elite that would keep the population in "perpetual childhood" by lording its power over them. The people can be easily misled, Jefferson and Adam recognized, but protective strata linked to the Western tradition of local liberty could keep them from being ruled over as subjects.

Although progressivism has dominated state and society for almost a century—whether through Wilsonian scientific administration, Dewey democratic emotionalism, or Rorty mystical intellectualism—its own political creation faces impending bankruptcy. Progressivism refuses to face this preeminent issue of our time.

Hayek captured the fatal flaw of progressive positivism:

> I believe people will discover that the most widely held ideas which dominated the twentieth century, those of a planned economy with a "just distribution," a freeing ourselves from repressive and conventional morals, of permissive education as a way to freedom, and the replacement of the market by a rational arrangement of a body with coercive powers, were all based on superstitions . . . an overestimation of what science has achieved. . . . What the age of rationalism—and modern positivism—has taught us to regard as senseless and meaningless formations due to accident or human caprice turn out in many instances to be the foundations on which our capacity for rational thought rests.[80]

An economist like Hayek might be expected to condemn an over-planned economy and coercive government regulation. His other two concerns about modern progressive intellectualism—the problems of "freeing ourselves from repressive and conventional morals" and of relying on "permissive education as a way to freedom"—may come as a surprise. But Hayek was an unusual economist; he considered tradition, history, law, and custom as essential moral and intellectual supports for a prosperous economy, a free society, and rationality itself.

In the mid-twentieth century, a new conservative stratum challenging these superstitions rose to contest progressive domination. For a while it prospered, but it became "slothful," as Bill Buckley himself put it. Another leader of the conservative stratum and a close Buckley associate wrote before the 2010 election, "The Movement—Bill Buckley's Movement, the struggle of the few, the happy few, the band of brothers—is over. It ended in 1980, when Ronald Reagan was elected president." The obvious decline in power of this explicitly antiprogressive and fusionist conservative stratum was not to be regretted, because the battle had ended and their "movement had won." He cited the large numbers of new conservative journals, think tanks, college organizations, radio talk shows, television programs, and speakers. He also claimed that conservative government policies had brought about "a generation—a whole generation!—of deregulation, privatization, and tax cuts."[81]

The major reason that this movement had won, he argued, was not its mass appeal—polls showed that as many self-described conservatives existed then as before the movement began—but "the number of intellectual operations there are, because they set the tone and shape the zeitgeist." In other words, the conservative movement had created an intellectual and social stratum committed to freedom and tradition that provided the dominant mystic glow for politics today. He did concede that "after the [Obama 2008] election it became clear that we need new formulations," but he added, "We always need new formulations."

These were optimistic views given that President Obama had already achieved so much of his ambitious transformational agenda and that progressives continued to dominate the most powerful cultural institutions. Even the Republican success in the 2010 congressional elections was widely understood as more a reaction against Democratic overreaching than support for a revived conservative dominance.[82] And Obama did not give ground after that, winning reelection in 2012. Well beforehand, regulation had grown, taxes had increased over the Reagan levels, and domestic spending had ballooned. Further, much (but by no means all) of the vaunted conservative infrastructure had accommodated itself to the GOP departures from orthodox Buckley conservatism, and some even led the cheering for the spending and regulatory apostasies of the two Bush presidencies.

After the retreats of these years, buyer's remorse led the vestiges of the movement to attempt to reinvigorate it with a new statement of principles, modeled on the Sharon Statement that young conservatives had drafted at Buckley's home in Connecticut back in 1960. A Mount Vernon Statement, a Manhattan Declaration, and a Pledge to America were all crafted in 2010. The fact that it was necessary to create more than one merely confirmed the difficulty.

These declarations were in fact statements of practical political coalition rather than of philosophical coherence such as the Sharon one. A coalitional statement allows those who cannot accept a fusionist "dualism" (as they would characterize its tension) to retain their monist social or foreign policy ideologies even as they might find it politically useful to support a statement of common principles. These 2010 declarations stretched broadly to reconcile neoconservatives and libertarians, in spite of the fact that Irving Kristol's manifesto specifically derided such a synthesis. Kristol explained that "neocons do not feel that kind of alarm or anxiety about the growth of the state in the past century" that is libertarianism's core.[83] Accepting the idea of coalition, however, does prepare the groups for the necessary compromises that will take place between the elements when the coalitional stratum holds power.

Although a coalition must be as inclusive as possible to build a political stratum, some center must exist around which its mystique can form.

Fusionists synthesize freedom and tradition not for coalitional purposes but because the two elements must be in constant tension for this to be their type of conservatism at all. As a matter of record it was fusionist leaders who primarily conceived, managed, and adopted these recent statements.[84] Only they have an intellectual and moral motivation for tradition and freedom to cohere.

In short, a true alternative protective stratum must at its core be motivated by principle and not simply by a desire for political success. This is precisely why any counterprogressive stratum requires some "happy band" deeply schooled in the Western tension between libertarian means and traditionalist ends and committed to constitutional institutions, experiences, and values. Otherwise, the movement will have no source of energy and no idea of its whole. Its raison d'être must be to free American creativity from the national government's "network of small complicated rules" to allow local people to shape their world with their more traditional values.[85] Providing the core for a new protective stratum will not necessarily require a majority, for as Lord Acton noted, "At all times sincere friends of freedom have been rare, and its triumphs have been due to minorities, that have prevailed by associating themselves with auxiliaries whose objects often differed from their own."[86]

A reconstituted fusionist conservative core would necessarily begin with the surviving Reagan happy band and the important institutions it created. Those original assets have been reinforced by newly energized Tea Party adherents. The core's greater social and business activism opens access to scores of thousands of such private groups nationally, as well as to independent centers at colleges, institutes, and academically inclined foundations. Homeschooling attracts perhaps two million of the most traditional but also the most individualist and best-educated students, as demonstrated by higher test scores and disproportionate victories in scholastic contests. Additional recruits may be found at the 28,000 private elementary and secondary schools and 2,400 independent colleges and universities, many of them religious.[87]

Can some critical core accept the high tension between truth and freedom that unleashed the creative energy of Western civilization? Can one hold to traditional truth without compelling it, without using government to impose that truth? Can Charles Murray's four values essential to freedom and social happiness—industriousness, honesty, marriage, and religion—all be openly defended? Can Reagan's values of God, family, freedom, neighborhood, and work? Can Buckley's values of freedom, individuality, the sense of community, the sanctity of the family, the supremacy of the conscience, the spiritual view of life, and political decentralization? Can one defend and promote freedom but also the fact that individuals need social groups like family, community, religion, associations, and corporations to live to the fullest? Can one defend a traditional family and childbearing without proscribing alternative arrangements? Can one demand that people be treated equally before the law but allow a freedom that necessarily produces inequality of outcomes?

Or must some single truth determine all? Truth may be said to be the highest traditionalist goal, but if it lacks tolerance and free exercise is it still truth? Perhaps love is the highest. Even the self-professed atheist Bertrand Russell made this value the indispensable motivation for a good social order:

> The root of the matter is a very simple and old-fashioned thing, a thing so simple that I am almost ashamed to mention it for fear of the derisive smile with which the wise cynic will greet my words. The thing I mean is love, Christian love, compassion. If you feel this you have a motive for existence, a guide for action, a reason for courage, an imperative necessity for intellectual honesty.[88]

But does not love itself require courage to confront the derisive smiles and a Western treasury of traditions and free means to live it? It simply is not possible to arrange this enormous variety of values in some authoritative hierarchy.

There is broad support for all these traditional values,[89] which suggests the possibility of success in recruiting and motivating the necessary core for a revitalized Western synthesis. The Western insight of a tension between the criterion principle of freedom and the good ends of a hard-won tradition is essential. Did it not provide the necessary energy before? Is not the current crisis actually the opportunity to transform the moribund welfare state into a truly vibrant free and good society?

The Great Adventure

It will not be easy to reenergize such a core when enervating progressivism commands the political and cultural ramparts, still promising that all will be well if only it is granted more power. "Remembrances of the fleshpots of enveloping security ever tugs insidiously at the souls of free men" to return to the comforting myth that the experts can impose a "design of perfection upon a world by its nature imperfect," as Frank Meyer warned. To live in a "state of tension, accepting both transcendence and the human condition with its freedom and imperfection," has long proved the more demanding task.[90] Can even a small band of individuals commit to this daunting responsibility? Fortunately someone with the necessary mystic glow showed the way, demonstrating how to live the tension and inspiring a movement to advance its principles in the process. That person was Ronald Reagan.

Primarily a man of action, Reagan could be surprisingly intellectual. As mentioned, he especially appreciated the thought of Russell Kirk, Friedrich Hayek, Henry Hazlitt, Milton Friedman, James Burnham, and Ludwig von Mises. He acknowledged Frank Meyer for revitalizing the synthesis that was the core of his beliefs. He read the major journals of the movement and often called Bill Buckley to ask his views. He did not have a straight-A college record but was a voracious reader of books. The late Robert Novak, a widely respected but cynical journalist, was taken aback in an early White House interview with the president because Reagan was quoting theorists like the economist Frédéric Bastiat whom he did not recognize. Leaving the meeting, Novak researched them and was so impressed with Bastiat's aptness to points the president was making that he thereafter took the former actor's intelligence very seriously.[91]

Ronald Reagan had a sophisticated philosophy of constitutional government and society. He expressed a deep "respect for law, an appreciation for tradition, and regard for the social consensus that gives stability to our public and private institutions." He loved the Constitution, which "is the guarantor of the greatest measure of individual freedom any people has ever known." Despite his reputation for being detached from his family other than his wife Nancy, his children, one by one, came to appreciate him as they matured, mostly after his death, probably the fate of most good fathers. His fine son Michael simply said, "I was a jerk" about his late appreciation of his father's loving but demanding ways.[92] The father was reserved, but this was undoubtedly a protection against his excessive generosity. He was religious, but he did not wear it on his sleeve.[93]

Contrary to the common progressive notion, Reagan did not even hate government. In his First Inaugural Address he did say: "In this present crisis, government is not the solution to our problem. Government is the problem. . . . It is no coincidence that our present troubles parallel and are proportionate to the intervention and intrusion in our lives that result from unnecessary and excessive growth of government." It might be too subtle for our dear progressive friends, but seeing government as the problem in a particular period of crisis is not the same as hating it. Most critics conveniently ignore the rest of what the president said:

> It is time to check and reverse the growth of government, which shows signs of having grown beyond the consent of the governed. It is my intention to curb the size and influence of the Federal establishment and to demand recognition of the distinction between the powers granted to the Federal Government and those reserved to the States or to the people. . . . Now, so there will be no misunderstanding, it is not my intention to do away with government. It is rather to make it work—work with us, not over us; to stand by our side, not ride on our back.[94]

Reagan's condemnation of the "unnecessary and excessive growth of government" and especially his desire to recognize "the distinction between the powers granted to the Federal Government and those reserved to the States or to the people" simply reflected constitutional government as the Founders understood it.

I saw President Reagan up close when he fired the air-traffic controllers. As director of the U.S. Office of Personnel Management, I had expressed my displeasure with the concessions that the Federal Aviation Administration (FAA) had made to the union; the FAA proposed major increases in pay and benefits when the controllers already received much higher rates than the rest of the workforce. Since the union was gaining advantages through the threat of disruptions and slowdowns, the inevitable result would be more of the same throughout the government. Luckily, the union was greedy, rejected the offer, and went on strike. The air-traffic controllers had crossed the line and President Reagan made history. At the subsequent White House meeting, the president was insistent. The controllers had violated their no-strike oath as federal employees and they had to go. That was that.[95]

The FAA head opposed the severity of the penalty. So on the way to the news conference announcing the move, Transportation Secretary Drew Lewis dropped off the FAA official. Lewis had initially favored the concessions but said it was now time to support the boss. All three of us wanted eventually to hire back the controllers (on our terms)—the worried personnel director for fear of an air incident during the time it would take to train the thousands of replacements needed. President Reagan, taking a broader view, would have none of it. As Secretary of State George Shultz later noted, it was Reagan's most important foreign policy message, since world leaders were impressed with a leader who would be so decisive.[96] House Speaker Tip

O'Neill's top staffer reported that this one act led the Democrat to respect Reagan as a serious political leader.[97] Business CEOs told me for years that President Reagan's actions in freezing employment, denying unnecessary pay and benefits increases, and especially firing the controllers steeled their resolve to slim their own bloated bureaucracies.

One day, while lolling around the White House Cabinet Room after making a presentation, I could feel that someone was waiting patiently behind me, just out of sight. The presentation had documented how the administration was faltering in one of its major promises by backfilling bureaucratic slots that had been cut during the first years of idealistic reform. Bragging to whoever would listen about the president's support for my plan to reverse the backsliding, I figured the guy behind me could wait. When I finally turned, there was the president of the United States of America patiently waiting to talk to the pompous civil service director.

Sensing my discomfort, he immediately put me at ease by saying, "Keep it up, fighting those bureaucrats, and don't give up." Smiling gently, he turned and went back to work. Here was the real Ronald Reagan—considerate, polite, decent, and letting you know he appreciated the job you were doing. But he was also focused like a laser, keeping to the task at hand, in this case trying to keep his promise to cut domestic government bureaucracy and red tape.

Reagan radiated kindness, but he could be firm and even courageous. From his earliest years he had rescued swimmers when he was a lifeguard, seventy-seven people from the treacherous Rock River. He especially showed his mettle when he was shot early in his presidency. He first refused to go to the hospital with a bullet lodged in his chest. After he woke in the hospital with a nurse holding his hand, he cracked: Don't let Nancy know about us. When he was awakened to be told he needed to undergo life-threatening surgery and delegate his powers to the vice president, he looked at the physicians and joked, "I hope you all are Republicans." (For once he was trumped: a surgeon replied, "We all are today, sir.") When Reagan finally recovered to see his wife, he comforted her by saying, "Sorry, Honey, I forgot to duck."[98]

From that day forward, he was convinced that God had a plan for keeping him alive when he easily could have died with the bullet so near his heart.[99] He even made a deal with the head of the "evil empire," Mikhail Gorbachev, when his closest associates told him he was being weak, but that decision eventually helped liberalize the Soviet regime, to the astonishment and benefit of the whole world.[100] He never gave up. In 1986, when I was advising Senator Robert Dole, the majority leader took a piece of paper from his desk and lofted it over to me. "Look what your friend is trying to get me to do." It read, "Do not forget about flattening the tax rates," plus a few suitable sentiments, and was signed Ron Reagan. "He is the only person in Washington who thinks this has a ghost of a chance of being adopted," said the senator. "What does he expect me to do?"

In less than a year, during a second term when supposedly nothing much can be accomplished, President Reagan signed a tax bill cutting the number of rates in half and reducing them to 15, 28, and 33 percent, the lowest then or since. The top marginal rate had gone from 70 percent to 33, the first substantial cut in a progressive tax system by a modern democratic government. His two-term record of economic prosperity, low taxes, reduced regulations and spending, and improved international security were accomplishments that even President Obama and Hillary Clinton conceded were unmatched in modern times.

However alone, Ronald Reagan never gave up. And neither, he thought, should anyone else. Americans were citizens, not subjects.[101] Reagan was convinced that one person could make an enormous difference, and the facts prove that he did. He even gave us an example that is especially appropriate for the crisis of our own times, in the person of Hayek-influenced economist Ludwig Erhard.[102] The failure of the German market system under Weimar was not corrected until an incredible three years after World War II ended, when Erhard, the German economic administrator for the American occupation forces in 1948, finally freed his country's economy by eliminating Hitler's wage and price controls. Over the next six months industrial production soared back by an incredible 50 percent and soon thereafter overtook the economies of victors Britain and France. This remarkable turnaround resulted because one courageous man acted against the will of the U.S. commander and the advice of the progressive economic experts.[103]

At my last cabinet meeting I reported that the administration was losing ground in its plans to reduce the federal bureaucracy and to transfer responsibilities to states and communities. After I finished, President Reagan urged his agency heads to renew their efforts to cut the size of government. He said that he understood how difficult the task was but that it was crucial. From his readings in history he knew that no nation had gone so far down as the United States the road toward the enervating bureaucracy and statism that Tocqueville described and still come back to freedom. The man with the pony story, however, was too optimistic to end there. He smiled and concluded, "Although no country has come back, I would like us to be the beginning. I would like us to be the first."

Ronald Reagan had a vision:

Our Founding Fathers began the most exciting adventure in the history of nations. In their debates with the principles of human dignity, individual rights, and representative democracy, their arguments were based on common law, separation of powers, and limited government. Their victory was to find a home for liberty. . . . We founded our society on the belief that the rights of men were ours by grace of God. That vision of our Founding Fathers revolutionized the world. Those principles must be reaffirmed by every generation of Americans, for freedom is never more than one generation away from extinction.[104]

That is his challenge. Who will enlist in this great adventure?

Notes

⇒◆⇐

Introduction: The Challenge

1. Ruth Marcus, "It's Been a Long Four Years," *Washington Post*, January 16, 2013, A15.
2. Peter G. Klein, *Biography of F. A. Hayek* (1899–1992), Ludwig von Mises Institute, mises.org/about/3234.
3. Frank S. Meyer, *The Molding of Communists* (New York: Harcourt, Brace, 1961).
4. Shailagh Murray. "Obama's Reagan Comparison Sparks Debate," *Washington Post*, January 17, 2008, voices.washingtonpost.com/44/2008/01/obamas-reagan-comparison-spark-1.html; "SC Debate Barack Obama: Hillary Clinton Praises Reagan," www.blip.tv/file/615671#.
5. F. A. Hayek, *The Constitution of Liberty* (Chicago: University of Chicago Press, 1960), 61.

Chapter 1: New Deal Faith Shattered

1. Paul Light, "The Real Crisis in Government," *Washington Post*, January 12, 2010.
2. *Report and Recommendations of the National Commission on the Public Sector* (Washington, DC: Government Printing Office, 1989), and National Commission on the Public Service, *Urgent Business for America: Revitalizing the Federal Government for the 21st Century* (Washington, DC: Government Printing Office, January 2003), www.washingtonpost.com/wp-srv/opinions/documents/Urgent_Business_for_America__Revitalizing_the_Federal_Government_for_the_21st_Century.pdf.
3. Andrew Kohut, "Americans Are More Skeptical of Washington Than Ever," *Wall Street Journal*, April 19, 2010, A19. See also a Fox News poll from about the same time that showed similar results: www.foxnews.com/projects/pdf/022610_govspending.pdf.
4. Light, "The Real Crisis in Government."
5. Ibid.
6. Max Weber, *Theory of Social and Economic Organization*, trans. A. M Henderson and Talcott Parsons (New York: Free Press, 1947; originally published in German in 1920), 343–55.
7. Ibid., 337.
8. Woodrow Wilson, *The Study of Administration* (Washington, DC: Public Affairs Press, 1955), 9, 12.
9. Ibid., 4, 12, 13.

10. Donald Devine, "American Culture and Public Administration," *Policy Studies Journal*, December 1992, 255–60. See also Herbert Croly, *The Promise of American Life* (New York: Macmillan, 1909).

11. *The Public Papers and Addresses of Franklin D. Roosevelt*, vol. 1, 1928–32 (New York: Random House, 1938), 647.

12. Murray Rothbard, *America's Great Depression* (Los Angeles: Nash Publishing, 1972, originally published 1963), ch. 5.

13. Gunnar Myrdal, *Beyond the Welfare State* (New Haven: Yale University Press, 1960).

14. President George W. Bush, Remarks to Ohio Operating Engineers, Labor Day, 2003.

15. Del Jones, "How's USA's First MBA President Doing?," *USA Today*, April 27, 2003.

16. Michael J. Gerson, *Heroic Conservatism* (New York: HarperOne, 2007), 62. The Roosevelt allusion is according to Karl Rove, in Richard Stevenson, "Interview with Karl Rove," *New York Times*, January 23, 2003.

17. E. J. Dionne Jr., "When Government Is Good," *Washington Post*, September 2, 2005, A29.

18. Bobby Jindal, "When Red Tape Trumped Common Sense," *Wall Street Journal*, September 8, 2005, A19.

19. John M. Barry, *Rising Tide: The Great Mississippi Flood of 1927 and How It Changed America* (New York: Touchstone, 1996).

20. E. J. Dionne Jr., "Higher Stakes for Roberts," *Washington Post*, September 6, 2005, A25.

21. Daniel Henninger, "To Understand Katrina's Problem, Read 9/11 Report," *Wall Street Journal*, September 2, 2005, A13.

22. Jeb Bush, Testimony before the House Committee on Homeland Security, October 19, 2005, 1.

23. Susan B. Glasser and Michael Grunwald, "DHS Disaster Plan Still a Work in Progress," *Washington Post*, September 4, 2005, A31.

24. "To the Gulf from around the Globe: After Katrina, U.S. Government Fumbled Foreign Aid," *Washington Post*, July 14, 2007.

25. Jeffrey Birnbaum, "Corporate Efforts for the Stricken Are Unprecedented," *Washington Post*, September 3, 2005, F1.

26. U.S. Senate Committee on Environment and Public Works, Full Committee Hearing on "The Role of Science in Environmental Policy," September 28, 2005.

27. Birnbaum, "Corporate Efforts for the Stricken," and "Amid Criticism Officials Blame Stolen Local Files," *Washington Post*, September 4, 2005, A24.

28. Barry, *Rising Tide*, and Ellen Ruppel, "A Confusion Lesson in Flood Control," *Washington Post*, September 4, 2005, B4.

29. Robert Block and Amy Schwartz, "Florida Beats Back Washington," *Wall Street Journal*, December 8, 2005, A1.

30. Department of Homeland Security, *National Incident Management System* (Washington, DC: Government Printing Office, March 1, 2004).

31. "About the National Incident Management System (NIMS)," FEMA.gov; Devlin Barrett, "ID Would Control Areas to Disaster Sites," *Washington Post*, September 4, 2007, A1.

32. Block and Schwartz, "Florida Beats Back Washington."

33. Greg Anrig, *The Conservatives Have No Clothes: Why Right-Wing Ideas Keep Failing* (Hoboken, NJ: John Wiley, 2007), ch. 1.

34. "FEMA Chief: Victims Bear Some Responsibility," CNN, September 1, 2005.

35. Veronique de Rugy, "Spending under President George W. Bush," Mercatus Center, George Mason University, March 2009, 1, mercatus.org/uploadedFiles/Mercatus/WP0904_GAP_Spending%20Under%20President%20George%20W%20Bush.pdf.

36. "Historical Tables," *The Budget for Fiscal Year 2009* (Washington, DC: Government Printing Office, 2007), 328–34. President Bush presents a table in his memoir, *Decision Points*, that suggests he spent less than Reagan and Clinton. But he uses total spending as a percentage of gross domestic product (GDP) and includes defense spending, which was greatly reduced as a percentage of GDP by the end of the Cold War. Domestic spending is the more appropriate

comparison, both mathematically and politically. See George W. Bush, *Decision Points* (New York: Crown, 2010).

37. Thomas Frank, *The Wrecking Crew: How Conservatives Ruined Government, Enriched Themselves, and Beggared the Nation* (New York: Metropolitan/Holt, 2008).

38. Anrig, *The Conservatives Have No Clothes.*

39. Ann Scott Tyson, "Army Disability Benefit Review System Feels Strain," *Washington Post*, March 13, 2007, A8; Ann Scott Tyson, "Apologies and Anger Expressed at Hearings at Walter Reed," *Washington Post*, March 6, 2007, A1; "Free Walter Reed," *Wall Street Journal*, March 10, 2007, A8.

40. Mimi Hall, "Airport Screeners Missed Weapons," *USA Today*, September 22, 2004; "Airline Screeners Fail Government Bomb Tests," MSNBC, March 17, 2006.

41. Spencer S. Hsu, "GAO Criticizes Homeland Security Efforts to Fulfill Its Mission," *Washington Post*, September 6, 2007, A10.

42. Clyde Wayne Crews, *Ten Thousand Commandments: An Annual Snapshot of the Federal Regulatory State* (Washington, DC: Competitive Enterprise Institute, 2012), 44; Eli Lehrer et al., Letter to President Bush, Competitive Enterprise Institute, October 31, 2008, cei.org/outreach-coalition-letters/letter-president-bush-midnight-regulations.

43. Robert J. Samuelson, "Bankrupt Economics," *Washington Post*, July 29, 2008.

44. "The Paulson Sale," *Wall Street Journal*, September 24, 2008, A16.

45. "The Beltway Crash," *Wall Street Journal*, September 30, 2008, A18.

46. E. J. Dionne Jr., "The Street on Welfare," *Washington Post*, March 18, 2008, A19.

47. "A Mortgage Fable," *Wall Street Journal*, September 22, 2008, A22.

48. Alan Greenspan, Testimony on Regulatory Reform of the Government-Sponsored Enterprises, U.S. Senate Committee on Banking and Urban Affairs, April 6, 2005.

49. Alan Reynolds, "Wall Street No Longer Exists," *Wall Street Journal*, September 23, 2008, A29.

50. Samuelson, "Bankrupt Economics."

51. Zachary Goldfarb, "The Talk," *Washington Post*, March 17, 2008; *Fox News Sunday*, March 16, 2008.

52. Milton Friedman and Anna Jacobson Schwartz, *A Monetary History of the United States* (Princeton: Princeton University Press, 1971; originally published 1965).

53. Boards of Trustees of Social Security and Medicare, *Annual Report*, March 23, 2005.

54. See "Statement of Actuarial Opinion," *2012 Annual Report of the Boards of Trustees of the Federal Hospital Insurance and Federal Supplementary Medical Insurance Trust Funds*; "Statement of Actuarial Opinion," *2010 Annual Report of the Boards of Trustees of the Federal Hospital Insurance and Federal Supplementary Medical Insurance Trust Funds*. See also "Richard Foster for President," *Wall Street Journal*, August 9, 2010, A16.

55. Mike Allen, "Hastert Doubtful on Social Security Bill," *Washington Post*, April 1, 2005, A4.

56. Light, "The Real Crisis in Government."

57. National Commission on the Public Service, *Urgent Business for America.*

58. Michael D. Shear and Jon Cohn, "Obama Leads, Pessimism Reigns among Key Group," *Washington Post*, August 4, 2008.

59. The essence of the solution is explored in chapters 8–10.

Chapter 2: Change Requires More Muscle

1. Maggie Rodriguez, CBS *Early Show*, January 19, 2009; Jim Acosta, CNN *American Morning*, January 13, 2009.

2. Andrea Mitchell, NBC *Nightly News*, January 20, 2009.

3. *A New Era of Responsibility: Renewing America's Promise* (Washington, DC: Office of Management and Budget, 2009) is a comprehensive and detailed statement of the Obama administration's first-year budget and policy proposals and the source for most of what follows.

4. Ben Smith, "Transformational Like Reagan: An Interview with Barack Obama in the *Reno Gazette*," *Politico*, January 16, 2008.

5. "Obama's Iraq Surprise," *Wall Street Journal*, April 8, 2009, A12; August Cole and Yochi Dreazon, "Pentagon Pushes Defense Cuts," *Wall Street Journal*, April 7, 2008, A1.

6. Press Conference, Executive Office of the President, February 26, 2009.

7. Center for Data Analysis, The Heritage Foundation, February 26, 2009.

8. Press Briefing by Treasury Secretary Tim Geithner, HUD Secretary Shaun Donovan, and FDIC Chairman Sheila Bair, Dobson High School, Arizona, February 18, 2009, C-Span, March 2, 2009; "Mortgage Relief Program Released," CBS News/AP, March 4, 2009, www.cbsnews.com/stories/2009/03/04/politics/100days/economy/main4842435.shtml.

9. It was still flat three years later. Meg Handley, "The Home Front: Is the Housing Recovery for Real?," *U.S. News & World Report*, October 10, 2012.

10. OMB director Peter Orszag and Council of Economic Advisers chair Christina Romer, Executive Office of the President, Fiscal Year 2010 Budget Overview, February 26, 2009, C-Span Video Library, www.c-spanvideo.org/program/Year2010B.

11. Ibid.

12. Ibid.

13. Mark Landler and Eric Dash, "Drama Behind a $250 Billion Banking Deal," *New York Times*, October 15, 2008, A1.

14. Liz Rappaport, "Lewis Testifies U.S. Urged Silence on Deal," *Wall Street Journal*, April 23, 2009, A1.

15. Ibid.

16. "The Extortion Economy," Center for Individual Freedom, April 29, 2008, www.cfif.org/htdocs/freedomline/current/in_our_opinion/The-Extortion-Economy.html.

17. David Cho, Tomoeh Murakami Tse, and Brady Dennis, "Major Banks Negotiate, Spin, Chafe at Stress-Test Results," *Washington Post*, May 8, 2009, A16.

18. Ibid.

19. "Deborah Solomon, "US Sets Plan for Toxic Assets," *Wall Street Journal*, March 21, 2009, A1. In fact, the costs were estimated to be lower, according to one source; see Lori Montgomery, "U.S. to Pay $250B for TARP, CBO Says," *Washington Post*, November 30, 2010, A18.

20. Massimo Calabresi, "Banks Balk at Selling Toxic Assets," *Time*, April 16, 2009.

21. "Chrysler Goes to Court," *Wall Street Journal*, May 1, 2009, A16.

22. Tomoeh Murakami Tse, "List of Objecting Creditors Shrinks in Chrysler Case," *Washington Post*, May 7, 2009, A17.

23. Peter Whoriskey, Brady Dennis, and Kendra Marr, "President Slams Holdout Creditors as Speculators," *Washington Post*, May 1, 2009, A1.

24. Serena Ng and Annelena Lobb, "U.S. Tactics Spark Worry over Lenders' Rights," *Wall Street Journal*, May 1, 2009, A13.

25. Deborah Solomon, Jonathan Weisman, and Laura Meckler, "At Treasury, Big White House Role," *Wall Street Journal*, May 1, 2009, A1.

26. George Melloan, "Basel's Capital Illusions," *Wall Street Journal*, September 14, 2010, A21.

27. Ralph Vartabedian and Tom Hamburger, "Crimes Suspected in 20 Bailout Cases," *Los Angeles Times*, April 21, 2009, A1.

28. "Happy Days Are Not Here Again," *Wall Street Journal*, October 8, 2012, A12.

29. Sheryl Gay Stolberg and Robert Pear, "Obama Signs Health Care Overhaul into Law," *New York Times*, March 23, 2010.

30. For the law details, see www.healthreform.gov. For the coverage data, including revisions for the effect of the Supreme Court decision, see Congressional Budget Office, *Estimates for the Insurance Coverage Provisions of the Affordable Care Act Updated for the Recent Supreme Court Decision*, July 2012, Table 3.

31. Orszag and Romer, Fiscal Year 2010 Budget Overview.

32. David S. Hitzenbath, "Wellness Incentives Could Create Health Care Loophole," *Washington Post*, October 16, 2009, A1.

33. Editorial, "No Mandate for Health Care," *Washington Times*, December 18, 2009.
34. Ricardo Alonso Zaldivar, "6 Million Uninsured Expected to Face Health-Care Penalty," *Washington Post*, September 20, 2012, A4.
35. Grace Marie Turner, "Obamacare: A Dozen (More) Damaging Disclosures," Forbes.com, April 27, 2012.
36. Scott Gottlieb, "Meet the Obamacare Mandate Committee," *Wall Street Journal*, February 16, 2012, A13.
37. Gina Colata, "Panel Recommends Mammograms at 50, Not 40," *New York Times*, November 16, 2009, A1.
38. Shailagh Murray, "Public Opinion May Be Highest Hurdle in Senate," and "Americans Worry about Costs Rising in the Future Across Party Lines," *Washington Post*, August 22, 2009, A1.
39. Emma Brown, "Chicago Pol Dan Rostenkowski Remembered," *Post Mortem*, WashingtonPost.com, August 11, 2010.
40. "Back Health Bill Even If It Hurts, Pelosi Tells Dems," *NewsMax*, February 28, 2010, www.newsmax.com/InsideCover/nancy-pelosi-support-Health/2010/02/28/id/351142; "Pelosi: Lawmakers Should Sacrifice Jobs for Health Care," FoxNews.com, February 28, 2010.
41. Shailagh Murray and Lori Montgomery, "On Health Care the Prognosis Is Compromise," *Washington Post*, July 6, 2009, A3.
42. David Brown, "U.S. Bishops Blast Obama's Contraception Compromise," *Washington Post*, February 11, 2011, A1.
43. Stolberg and Pear, "Obama Signs Health Care."
44. Timothy Carney, "Obama Gives Sugar Plums to Special Interests," *Washington Examiner*, March 24, 2010, www.washingtonexaminer.com/politics/Obama-gives-sugar-plums-to-the-special-interests-88958037.html#ixzz0j6qAQBpR.
45. E. J. Dionne Jr., "An Ebullient Pelosi," *Washington Post*, March 23, 2010.
46. "ObamaCare Day One," *Wall Street Journal*, March 25, 2010, A20.
47. "The ObamaCare Writedowns," *Wall Street Journal*, March 27, 2010, A14.
48. Miles Mogulescu, "NY Times Reporter Confirms Obama Made Deal to Kill Public Option," *Huffington Post*, March 16, 2010, www.huffingtonpost.com/miles-mogulescu/ny-times-reporter-confirm_b_500999.html.
49. Chris Frates, "Payoffs for States Get Harry Reid to 60 Votes," *Politico*, December 19, 2009.
50. "Passion Fuels Opposition to Health Care Law," *Washington Post*, March 28, 2010, A1.
51. Robert J. Samuelson, "Bernanke on the Brink," *Washington Post*, September 17, 2012, A15.
52. Alan S. Blinder and Mark Zandi, "How the Great Recession Was Brought to an End," self-published, July 27, 2010.
53. Lawrence B. Lindsey, "Did the Stimulus Stimulate?," *Weekly Standard*, August 16, 2010, 9–12. See also John F. Cogan and John B. Taylor, "The Obama Stimulus Impact? Zero," *Wall Street Journal*, December 9, 2010, A23.
54. Anita Dunn, "The Truth about Czars," The White House Blog, September 16, 2009.
55. Douglas Feith, *War and Decision* (New York: HarperCollins, 2008), 509–20.
56. Donald Devine, *Reagan's Terrible Swift Sword* (Ottawa, IL: Jameson Books, 1991), 195–202.
57. Jackie Calmes, "Obama Seeks Spending Freeze," *New York Times*, January 25, 2010, A1; "On Presidential Rhetoric," *Wall Street Journal*, April 22, 2010, A22.

Chapter 3: Why Can't We All Agree?

1. President Barack Obama, Radio Address, May 16, 2009; Obama also used the phrase on May 6, 12, and 17, among other occasions.
2. Jesse Lee, "President Obama Follows Up on Thursday's Bipartisan Meeting on Health Reform," The White House Blog, March 2, 2010, www.whitehouse.gov.

3. President Barack Obama, "Let's Find Those Areas Where We Can Agree," White House Press Conference, November 3, 2010, www.whitehouse.gov/blog/2010/11/03/president-obama-s-press-conference-lets-find-those-areas-where-we-can-agree.

4. Jeff Israely, "Will Pope and Obama Clash over Abortion?," *Time*, November 18, 2008; Congressional Research Service description of H.R. 1964.

5. Patricia Zapore, "Bishops Cite Abortion Fears," Catholic News Service, November 14, 2008.

6. Peter Finney Jr., "On Life Issue Cardinal Says Obama on Wrong Side of History," Catholic News Service, April 21, 2009. His successor was not as observant; see John L. Allen Jr., "Bishops Are Not Obama Haters, Dolan Insists," *National Catholic Reporter*, February 14, 2012, ncronline.org/blogs/ncr-today/bishops-are-not-obama-haters-dolan-insists.

7. Associated Press, "Obama: Don't Jump to Conclusions," CBS News, November 6, 2009.

8. "Army Chief: Fort Rampage a 'Kick in the Gut,'" MSNBC.com, November 8, 2009.

9. Joe Klein, "In the Arena: Bigoted Religious Extremists," *Time*, November 9, 2009, swampland.time.com/2009/11/07/bigoted-religious-extremists/.

10. Daniel Zwerdling, "Walter Reed Officials Asked: Was Hasan Psychotic?," National Public Radio, November 11, 2009.

11. Zwerdling, "Walter Reed Officials."

12. Charles Krauthammer, "Medicalizing Mass Murder," *Washington Post*, November 13, 2009, A21.

13. Ann Scott Tyson and Dana Priest, "Army Sought Ways to Chanel Hasan's Absorption with Islam," *Washington Post*, November 11, 2010, A1.

14. Zwerdling, "Walter Reed Officials."

15. Laurence Bergreen, *Marco Polo* (New York: Vintage, 2007), 131.

16. Donald J. Devine, *The Political Culture of the United States* (Boston: Little Brown, 1972), ch. 1.

17. Eagle Man, "We Are All Related," in Ed McGaa, ed., *Mother Earth Spirituality* (New York: HarperCollins, 1990). For a more modern specification, see Aldo Leopold, *A Sand Country Almanac* (New York: Oxford University Press, 1949).

18. Donald Devine, *In Defense of the West* (Lanham, MD: University Press of America, 2004), 2–3.

19. Will Durant, *The Life of Greece*, vol 2, *The Story of Civilization* (New York: MJF Books, 1997).

20. David Maybury-Lewis, "Tribal Wisdom," in David Maybury-Lewis, *Millennium* (London: Biniman, 1992).

21. Karl A. Wittfogel, *Oriental Despotism* (New Haven: Yale University Press, 1957).

22. Rodney Stark, *Discovering God* (New York: HarperOne, 2007), 105–12.

23. Paul A. Rahe, *Montesquieu and the Logic of Liberty* (New Haven: Yale University Press, 2009), 1:1–2, 31–39.

24. Frank S. Meyer, *In Defense of Freedom and Related Essays* (Indianapolis: Liberty Fund, 1996), 209–24.

25. Rodney Stark, *One True God* (Princeton: Princeton University Press, 2007), 35.

26. John Emerich Edward Dalberg Acton, "The History of Freedom in Antiquity," in *The History of Freedom and Other Essays* (Indianapolis: Liberty Classics, 1986), 5–28.

27. Meyer, *In Defense of Freedom*, 212–16.

28. Ibid.

29. Devine, *In Defense of the West*, 18.

30. Herbert Butterfield, "Originality in the Old Testament," in C. Thomas McIntire, ed., *Writings on Christianity and History* (New York: Oxford University Press, 1979).

31. Meyer, *In Defense of Freedom*, 223.

32. 2 Samuel 11; 1 Samuel 8.

33. Meyer, *In Defense of Freedom*, 219.

34. Acton, "The History of Freedom in Christianity," 28, and Meyer, *In Defense of Freedom*, 221.

35. Fareed Zakaria, *The Future of Freedom* (New York: Norton, 2003), 34.

36. Acton, "The History of Freedom in Christianity," 30.

37. Meyer, *In Defense of Freedom*, 92–93.
38. Acton, "The History of Freedom in Christianity," 29–53.
39. Niccolò Machiavelli, *The Art of War*, trans. Ellis Farnsworth, ed. Neal Wood (Cambridge, MA: DaCapo Press, 1965), 2:79.
40. Jean-Jacques Rousseau, "The Social Contract," in *The Social Contract and Other Essays*, trans. G. D. H. Cole (New York: Everyman's Library, 1950), 320–33.
41. Meyer, *In Defense of Freedom*, 220. The reference is to the First Lateran Council of 1123, which officially declared the separation of ecclesiastical and temporal authority.
42. Christopher Dawson, *Religion and the Rise of Western Civilization* (Garden City, NY: Image Books, 1958), chs. 7–8.
43. F. A. Hayek, "The Origins of the Rule of Law," in *The Constitution of Liberty* (Chicago: University of Chicago Press, 1960), ch. 11.
44. Stark, *One True God*, 220, and Chris Wickham, *The Inheritance of Rome: A History of Europe from 400 to 1000* (New York: Viking, 2009), 172. According to Max Weber, it was this very "laxity" in doctrine and performance before the Reformation that led Protestants to proclaim the need for a reformed Church. See Stark, *One True God*, 220–21, and Eric Hoffer, "The Readiness to Work," in *Between the Devil and the Dragon* (New York: HarperCollins, 1982).
45. Jean Gimpel, *The Medieval Machine: The Industrial Revolution of the Middle Ages* (New York: Barnes & Noble, 1976), 1.
46. Ibid., 229.
47. Ibid., 10; Acton, "The History of Freedom in Christianity," 27.
48. Wickham, *The Inheritance of Rome*, 543–44. See also Derek Thompson, "The Economic History of the Last 2000 Years: Part II," *The Atlantic*, June 20, 2012, www.theatlantic.com/business/archive/2012/06/the-economic-history-of-the-last-2000-years-part-ii/258762/.
49. Gimpel, *The Medieval Machine*, 199.
50. Donald Devine, "The Post Westphalian State System and Its Universalistic Challenges," State of the World Conference on Globalism, Brussels, June 18, 2003.
51. Dawson, *Religion and the Rise of Western Civilization*, 215; Christopher Dawson, *The Dividing of Christendom* (San Francisco: Ignatius Press, 2008, originally published 1965), 118–30.
52. Robert Filmer, *Patriarcha and Other Writings*, ed. Johann Sommerville (Cambridge: Cambridge University Press, 1991), 1–68.
53. Rahe, *Montesquieu and the Logic of Liberty*, 6.
54. Meyer, *In Defense of Freedom*, 216–17.
55. Plato, *The Republic*, Book V.
56. Rousseau, "The Social Contract," 330.
57. Lord Acton, "Nationalism," in *Essays in the History of Liberty* (Indianapolis: Liberty Classics, 1985), 409–33.
58. John Lukacs, *The Passing of the Modern Age* (New York: Wiley, 1970), 17.
59. R. J. Rummel, *Death by Government* (New Brunswick, NJ: Transaction, 1994), 4, 70ff., and Matthew White, "Selected Death Tolls for Wars, Massacres, and Atrocities before the Twentieth Century," necrometrics.com/pre1700a.htm.
60. Meyer, *In Defense of Freedom*, 221, 224.
61. Ibid.
62. Seymour Martin Lipset, *The First New Nation* (Garden City, NY: Anchor/Doubleday, 1967), 107; Devine, *The Political Culture of the United States*, 43–58.
63. Hector St. John de Crevecoeur, "What Is an American?," *Letters from an American Farmer and Sketches of 18th-Century America* (New York: New American library, 1963), 246–52.
64. Meyer, *In Defense of Freedom*, 224.
65. Alexis de Tocqueville, *Democracy in America*, trans. Henry Reeve (London: Saunders & Otley, 1835, 1840), 253–57.
66. Ibid., 256.

67. David C. Hendrickson, *Union, Nation, or Empire?* (Lawrence: University Press of Kansas, 2009), chs. 26–27. See also Acton, "The American Revolution," in *Essays in the History of Liberty*, 189–97.
68. Woodrow Wilson, *Congressional Government* (New York: Meridian Books, 1956, originally published 1885), 187.
69. Wilson, *The Study of Administration*.
70. "If we judge events by their consequences, the great world revolutionary was Wilson rather than Lenin." Lukacs, *The Passing of the Modern Age*, 22.
71. Lukacs, *The Passing of the Modern Age*, 23.
72. James McGregor Burns, *Deadlock of Democracy* (New York: Prentice Hall, 1963). See also Robert Samuelson, "The Deadlock of Democracy," *Washington Post*, November 1, 2004, A21, and F. A. Hayek, "The Political Order of a Free People," *Law, Legislation, and Liberty*, vol. 3 (Chicago: University of Chicago Press, 1979), 93.
73. See E. E. Schattschneider, *Party Government* (Westport, CT: Greenwood Press, 1942).
74. "Science and the Drilling Ban," *Wall Street Journal*, November 20, 2010, A16.

Chapter 4: Superseding Tradition?

1. U.S. Bureau of the Census, *Historical Statistics of the United States: Colonial Times to 1970* (Washington, DC: U.S. Government Printing Office, 1975), vol. 2, Y308–17, 332–34, 335–38, 682–709; Devine, "American Culture and Public Administration," 255–56; *A Biography of an Ideal: A History of the Civil Service* (Washington DC: U.S. Government Printing Office, 2003), ch. 1,
2. Leonard K. Nash, *The Nature of the Natural Sciences* (Boston: Little Brown, 1963), 105–7.
3. Ralph Henry Gabriel, *The Course of American Democratic Thought* (New York: Meridian Books, 1956; originally published 1940), 247.
4. Ibid., 352–53.
5. Woodrow Wilson, "The Study of Administration," 3.
6. Ibid., 10.
7. R. Sam Garrett, James A. Thurber, A. Lee Fritschler, and David H. Rosenbloom, "Assessing the Impact of Bureaucracy Bashing by Political Campaigns," *Public Administration Review*, March 2006, 226–40. See also Vincent Ostrom, *The Intellectual Crisis in American Public Administration* (Tuscaloosa, AL: University of Alabama Press, 1973); Devine, "American Culture and Public Administration," 258–59.
8. Devine, *Reagan's Terrible Swift Sword*, chs. 8–9.
9. Donald Devine, "Managing the Largest Corporation in the World," in Alvin S. Felzenberg, ed., *The Keys to a Successful Presidency* (Washington, DC: The Heritage Foundation, 2000), 116–34; Devine, *Reagan's Terrible Swift Sword*, 83–85. One estimate is that there were an average of three hundred serious union work actions annually before the air controller strike and thirty afterward. See Joe Davidson, "Reagan's Complicated Legacy for Federal Workers," *Washington Post*, February 7, 2011, B7. See also Joseph A. McCartin, "The Strike That Busted Unions," *New York Times*, August, 3, 2011, A25.
10. George Nesterczuk and Donald Devine, "Taking Charge of Federal Personnel," *Heritage Foundation Backgrounder*, January 10, 2001.
11. Donald Devine, "The Future of Labor Relations in the Public Sector," *Journal of Labor Research*, Winter 2004, 9–18.
12. Randal O'Toole, *The Best-Laid Plans* (Washington, DC: The Cato Institute, 2007), ch. 1.
13. Ibid,. chs. 2–5.
14. Ibid., Part IV.
15. Ibid., ch. 8.
16. See also James Q. Wilson, *Bureaucracy: What Government Agencies Do and Why* (New York: Basic Books, 1989), ch. 20.

17. O'Toole, *The Best-Laid Plans*, part 7.
18. Bob Davis, Damian Paletta, and Rebecca Smith, "Unraveling Reagan: Amid Turmoil, U.S. Turns Away from Decades of Deregulation," *Wall Street Journal*, July 25, 2008, A1.
19. Stephen Dinan, "Rocky Kickoff to Changes for Student Loans," *Washington Times*, March 31, 2010, A1.
20. Ludwig von Mises, *Bureaucracy* (New Haven: Yale University Press, 1944).
21. Donald Devine, "Public Administration: The Right Way," in Robert Rector and Michael Sanera, eds., *Steering the Elephant* (New York: Universe Books, 1987). See also Devine, "Managing the Largest Corporation in the World," 116–34.
22. Devine, *Reagan's Terrible Swift Sword*, 105.
23. Theodore Lowi, "The Public Philosophy: Interest Group Liberalism," *Journal of Politics*, March 1967, 5–24.
24. Grace-Marie Turner, "ObamaCare Danger Signs," *National Review Online*, April 23, 2010.
25. "The New Lords of Finance," *Wall Street Journal*, May 24, 2010, A16.
26. "So Much for the Volcker Rule," *Wall Street Journal*, October 24, 2011, A14.
27. F. A. Hayek, "The Theory of Complex Phenomena," in *Studies in Philosophy, Politics, and Economics* (Chicago: University of Chicago Press, 1967), ch. 2.
28. Hayek, *Law, Legislation, and Liberty*, vol. 3, 176.
29. H. L. Mencken, "The Monkey Trial: A Reporter's Account," University of Kansas Law School, July 18, 1925, law2.umkc.edu/faculty/projects/ftrials/scopes/menk.htm.
30. H. L. Mencken, "In Tennessee," *The Nation*, July 1, 1925.
31. Michael Powell, "Judge Rules Against 'Intelligent Design,'" *Washington Post*, December 21, 2005.
32. *Kitzmiller v. Dover Area School District*, U.S. District Court for the Middle District of Pennsylvania, Case 4:04-cv-02688-jej, Document 342, Filed December 20, 2005, 63.
33. Ibid., 71–72.
34. Ibid., 43.
35. Alvin Plantinga, *Where the Conflict Really Lies* (Oxford: Oxford University Press, 2011), chs. 1, 2, 6.
36. Rodney Stark, *For the Glory of God* (Princeton: Princeton University Press, 2003), 198–99.
37. *Kitzmiller v. Dover Area School District*, 65–71.
38. David Brown and Rick Weiss, "Defending Science by Defining It," *Washington Post*, December 21, 2005, A20.
39. Karl R. Popper, *The Logic of Scientific Discovery* (New York: Harper & Row, 1965; originally published in German, 1934; in English, 1958), 34–39.
40. *Kitzmiller v. Dover Area School District*, 83, 87–88.
41. Popper, "Preface to the English Edition, 1955," *The Logic of Scientific Discovery*, 15.
42. See Plantinga, *Where the Conflict Really Lies*, 121, which also claims that that belief is under challenge today.
43. Alfred de Grazia, *The Velikovski Affair: The Warfare of Science and Scientism* (New York: Citadel Press, 1996). Again, Judge Jones did concede Darwinism was "imperfect." See *Kitzmiller v. Dover Area School District*, 137.
44. Plantinga, *Where the Conflict Really Lies*, 123. See also Thomas Nagel, *Mind and Cosmos: Why the Materialist Neo-Darwinian Conception of Nature Is Almost Certainly False* (Oxford: Oxford University Press, 2012), 122–23.
45. Brown and Weiss, "Defending Science by Defining It," A20.
46. *Kitzmiller v. Dover Area School District*, 70.
47. American Association for the Advancement of Science et al., "Letter to the U.S. Senate," October 21, 2009, www.aaas.org/spp/cstc/climateletterfinal.pdf.
48. Celia Cole, "Leading Scientists Condemn Political Assaults on Climate Researchers," *The Guardian*, May 26, 2010.
49. Claude Allegre et al., "No Need to Panic about Global Warming," *Wall Street Journal*, January 27, 2012.

50. "A National Survey of Television Meteorologists about Climate Change Education," Center for Climate Change Communication, June 30, 2011, www.climatechangecommunication. org/images/files/2011_Mason_AMS_NWA_Weathercaster_Survey_Report_NA_doc_ pdf%281%29.pdf; Leslie Kaufman, "Among Weathercasters, Doubt on Warming," *New York Times*, March 30, 2010, A1.

51. Lydia Saad, "In U.S., Global Warming Views Steady Despite Warm Winter," *Gallup Politics*, March 30, 2012, www.gallup.com/poll/153608/global-warming-views-steady-despite-warm-winter.aspx.

52. Jeffrey Ball, "Climate Panel Faces Heat: Investigation Calls for 'Fundamental Reform' at UN group on Global Warming," *Wall Street Journal*, September 1, 2010, A1.

53. Popper, *The Logic of Scientific Discovery*, 106.

54. Lincoln Barnett, *The Universe and Dr. Einstein*, rev. ed. (New York: William Morrow, 1948), esp. ch. 3.

55. Michael Scriven, "The Covering Law Position: A Critique and an Alternative Analysis," in Leonard I. Krimerman, ed., *The Nature and Scope of Social Science* (New York: Appleton-Century-Crofts, 1969), 107.

56. Nash, *The Nature of the Natural Sciences*, 125–27.

57. Michael Polanyi, Personal Knowledge (Chicago: University of Chicago Press, 1958), 384, 41–47; and Ernst Mayr, "Cause and Effect in Biology," in Daniel Lerner, ed., *Cause and Effect* (New York: Free Press, 1965), 49.

58. Walter Clark Hamilton, *Statistics in Physical Science* (New York: Ronald Press, 1964), v.

59. Richard Rudner, "The Scientist Qua Scientist Makes Value Judgments," *Philosophy of Science* (January 1953), 3. See also Barnett, *The Universe and Dr. Einstein*, 30.

60. First, the index or measure must be categorized. Yet the type of scale necessary is not always obvious; nor is it always available. And the boundaries of categories are never absolute but must be decided by the investigator. Second, the data must be collected and one must be concerned whether the sample is representative of phenomena to be measured. But one can never obtain all cases, and even if the most refined techniques are on hand and a random sample is used, error still remains, as the sample still has a range of sampling error and a confidence probability that the whole sample is unreliable. Third, no matter how precise a measurement instrument is used, there will be some difficulty in reproducing the measurement with different investigators, as different people will see the instrument somewhat differently. Fourth, some data are almost always unavailable for some analysis purposes, and this always causes some distortion. Fifth, there is a circularity to measurement, because if one corrects for one instrument with another, that instrument has to be corrected with another, and the second with a third, etc.; and any reading must be compared ultimately with some subjective reference. Sixth, when measurements are made on very small or very large (or very complex) phenomena, error seems to increase because of the nature of the complexity; for example, light-years in distance is not even assumed to have the accuracy of feet or yards. Finally, there are some concepts that are in principle unmeasurable—as exotic as subatomic particles but also as mundane as "water" temperature below 265 degrees Celsius. See Nash, *The Nature of the Natural Sciences.*

61. Popper, *The Logic of Scientific Discovery*, 61; Hubert M. Blalock Jr., *Causal Inferences in Non-experimental Research* (Chapel Hill: University of North Carolina Press, 1961), 15. Statistical hypothesis testing attempts to objectify the selection of explained hypotheses by eliminating the fallacy of affirming the consequent (type II error) through empirically testing null hypotheses and setting an absolute alpha level at which the null can be rejected. Yet not only can the alpha level be "adjusted" to fit the results, but also the alpha level itself is the probability of the error (type I) that the null should not have been rejected. Error, therefore, is an inherent part of statistical hypothesis testing whether the null hypothesis is rejected or not. Moreover, the alpha levels most used in testing (i.e., .05, .01, and .001) do not seem very demanding and are greatly affected by sample size. At the end, the scientist must make

the decision that the evidence is sufficiently strong or the probability is sufficiently high to warrant the acceptance of the hypothesis. Hypothesis testing is not avoided by saying a hypothesis is not being tested but that only a range of probability is being specified, since any specification is a limit test. A two-tailed test does not avoid the problem either, as limits are still imposed and in addition it is a sterile replacement for the rich meaning of asymmetry, which can be associated with causality. Using probability of hypothesis criteria in the Bayesian sense can be useful as a complement to hypothesis testing in specifying them further or in helping decide on alpha levels and sample size, but the approach does not change the essentially subjective nature of the process. Although the assignment of prior probabilities is not arbitrary, it is necessarily subjective and based on personal experience and intuition; there certainly is no guarantee that the decision will be any better than the initial guesses. It also seems clear that fitting nonlinear curves does not necessarily solve any of the major problems but introduces a much greater problem, because it is possible to fit a very large number of curves to any given data. Moreover, the fact that so many different forms are available encourages unique explanations for every different set of data, as a formula for some shape can be derived by anyone with enough mathematical sophistication to fit any data points. Significantly, with N-1 curves any set of data can be explained perfectly even though the description seems meaningless.

62. Warren Weaver, "A Scientist Ponders Faith," *Saturday Review,* January 3, 1959; Karl R. Popper, "On the Sources of Knowledge and Ignorance," in *Conjectures and Refutations* (New York: Harper & Row, 1968), ch. 1.

63. See Carl G. Hempel, "The Covering Law Position: A Reply to Critics," in Krimerman, *The Nature and Scope of Social Science,* 135–36.

64. Polanyi, *Personal Knowledge,* 4.

65. Gautam Naik, "Mistakes in Scientific Journals Surge," *Wall Street Journal,* August 10, 2011, A1.

66. Nash, *The Nature of the Natural Sciences,* 298–318, and de Grazia, "The Scientific Reception System," in *The Velikovski Affair,* 106–12. Of course, Galileo was wrong, and the much earlier Cardinal Nicholas of Cusa was more correct that the sun was not the center but that "the fabric of the world will quasi have its center everywhere and circumstance nowhere." Palolo Palmieri, "Galileus Deceptus," *Journal for the History of Astronomy,* November 2008, 425–52.

67. Daniel B. Botkin, "Absolute Certainty Is Not Scientific," *Wall Street Journal,* December 2, 2011, A19.

68. Dennis Avery, "Energy Secretary Admits We Don't Understand Climate Change," *Canada Free Press,* March 29, 2010.

69. Herbert Croly, *The Promise of American Life* (New York: Macmillan, 1912).

70. Gabriel, *The Course of American Democratic Thought,* 335.

71. Edwin Arthur Burtt, *The Metaphysical Foundations of Modern Physical Science* (London: Routledge and Kegan Paul, 1932); Popper, *The Logic of Scientific Discovery,* 19, 38, 262; and Nash, *The Nature of the Natural Sciences,* ch. 7.

72. Barnett, *The Universe and Dr. Einstein,* 22.

73. Bertrand Russell, *Problems of Philosophy* (London: Oxford University Press, 1912), 23; Alfred North Whitehead, *Science and the Modern World* (New York: Macmillan, 1925), 4.

74. Nash, *The Nature of the Natural Sciences,* 29–31.

75. Ibid., 43–62.

76. Friedrich Nietzsche, *Twilight of the Idols and the Anti Christ,* trans. R. J. Hollingdale (Baltimore: Penguin, 1968), 36, 189–90; and *The Will to Power,* trans. Anthony M. Ludovice (New York: Russell & Russell, 1964), 2:515, 29–30.

77. Morris R. Cohen, *Reason and Nature* (New York: Harcourt, Brace, 1931), 224.

78. R. M. MacIver, *Social Causation* (New York: Harper & Row, 1942), 62–68.

79. Ernest Nagel, *The Structure of Science* (New York: Harcourt, Brace and World, 1961), 324.

80. Popper, *Conjectures and Refutations,* 62.

81. James Gleick, *Chaos* (New York: Penguin Books, 1987), 103.

82. Polanyi, *Personal Knowledge.*

83. Whitehead, *Science and the Modern World*, 16.

84. Rudner, "The Scientist Qua Scientist Makes Value Judgments," 758.

85. Edward Fesser criticizes Popper's (and John Locke's) rejection of essentialism and finds this basis for essences too frail, arguing that a more objective basis in essentialism is essential. See his *Locke* (Oxford: Oneworld Publications, 2007), ch. 6. But this is a large call that he promises to remedy in a future book. Popper actually suggests a "third way" between essentialism and nominalism, distinguishing between "methodological nominalism," which covers the scientific and mathematical realm where forms are simply subjectively defined by the investigator for analytical purposes, and "metaphysical realism" in the real world realm, where there are essences that are embedded in reality and available to common sense, even if only in a probabilistic manner. See Popper, *Conjectures and Refutations*, 62–65, 114–19, 173–74.

86. Richard M. Weaver, "Relativism and the Crisis of Our Times," in Ted J. Smith III, ed., *In Defense of Tradition* (Indianapolis: Liberty Fund Books, 1963), 103.

87. Plantinga, *Where the Conflict Really Lies*, ch. 9; Stark, *For the Glory of God*, ch. 2.

88. Karl R. Popper, "Towards a Rational Theory of Tradition," in *Conjectures and Refutations*, 129.

89. Ibid., 130–31.

Chapter 5: Why Freedom?

1.   Food and Drug Administration website: www.fda.gov/RegulatoryInformation/Legislation/default.htm; www.fda.gov/AboutFDA/WhatWeDo/History/Origin/ucm124403.htm.

2.   www.fda.gov/AboutFDA/WhatWeDo/History/Origin/ucm054819.htm.

3.   FDA Press Conference, August 16, 2007, www.fda.gov/downloads/NewsEvents/Newsroom/MediaTranscripts/ucm123583.pdf.

4.   Anna Wilde Matthews, "In Milestone, FDA Pushes Genetic Tests Tied to Drugs," *Wall Street Journal*, August 16, 2007, A1.

5.   Rick Weiss, "Fungus Infected Woman Who Died After Gene Therapy," *Washington Post*, August 17, 2007, A8.

6.   Ibid., A10.

7.   John R. Graham, "Leviathan's Drug Problem," Pacific Research Institute, July 29, 2010; "How about a Kianna's Law?," *Wall Street Journal*, March 24, 2005, A14.

8.   Marc Kaufman, "Painkiller Decision Suggests Shift in FDAs Risk-Benefit Equation," *Washington Post*, March 18, 2005, A10.

9.   "FDA Panel Urges Ban on Vicodin and Percocet," *Health Day News*, June 30, 2009, www.prohealthcare.org/wellness/health-news/general-wellness/fda-panel-urges-ban-on-vicodin-percocet.aspx.

10. Gautam Naik, "Scientists' Elusive Goal: Reproducing Study Results," *Wall Street Journal*, December 2, 2011, A14; Naik, "Mistakes in Scientific Studies Surge."

11. Naik, "Mistakes in Scientific Studies Surge."

12. Ibid.

13. FDA Press Conference.

14. www.fda.gov/AboutFDA/WhatWeDo/History/Origin/ucm054819.htm.

15. Chris Buckley, "China Calls Official Execution a Warming Siren," Reuters, July 11, 2007, www.reuters.com/article/idUSSP32731420070711.

16. Charles Ornstein and Hagit Limor, "Where's the Openness, Mr. President?" *Washington Post*, April 1, 2011, A15.

17. David Paschal, "Irregular Warfare," *USAWC Strategy Research Project* (Carlisle Barracks: U.S. Army War College, 2006).

18. Timothy Carney, "Big Government Gets in Your Food," *Washington Examiner*, July 30, 2009.

19. Walter Pincus and Peter Baker, "Dissent on Intelligence Critical, Report Says," *Washington Post*, March 30, 2005, A1.

20. Michael O'Hanlon, Jack Keane, and Robert M. Morgenthau, "We Needed the Veterans— Now They Need Us," *Wall Street Journal*, July 6, 2012, A13; Christian Davenport, "Mystery Involving Arlington Grave Sites Grows," *Washington Post*, September 2, 2010, A1; Christian Davenport, "Remains of 8 People Found in One Arlington Grave," *Washington Post*, December 3, 2010, A1.

21. Ashley Halsey III, "2 Watchdogs Question FAA Error Data at House Hearing," *Washington Post*, April 26, 2012, A5.

22. Andy Pasztor, "Air Traffic Errors Stay Flat After Surge," *Wall Street Journal*, February 22, 2012, A2.

23. Robert Poole, "Lessons from Sleeping Controller Incident," *ATC Reform Newsletter*, The Reason Foundation, March 26, 2011.

24. Pasztor, "Air Traffic Errors Stay Flat After Surge."

25. Matthew Bigg, "No Magic Solution for Oil Spill," Reuters, March 24, 2010, www.reuters.com/article/idUSN0322326220100603?type=marketsNews.

26. "U.S. Keeps 'Boot on Neck' of BP," Reuters, May 24, 2010, http://www.reuters.com/article/2010/05/24/us-oil-rig-leak-idUSTRE6430AR20100524.

27. Mike Kunzelman and Greg Bluestein, "Criminal Investigation Launched by Feds," Associated Press, June 1, 2010, www.huffingtonpost.com/2010/06/01/bp-criminal-investigation_n_596626.html.

28. F. A. Hayek, "The Political Order of a Free People," *Law, Legislation, and Liberty* (Chicago: University of Chicago Press, 1979), 3:68, and "The Uses of Knowledge in Society," in *Individualism and Economic Order* (London: Routledge & Kegan Paul, 1949); Ludwig von Mises, "Economic Calculation in the Socialist Commonwealth," in F. A. Hayek, ed., *Collectivist Economic Planning* (London; George Rutledge & Son, 1935).

29. Leonard E. Reed, *I Pencil* (Irvington-on-Hudson, NY: Foundation for Economic Education, n.d.).

30. Adam Smith, *An Inquiry into the Nature and Causes of the Wealth of Nations* (New York: Modern Library, 1937), 4:9, 51, 651.

31. Ibid., 4:2, 9, 423.

32. Ibid., 4:9, 51.

33. See also Hayek, "The Political Order of a Free People," 60.

34. Smith, "Wealth of Nations," 5:126–7, 1:715.

35. "Triumph of the Regulators," *Wall Street Journal*, June 28, 2010, A20.

36. Anthony Faiola, "Ex-Barclays Head Faults Regulators," *Washington Post*, July 5, 2012, A10; "New York Fed to Barclays: Mm . . . hum," *Wall Street Journal*, July 17, 2012, A14.

37. Bradley Dennis, "Senate Passes Financial Regulation Bill," *Washington Post*, May 21, 2010, A1.

38. Robert A. Dahl and Charles Lindblom, *Politics, Economics, and Welfare* (New York: Harper, 1952), ch. 1.

39. Rothbard, *America's Great Depression*, esp. section 8; and "Books: A President's Ordeal," *Time*, September 8, 1952 (www.time.com/time/magazine/article/0,9171,935714–1,00.html).

40. Amity Shlaes, *The Forgotten Man: A New History of the Great Depression* (New York: Harper-Collins, 2007); Henry Hazlitt, *The Failure of the New Economics* (Princeton: Van Nostrand, 1959), ch. 28.

41. Annelena Lobb, "Looking Back on Black Monday: A Discussion with Richard Sylla," *Wall Street Journal*, October 14, 2007.

42. Robert J. Barro, "Stimulus Spending Keeps Failing," *Wall Street Journal*, May 5, 2012, A15.

43. Terry Miller, Kim R. Holmes, and Edwin J. Feulner, 2012 *Index of Economic Freedom* (Washington, DC: The Heritage Foundation and Dow Jones, 2012), table 2.

44. Devine, *Does Freedom Work?*, 44–62.

45. Freedom House, "Combined Average Ratings," *Freedom in the World* (New York: Freedom House, 2001), 660–61.

46. David Dollar and Aart Kraay, "Democracy and Rule of Law in Supporting Economic Growth," in *Property Rights, Political Rights, and the Development of Poor Countries in the Post-Colonial World* (World Bank, 2000), www.worldbank.org/research/growth. These measures have remained rather stable over time; see Daniel Kaufmann, Aart Kraay, and Massimo Mastruzzi, "Aggregate and Individual Governance Matters, 1996–2008," World Bank Development Research Group, June 2009. See also Robert J. Barro, "Rule of Law, Democracy, and Economic Performance," in Gerald P. O'Driscoll, Kim R. Holmes, and Melanie Kirkpatrick, *2000 Index of Economic Freedom* (Washington, DC: The Heritage Foundation and the Wall Street Journal, 2010), 31–50.

47. Wickham, *The Inheritance of Rome*, ch. 8.

48. Tom Bethell, *The Noblest Triumph: Property and Prosperity Through the Ages* (New York: Palgrave, 1998), 230–42, 285–89. For a Muslim confirmation, see Amin Maalouf, *The Crusades Through Arab Eyes*, trans. Jon Rothschild (New York: Schocken Books, 1984), 263. See also Victor Davis Hanson, *The Other Greeks* (New York: Free Press, 1995).

49. Victor Davis Hanson, *Carnage and Culture* (New York: Doubleday, 2001), esp. 441–44.

50. Harold J. Berman, *Law and Revolution: The Formation of the Western Legal Tradition* (Cambridge, MA: Harvard University Press, 1983), ch. 2; Angus Maddison *The World Economy: Historical Statistics* (Brussels: OECD Publishing, 2003), vol. 2, 92, as combined by Michael Cembalest in Derek Thompson, "The Economic History of the Last 2,000 Years, Part II," *The Atlantic*, June 20, 2012. Secondary analysis that does not find the evidence of the West's "first industrial revolution" in the Middle Ages—such as Tom G. Palmer, "Poverty, Morality, and Liberty," in Tom G. Palmer, ed., *After the Welfare State* (Ottawa, IL: Jameson Books, 2012)—rely on scales with too large intervals to catch the earlier wealth rise (figure on page 113), although even there the uncommented-upon raw data for the year 1500 (after declines from the earlier Black Death plague) show the West far ahead of the rest of the world already, especially but not only Italy (table 1 on p. 112).

51. Al Shafi'i, "Treatise on the Roots of Jurisprudence," in F. E. Peters, ed., *Judaism, Christianity, and Islam* (Princeton: Princeton University Press, 1990), 306–7.

52. Bethell, *The Noblest Triumph*, ch. 15; Hernando de Soto, "Egypt's Economic Apartheid," *Wall Street Journal*, February 3, 2011, A19.

53. David Wessel, "The Legal DNA of Good Economies," *Wall Street Journal*, September 6, 2001, A1.

54. Michael Novak, *The Fire of Invention* (Lanham, MD: Rowman & Littlefield, 1997), esp. 53–67.

55. John Haltiwanger, Ron Jarmin, and Javier Miranda, "Who Creates Jobs: Small vs. Large vs. Young," July 2009, siteresources.worldbank.org/INTFR/Resources/HaltiwangerJarminMirandaWhoCreatesJobsjuly8.pdf.

56. Robert J. Samuelson, "Engineering Our Own Recovery," *Washington Post*, October 4, 2010, A17.

57. Alan Reynolds, "Taxes and the Top Percentile Myth," *Wall Street Journal*, December 23, 2010, A17.

58. Freedom House, "Combined Average Ratings," list of most free nations with the score of 1.0.

59. Karl Marx and Friedrich Engels, *The Communist Manifesto*, trans. Samuel Moore with F. Engels (Chicago: Kerr, 1913). See Devine, *In Defense of Freedom*, 78–81.

60. Joseph A. Schumpeter, *Capitalism, Socialism, and Democracy*, 3rd ed. (New York: Harper & Row, 1950), ch. 7.

61. Ibid., ch. 8.

62. Herbert Kaufman, *The Administrative Behavior of Federal Bureau Chiefs* (Washington, DC: The Brookings Institution, 1981).

63. Peter Drucker, *Innovation and Entrepreneurship* (New York: Harper & Row, 1985), 259.

64. Schumpeter, *Capitalism, Socialism, and Democracy*, 134, 162.

65. Ralph Waldo Emerson, "Self-Reliance," in *Essays* (Boston: Munne, 1841).

66. Henry David Thoreau, *Resistance to Civil Government* (New Haven: Rollins, 1928).

67. Friedrich Nietzsche, *The Anti-Christ*, trans. H. L. Mencken (New York: Knopf, 1920), 4–7, 13, 15, 18.
68. Thomas Hobbes, *Leviathan* (New York: Penguin Books, 1985), 186.
69. Alexis de Tocqueville, *Democracy in America*, trans. Henry Reeve (London: Saunders & Otley, 1840), 2:2, v.
70. Ibid., 1:v.
71. Ibid,, 2:4, vi.
72. Ibid., 2:xiii.
73. Ibid., 1:xvii.

Chapter 6: Rule of Law

1. Terry Miller and Kim R. Holmes, *2010 Index of Economic Freedom* (Washington, DC: The Heritage Foundation and the Wall Street Journal, 2010), and Terry Muth, "The U.S. Isn't as Free as It Used to Be," *Wall Street Journal*, January 20, 2010, A16. In the *2011 Index of Economic Freedom*, the United States slipped further in the ratings, from seventh to eighth place, and in 2012 it fell to tenth place.
2. Hans Eicholz, "Pufendorf, Grotius, and Locke: Who Is the Real Father of America's Founding Political Ideas?," *Independent Review* (Winter 2009): 447–54.
3. John Locke, "Second Treatise on Government," in Ernest Baker, ed., *Social Contract* (New York: Oxford University Press, 1962), ch. 6, sec. 66. This view of Locke has been questioned, and the author has given a detailed justification of his interpretation at Donald J. Devine, "John Locke: His Harmony between Liberty and Virtue," *Modern Age* (Summer 1978): 246–56. See also Sterling Power Lamprecht, *The Moral and Political Philosophy of John Locke* (New York: Russell & Russell, 1952; originally published 1914). Even critics have to make large concessions to alternative conclusions; see John Courtney Murray, *We Hold These Truths* (New York: Sheed and Ward, 1960), 313.
4. Locke, "Second Treatise on Government," ch. 2, sec. 6. See also Devine, *In Defense of the West*, 37–38.
5. Locke, "Second Treatise on Government," ch. 9, sec. 124–42.
6. F. A. Hayek, "Economic Policy and Rule of Law," *The Constitution of Liberty* (Chicago: University of Chicago Press, 1960), ch. 15.
7. Ibid.
8. Jeremy Bentham, *A Comment on the Commentaries and a Fragment on Government*, ed. J. H. Burns and H. L. A. Hart (London: The Athlone Press, 1977).
9. H. L. A. Hart, *The Concept of Law*, 2nd edition, ed. P. Bullock and J. Raz (Oxford: Clarendon Press, 1994, 1st ed. 1961), 116.
10. Ibid., 117.
11. Stanislav Dolgopolov, "Insider Trading," *The Concise Encyclopedia of Economics*, www.econlib.org/library/Enc/InsiderTrading.html.
12. Brody Mullins, Tom McGinty, and Jason Zweig, "Congress Staffers Gain from Trading in Stocks," *Wall Street Journal*, October 12, 2010, A1; Robert Pear, "Insider Trading Ban for Lawmakers Clears Congress," *New York Times*, March 22, 2012.
13. Alan Reynolds, "Martha's Mistrial," *Financial Post and FP Investing*, March 9, 2004, www.cato.org/research/articles/reynolds-040309.html; Paul Craig Roberts, "Punishing the Innocent, Excusing the Guilty," LewRockwell.com, www.lewrockwell.com/roberts/roberts58.html.
14. Holman W. Jenkins Jr., "The High Cost of Ignorant Stock Prices," *Wall Street Journal*, December 1, 2012, A15.
15. Reynolds, "Martha's Mistrial."
16. Sebastian Mallaby, "The Trouble with Torts," *Washington Post*, January 10, 2005, A17; and "Better Than Lawsuits," *Washington Post*, January 17, 2001, A17.

17. Towers, Perrin, Tillinghast, "U.S. Tort Costs and Cross-Border Prospects," Washington, DC, 2005 update,

18. Mallaby, "The Trouble with Torts."

19. Samuel R. Gross and Michael Shaffer, *Exonerations in the United States, 1989–2012*, National Registery of Exonerations (a joint project of Michigan Law and Northwestern Law), June 2012, www.law.umich.edu/special/exoneration/.

20. Ibid.

21. Carrie Johnson and Brooke Masters, "Fraud Cases Focus on Top Executives," *Washington Post*, January 19, 2005, A1.

22. Ibid.

23. Schulte, Roth & Zibel LLP, "Federal Judge Declares Unconstitutional Government's Practice of Pressuring Corporations," *Alert*, July 12, 2006, www.srz.com/Federal-Judge-Declares-Uncon-stitutional-Governments-Practice-of-Pressuring-Corporations-to-Cut-off-Employees-Legal-Fees-07-12-2006/.

24. "Mutual Displeasure," *Wall Street Journal*, January 17, 2005, A14.

25. Zachary A. Goldfarb, "The Madoff Files: A Chronicle of SEC Failure," *Washington Post*, September 3, 2009, A1.

26. "The SEC's Impeccable Timing," *Wall Street Journal*, April 20, 2010, A20.

27. Kara Scanall, Liz Rappaport, and Thomas Catan, "SEC Blasted on Goldman," *Wall Street Journal*, September 28, 2010, A1.

28. Johnson and Masters, "Fraud Cases Focus on Top Executives."

29. Jeff Coen, Rick Pearson, and David Kidwell, "Blagojevich Arrested: Fitzgerald Calls It a 'Political Corruption Crime Spree,'" *Chicago Tribune*, December 13, 2008, A1.

30. Victoria Toensing, "Fitzgerald Should Keep His Opinions to Himself," *Wall Street Journal*, December 15, 2008, A13.

31. Ibid.

32. Ibid.

33. Barbara F. Hollingsworth, "The Blago File," *Weekly Standard*, October 29, 2012, 32.

34. "Blagojevich 23, Fitzgerald 1," *Wall Street Journal*, August 19, 2010, A16.

35. Douglas Balkin and Steven Blanchero, "Blagojevich Convicted on Corruption Charges," *Wall Street Journal*, June 28, 2011, A3.

36. U.S. Attorney Fitzgerald Media Conference, C-Span, December 12, 2008.

37. Berman, *Law and Revolution*, 188.

38. Kevin Jon Heller, "Conspiracy," in E. Paul Finkelman, ed., *Encyclopedia of Civil Liberties* (New York: Taylor and Francis, 2006), 1:351–52. The Obama Justice Department did not bring suit under international war crimes doctrine for bin Laden's son-in-law because international law finds U.S. interpretation of conspiracy too vague: Steve Inskeep and Dina Temple-Raston, "Bin Laden's Son-in-Law to Appear in U.S. Court," *Morning Edition*, NPR, March 8, 2013.

39. Paul Craig Roberts and Lawrence M. Stratton, *The Tyranny of Good Intentions* (Rosedale, CA: Prima, 2000).

40. Gary Fields and John R. Emshwiller, "A Surge Blunder Earns Engineer a Criminal Record," *Wall Street Journal*, December 12, 2011, A1.

41. Gary Fields and John R. Emshwiller, "As U.S. Federal Criminal Laws Proliferate, More Are Ensnarled," *Wall Street Journal*, July 23, 2011, A1, A10.

42. Gary Fields and John R. Emshwiller, "Criminal Code Is Overgrown," *Wall Street Journal*, December 14, 2011, A8.

43. Spencer S. Hu, "Defendants Left Unaware of Flaws Found in Cases, *Washington Post*, April 17, 2012, A1.

44. Carl Bialik, "Matching Science of DNA with Art of Identification," *Wall Street Journal*, May 7, 2011, A2.

45. Brendan V. Sullivan Jr., "No Justice for 'Reckless' Prosecutors," *Wall Street Journal*, July 6, 2012, A15.

46. Harvey A. Silverglate, *Three Felonies a Day: How the Feds Target the Innocent* (New York: Encounter Books, 2009), esp. ch. 4. See also William J. Stuntz, *The Collapse of American Criminal Justice* (Cambridge, MA: Harvard University Press, 2011).

47. James Madison, Alexander Hamilton, and John Jay, *The Federalist Papers* (New York: New American Library, 1961), No. 62.

48. Hayek, *Constitution of Liberty*, 228–33, 244–49, chs. 17–24.

49. Berman, *Law and Revolution*, 292–94.

50. *The Collected Works of F. A. Hayek*, ed. W. W. Bartley III, vol. 1, *The Fatal Conceit* (Chicago: University of Chicago Press, 1988), 137.

51. Berman, *Law and Revolution*, 336–41.

52. Hayek, *Constitution of Liberty*, 61, 160, 163

53. Berman, *Law and Revolution*, 338, 538–58.

54. Schumpeter, *Capitalism, Socialism, and Democracy*, 139.

55. Marx and Engels, *Communist Manifesto*, 1.

56. Svetozar Pejovich, *Law, Informal Rules, and Economic Performance: The Case for Common Law* (Cheltenham: Edward Elgar Publishing, 2008), with contributions from Enrico Colombatto.

57. Fareed Zakaria, *The Future of Freedom* (New York: Norton, 2003), 34.

58. Pejovich, *Law, Informal Rules, and Economic Performance*, 43–44; and Berman, *Law and Revolution*, ch. 2.

59. Ljubomir Madzar, review of *Law, Informal Rules, and Economic Performance*, ms.

60. David Bruce, *Voltaire's "Candide": A Discussion Guide*, docs.google.com/viewer?a=v&q=cache:9JbYRWxVqIsJ:www.lulu.com/items/volume_65/2821000/2821281/10/print/2821281.pdf+&hl=en&gl=us&pid=bl&srcid=ADGEESgSQah6ni9FKrHdPdvX2c1_HU_9c-jT5F-wyn4s1x6MrKNV3SdSKAgsNtlvUBa9uCN2DWigR6wxLXp7eIw24xZPUs0m8GwucIJ-FyMFZ3pa-_tQ8wBGcQNBQqeA6RYafBr3UdL7wA&sig=AHIEtbSoNlFnX4kLT9vNTZi-nHqWEZJdFQ&pli=1, 2.

61. Marx and Engels, *Communist Manifesto*, 1.

62. The *Der Spiegel* series, authored by Mario Kaiser, Ansbert Kneip, and Alexander Smoltczyk and translated by Christopher Sultan and Damien McGuiness, can be found at www.spiegel.de/international/spiegel/0,1518,370072,00.html. See also John Stackhouse, "Where Religion Matters," *American Outlook* 5 (Fall 2002); Pippa Norris and Ronald Inglehart, *God, Guns, and Gays: Religion and Politics in the U.S. and Western Europe* (Boston: Harvard University Kennedy School of Government, 2004); Population Division of the Department of Economic and Social Affairs of the United Nations Secretariat, *World Population Prospects*, 2002 revision.

63. Rodney Stark, *One True God*, 66–78.

64. Norris and Inglehart, *God, Guns, and Gays*, 27.

65. Kaiser et al., "When the German Pope Returns Home, He'll Find an Un-Christian Land," 13; Shannon Smiley, "Sea of Youth Embrace New Pope," *Washington Post*, August 22, 2005, A10; and Craig Whitlock, "Pope Welcomed Home to Germany," *Washington Post*, August 19, 2005, A12.

66. Andrew Higgins, "In Europe God Is (Not) Dead," *Wall Street Journal*, July 14, 2007, A1.

67. Ibid., A8.

68. United Nations Office on Drugs and Crime, Centre for International Crime Prevention. "Total Crimes by Country," *The Eighth United Nations Survey on Crime Trends and the Operations of Criminal Justice Systems* (2002), www.nationmaster.com. Finland, Denmark, and the United Kingdom have higher per capita crime rates, primarily among immigrants.

69. Baro, "Rule of Law, Democracy and Economic Performance," 31–50.

70. Berman, *Law and Revolution*, 166–67.

71. Charles Van Doren, *History of Knowledge* (New York: Ballantine Books, 1991), 121–24; Christopher Dawson, *The Formation of Christianity* (San Francisco: Ignatius Press, 2008; originally published 1965), 253–55.

72. Acton, "The History of Freedom in Christianity," 42–49; Devine, "John Locke," 246–56; Eicholz, "Pufendorf, Grotius, and Locke."

73. See F. A. Hayek, "Kinds of Rationalism," in *Studies in Philosophy, Politics, and Economics* (Chicago: University of Chicago Press, 1967), 399–401.

74. Leo Strauss, *Natural Right and History* (Chicago: University of Chicago Press, 1953), 74.

75. Ibid., 8. In spite of these statements, it is interesting that a modern admirer attempts to identify Strauss with the concepts of tension and balance: Kenneth L. Deutsch, "Leo Strauss's Friendly Criticism of American Liberal Democracy," in Kenneth L. Deutsch and Ethan Fishman, *The Dilemmas of American Conservatism* (Lexington: University of Kentucky Press, 2010), esp. 57–59. Actually Strauss recognized the importance of the tension to the development of Western civilization but concluded it only "pretends to be a synthesis of both. But every one of us can and ought to be one or the other." Leo Strauss, *The Rebirth of Classical Political Rationalism*, ed. Thomas Pangle (Chicago: University of Chicago Press, 1989), 270.

76. John Courtney Murray, *The Problem of God* (New Haven: Yale University Press, 1964), 181–82.

77. Hayek, "Kinds of Rationalism," 401. See also Michael Polanyi, *Personal Knowledge* (Chicago: University of Chicago Press, 1958).

78. Hayek, "Kinds of Rationalism."

79. Frank Meyer, *In Defense of Freedom*, 80; regarding "tension," see 98.

80. This synthesis differs most from the Hegelian/Marxist one in that in the latter the two separate theses disappear into a new synthesis, whereas the Meyer/Medieval synthesis retains its constituent elements, with only God as the possible single higher ideal unifying them in another realm entirely. See John Courtney Murray, "The Medieval Synthesis," in *The Problem of God*, ch. 3; and Hayek, "Kinds of Rationalism."

81. Meyer, *In Defense of Freedom*, 85.

82. See also Devine, *The Political Culture of the United States*, ch. 1.

83. See E. J. Dionne Jr., *Why Americans Hate Politics* (New York: Simon & Schuster, 1991), 161.

84. Russell Kirk, "The Problem of Tradition," in *A Program for Conservatives* (Washington, DC: Regnery, 1954), 35–38. Meyer conceded that Kirk's defense of "natural liberty" was "excellent"; see Meyer, *In Defense of Freedom*, 125.

85. Meyer, *In Defense of Freedom*, 150.

Chapter 7: Moral Power and Creative Energy

1. C. J. Chivers, "Putin Calls for Steps to End Drop in Population," *New York Times*, May 10, 2006, A1; "Putin Population Plan," *Washington Times*, June 6, 2006, A1.

2. This and most of the following data are from *World Fertility Report 2003* (New York: United Nations, 2003).

3. *World Fertility Report 2008* (New York: United Nations, 2008).

4. Todd Johnson, "Christianity in Global Context: Trends and Statistics" (Pew Forum on Religion and Public Life, 2005), www.pewforum.org/uploadedfiles/Topics/Issues/Politics_and_Elections/051805-global-christianity.pdf.

5. Alan Carlson, "What Went Wrong: The Decline of the Natural Family," The Howard Center, October 19, 2010, www.profam.org/docs/acc/thc_acc_dectnf.htm; Phillip Longman, *The Empty Cradle* (New York: Basic Books, 2004), ch. 12.

6. *World Fertility Report 2008*.

7. United Nations press release, January 25, 2005, www.un.org/News/Press/docs/2005/pop917.doc.htm.

8. Population Profile of the United States, U.S. Census Bureau, www.census.gov/population/www/pop-profile/natproj.html.

9. Gretchen Livingston and D'Vera Cohn, *U.S. Birth Rate Falls to Record Low*, Pew Research Center, November 29, 2012.

10. Phillip Longman, "The Return of Patriarchy," *Foreign Policy,* March 1, 2006, www.newamerica. net/publications/articles/2006/the_return_of_patriarchy.

11. Longman, "The Return of Patriarchy"; Longman, *The Empty Cradle,* 20–21.

12. Richard Dawkins, *The Selfish Gene* (Oxford: Oxford University Press, 1989).

13. Channel 4 news release, "The Root of All Evil? Part 1; Richard Dawkins, "The Root of All Evil: The God Delusion," May 10, 2006, richarddawkins.net/videos/107-root-of-all-evil-part-1-the-god-delusion.

14. Dawkins, "The Root of All Evil?"

15. Channel 4 News release, "Root of All Evil?," May 19, 2006, richarddawkins.net/videos/107-root-of-all-evil-part-1-the-god-delusion.

16. Plato, *The Republic,* trans. Benjamin Jowett (New York; Scribner, 1871); Devine, *In Defense of the West,* 16–24.

17. James Davison Hunter, *The Death of Character* (New York: Basic Books, 2000), 60, 84, 164, 184, 205.

18. Richard Dawkins, "Banishing the Green-Eyed Monster: Is Sex Outside Marriage a Sin?," On Faith, WashingtonPost.com, newsweek.washingtonpost.com/onfaith/panelists/richard_dawkins /2007/11/banishing_the_greeneyed_monste.html.

19. David Maybury-Lewis, "Tribal Wisdom," *Millennium* (London: Biniman, 1992), 10.

20. Schumpeter, *Capitalism, Socialism, and Democracy,* 157.

21. Berman, *Law and Revolution,* 226–30.

22. Longman, *The Empty Cradle,* ch. 7. Charles Murray sums it up that the modern welfare state simply "drains too much of the life from life." See Murray, *In Our Hands* (Washington, DC: American Enterprise Institute, 2006), 120–24.

23. Lisa Sandberg and Teri Langford, "Texas Appeals Court Rules State Had No Right to Seize Kids," *Houston Chronicle,* May 22, 2008, A1; "Appeals Court Rules YFZ Ranch Raid Unwarranted," *Jasper Newsboy,* May 28, 2008, A1; William Murchison, "Did Texas Go Too Far?," *Dallas Morning News,* May 28, 2008.

24. "Polygamy's Practice Stirs Debate in Israel," *Salt Lake Tribune,* December 8, 2001, A1.

25. Christopher Dawson, *The Dividing of Christendom* (San Francisco: Ignatius Press, 2008, originally published 1965), 106; Martin Luther, *The Life of Luther Written by Himself,* trans. William Hazlitt (London: George Bell and Sons, 1904), 251.

26. Katha Pollitt, "Polymaritally Perverse," *The Nation,* October 4, 1999.

27. Lionel Tiger, "Civilization and the Texas Cult," *Wall Street Journal,* May 21, 2009, A15.

28. Hayek, *Constitution of Liberty,* 61.

29. Virginia Woolf, "Professions for Women," in *Death of the Moth and Other Essays* (New York: Harcourt, 1942), 507–9.

30. Donna St. George, "Despite 'Mommy Guilt,' Time with Kids Increasing," *Washington Post,* March 20, 2007, A1.

31. Suzanne M. Bianchi, John Robinson, and Melissa Milkie, *Changing Rhythms of American Family Life* (New York: Russell Sage Foundation, 2006), ch. 6.

32. Bianchi et al., *Changing Rhythms,* ch. 4.

33. St. George, "Despite 'Mommy Guilt.'"

34. Bianchi et al., *Changing Rhythms,* ch. 4.

35. "Married and Single Parents Spending More Time with Children, Study Finds," *New York Times,* October 16, 2006.

36. Steven E. Rhoads, *Taking Sex Differences Seriously* (San Francisco: Encounter, 2004), 134–58.

37. Longman, "The Return of Patriarchy."

38. Kaiser et al., "When the German Pope Returns Home, He'll Find an Un-Christian Land."

39. John D. Mueller, *Redeeming Economics: Rediscovering the Missing Element* (Wilmington, DE: ISI Books, 2010).

40. Patrick Fagan, "Why Religion Matters Even More: The Impact of Religious Practices on Social Stability" (Washington, DC: The Heritage Foundation, December 16, 2006); Patrick

Fagan, "95 Social Science Reasons for Religious Worship and Practice," *Mari Research*, October 16, 2012.

41. Hana Levi Julian, "Orthodox Judaism Growing Among American Jews," *Arutz Sheva*, May 9, 2006.

42. Stark, *One True God*, 1–2.

43. Bryan Appleyard, "The God Wars," *New Statesman*, February 28, 2012.

44. Robert Marquand, "China Opens Door to Christianity, of a Patriotic Kind," *Christian Science Monitor*, March 8, 2004.

45. Michael Slackman, "Bin Laden Says West Is Waging War Against Islam," *New York Times*, April 24, 2008, A1.

46. David G. Paschal, "Irregular Warfare," *USAWC Strategy Research Project* (Carlisle Barracks: U.S. Army War College, 2006).

47. Robert Nisbet, *History and the Idea of Progress* (New York: Basis Books, 1980), 150; Robert W. Merry, *Sands of Empire* (New York: Simon & Schuster, 2005), chs. 1–4.

48. Merry, *Sands of Empire*, 53–56; Dinesh D'Souza, *The Enemy at Home: The Cultural Left and Its Responsibility for 9/11* (New York: Doubleday, 2006).

49. U.S. Bureau of the Census, *Historical Statistics of the United States: Colonial Times to 1970* (Washington, DC: U.S. Government Printing Office, 1975), 1–43; *Statistical Abstract of the U.S.* (Washington, DC: U.S. Government Printing Office, 2010), Tables 128–29.

50. *World Fertility Report 2008*.

51. Johnson, "Christianity in Global Context."

52. Hunter, *The Death of Character*, 60. See also Stark, *One True God*, 78–85.

53. Appleyard, "The God Wars."

54. Schumpeter, *Capitalism, Socialism, and Democracy*, 134–39.

55. Kaiser et al., "When the German Pope Returns Home, He Will Find an Un-Christian Land."

56. Michelle Boorstein, "15 Percent of Americans Have No Religion," *Washington Post*, March 9, 2009, A1; American Religious Identification Survey, *Christianity and Religion Decline in U.S.* (Hartford, CT: Trinity College, 2009), www.americanreligioussurvey-aris.org/reports/ARIS_REPORT_2008.

57. Pew Forum on Religion and Public Life, *Religion in America Report*, May–August 2007, religions.pewforum.org/reports, where the religiously "unaffiliated" are divided among the existing religious affiliations.

58. Robert D. Putnam and David E. Campbell, *American Grace: How Religion Divides and Unites Us* (New York: Simon & Schuster, 2010), 122–48.

59. "Among Wealthy Nations, U.S. Stands Alone," Pew Research Center, December 19, 2002, people-press.org/report/167/among-wealthy-nations-%E2%80%A6; Putnam and Campbell, *American Grace*, 7–10.

60. Pew Research Center, "'Nones' on the Rise," Pew Forum on Religion and Social Life, October 9, 2012, public executive summary, www.pewforum.org/unaffiliated/nones-on-the-rise.aspx.

61. Putnam and Campbell, *American Grace*, chs. 11–15.

62. Pew Research Center, "'Nones' on the Rise," full report, 78.

63. Cathy Lynn Grossman, "83 Percent Say God Answers Prayers," *USA Today*, May 4, 2010; "How Important Is Religion?" Gallup 2009, www.gallup.com/poll/1690/religion.aspx#1; and Devine, *The Political Culture of the United States*, 221–28. There seems a slight tendency over time for church attendance to decline, perhaps one week less per decade, but that is somewhat offset by an increase in church attendance as a person ages.

64. "Christmas Strongly Religious," Gallup, December 24, 2010, www.gallup.com/poll/145367/christmas-strongly-religious-half-celebrate.aspx; "110 Million Eyes Glued to Tube to Watch Super Bowl," *Mill Blog*, February 6, 2012, www.themill.com/blog/2012/february/6/110-million-eyes-glued-to-tube-watching-super-bowl-xlvi-.aspx.

65. Putnam and Campbell, *American Grace*, 19, 463–79.

66. Higgins, "In Europe God Is (Not) Dead," A8.

67. Stark, *For the Glory of God*, 374–75.
68. Ibid., 372–74.
69. Rodney Stark, *The Victory of Reason* (New York: Random House, 2005), 29.
70. Stark, *For the Glory of God*, 328–29.
71. Tocqueville, "Present and Future Conditions of the Negro," xvii.
72. Stark, *For the Glory of God*, 375.
73. Putnam and Campbell, *American Grace*, ch. 13.
74. Charles Murray, *Coming Apart* (New York: Crown Forum, 2012), parts 1 and 2, esp. 87.
75. Appleyard, "The God Wars."
76. Kaiser et al., "When the German Pope Returns Home, He'll Find an Un-Christian Land."
77. Stark, *For the Glory of God*.
78. Brian Murray, "Miami Vise," *Weekly Standard*, December 3, 2012, www.weeklystandard.com/articles/miami-vise_663822.html.
79. Joseph Ratzinger, *Truth and Tolerance* (San Francisco: Ignatius Press, 1994), ch. 1.
80. There is also the perplexing fact that the greatest period of witchcraft persecution was during the Enlightenment. See Stark, *For the Glory of God*, 221. On the other hand, major segments of Christianity consider the Enlightenment to have had positive attributes. Orthodox Patriarch Bartholomew specifically raised the near equivalence between reason and revelation in Catholicism as an obstacle to unification. See rumkatkilise.org/dialogue_in_action.htm.
81. Nietzsche, *The Anti-Christ*, 6–18.
82. Weber, *The Theory of Social and Economic Organization*, 320–39.
83. Rahe, *Montesquieu and the Love of Liberty*, 224–41.
84. Putnam and Campbell, *American Grace*, 12.
85. Stark, *One True God*, 98–104.
86. Ibid., 105.
87. Andrew G. Biggs and Jason Richwine, "The Underworked Public Employee," *Wall Street Journal*, December 5, 2012, A17.
88. Rodney Stark, *Discovering God* (New York: HarperCollins, 2007), 188–202. Even Zoroaster's influence may be seen as continuing through its influence on Judaism and Christianity.
89. Novak, *The Fire of Invention*, 21–44.
90. The Crusades, of course, were not initiated until after Islam had conquered Jerusalem and not until the whole Christian Eastern Byzantine Roman Empire was tottering and its Holy Land religious sites were desecrated (see Malcolm Billings, *The Crusades* [New York: Sterling, 1996], ch. 1). Muslim tolerance is often contrasted with Christian prejudice (see, e.g., Maria Rosa Menolal, *The Ornament of the World* [Boston: Little Brown, 2002], esp. 72–73). But severe restrictions were imposed on Christians, including regulations against new churches or wearing distinctive dress or identifications, higher taxation, and the inability to participate in political life (see Devine, *In Defense of the West*, 157). By actual count both Islam and Christianity had minimal conflict with Jews, as Jews were often restricted to segregated communities, until the two went into combat with each other over control of Europe and Jews had to choose sides, when both Islam and Christianity turned against them. Persecution from both then continued as long as the outcome was in doubt (see Stark, *One True God*, 129–33, 169–70). When the Christians won in Spain, they did expel the Jews, but this merely mirrored the Muslim expulsion of the Jews in 1148. Maimonides, often cited for his anti-Semitism charges against Christians and support for Muslims, actually escaped Spain from Moorish rather than Christian persecution and was forced to hide his Judaism in Arabia to protect himself, and his family only pretended to convert to Islam to escape expulsion or possible death (see Stark, *One True God*, 169–71). As is well documented, anti-Semitic assaults in Europe were popular uprisings and were usually opposed by elitist popes and bishops alike, the latter often providing refuge at some cost to their own safety (see Stark, *One True God*, 153–56; Billings, *The Crusades*, 15–16).
91. Stark, *For the Glory of God*, 257.

92. R. J. Rummel, *Death by Government* (New Brunswick, NJ: Transaction, 1994), 4, 70ff. See also Matthew White, Selected Death Tolls, necrometrics.com/pre1700a.htm.

93. Dawson, *The Dividing of Christendom*, 142, 171.

94. Stark, *For the Glory of God*, 83–90; Rodney Stark, *The Victory of Reason* (New York: Random House, 2005), 202.

95. Dawson, *The Formation of Christendom*, 233.

96. John A. Crow, *Spain: The Root and the Flower* (Berkeley: University of California Press, 1963), 145, 170, 153.

97. Acton, "The History of Christianity," 29–53.

98. Rodney Stark, *The Triumph of Christianity* (New York: HarperCollins, 2011), ch. 22.

99. Whitehead, *Science and the Modern World*, 12–13. See also Stark, *Discovering God*, 396–99, and *For the Glory of God*, 154–58. Islam's claim to scientific expertise is almost all second-hand from Europe, as Islam used captured or paid Europeans and their writings.

100. Rodney Stark, *The Rise of Christianity* (Princeton: Princeton University Press, 1996), 82–88.

101. Robert B. Reich, *Tales of a New America* (New York: Times Books, 1987), 588–91.

102. Andrew Flew and Garry Habermas, "My Pilgrimage from Atheism to Theism: An Interview with Andrew Flew," December 4, 2004, www.biola.edu/antonyflew/flew-interview.pdf.

103. Plantinga, *Where the Conflict Really Lies*, esp. ch. 9.

104. Blaise Pascal, *Pascal's Pensées* (New York: Dutton, 1858), 3:227–41. See also Paul Saka, "Pascal's Wager about God," *Internet Encyclopedia of Philosophy: A Peer-Reviewed Academic Resource*, www.iep.utm.edu/pasc-wag. Some observers object that logic cannot or should not force belief, that the possibility of multiple gods undermines the argument, and that decision-logic itself may be faulty. But why should logic not force the more logical conclusion? Why does not infinity on the side of God regardless of the number of gods still not determine the matter? Why are limits to the decision-making model any different from differences in thinking generally? The argument is probabilistic, after all. See also Rahe, *Montesquieu and the Love of Liberty*, 104–13.

105. Christianity was the predominant belief among Locke and the Founders but not necessarily unanimously or with a single orthodoxy. See Devine, "John Locke," 248–50; Jeremy Waldron, *God, Locke, and Equality* (Cambridge: Cambridge University Press, 2002); and even Steven Waldman, *Founding Faith* (New York: Random House, 2008), 26, 43–44.

106. Meyer, *In Defense of Freedom*, 217.

107. Frank S. Meyer, "Champion of Freedom," *National Review*, May 7, 1960, 304–5.

108. Hayek, "The Political Order of a Free People," 3:176.

109. Hayek, *The Fatal Conceit*, 137.

110. Meyer, *In Defense of Freedom*, 219–20.

Chapter 8: The Constitutional Miracle

1. *Federalist* No. 10.

2. 1 Samuel 8:3.

3. *Federalist* No. 10.

4. *Federalist* No. 51.

5. Samuel P. Huntington, *Political Order in Changing Societies* (New Haven: Yale University Press, 1968), 96–97.

6. *Federalist* No. 10.

7. Michael Barone, "Obama Thuggery Is Useless in Fighting Spill," *Washington Examiner*, June 20, 2010.

8. Ashby Jones, "The Government Wants BP to Put Up $20 Billion, but Can It Order It?" Law Blog: *WSJ* Blogs, June 15, 2010.

9. David A. Broder, "A GOP Gift in the Gulf," *Washington Post*, June 20, 2010, A19.

10. Jess Bravin, "Court Backs Shilling Appeal: Justices Narrow Fraud Statutes Used in Several High-Profile Convictions," *Wall Street Journal*, June 25, 2010, A1; and "Conrad Black's Revenge," June 25, 2010, A12.

11. Bloomberg News, "Tax Court Rules for Deceased Enron Chief," *Washington Post*, August 30, 2011, A11; "Spitzer's Latest Loss," *Wall Street Journal*, August 2, 2011, A12; Brent Kendall, "Probe Finds Misconduct in Case against Senator," *Wall Street Journal*, November 22, 2011.

12. Bravin, "Court Backs Shilling Appeal," A6.

13. Katrina Vanden Heuvel, "A Free Pass for the Corrupt," *Washington Post*, June 26, 2010, A15.

14. Bravin, "Court Backs Shilling Appeal," A5.

15. "Constitutional Power Hour," *Wall Street Journal*, January 6, 2011, A16.

16. *Federalist* No. 78.

17. Robert Bork, "Individual Liberty and the Constitution," *American Spectator*, June 2008, 30.

18. Woodrow Wilson, *Constitutional Government in the United States* (New York: Columbia University Press, 1908), 167–68, 193.

19. C-Span, June 25, 2008.

20. Bork, "Individual Liberty and the Constitution," 28–35.

21. Ibid., 29.

22. Although the quotation is sometimes disputed, it is close enough to the preferred alternative: "The decision of the Supreme Court has fell still born and they find they cannot coerce Georgia to yield to its mandate." Paul F. Boller and John H. George, *They Never Said It* (New York: Oxford University Press, 1989), 53.

23. *Worcester*, 31 US, 6 Pet., 515 (1832). On the property claim, see *Johnson v. M'Intosh*, 21US, 8 Wheat, 543 (1888).

24. Robert A. Dahl, "Decision-Making in a Democracy," *Journal of Public Law*, Fall 1957, 279–93.

25. Leon Friedman, "Overruling the Court," *American Prospect*, December 19, 2001, prospect.org/article/overruling-court. The first case was *Grove City College v. Bell*.

26. Dana Milbank, "If at First You Don't Secede, Try, Try Again," *Washington Post*, August 8, 2010.

27. Alec MacGillis, "Health Law Opponents Point to Missouri Vote," *Washington Post*, August 6, 2010, A6.

28. *Federalist* No. 51.

29. James Madison had anticipated the idea of interposition even before the Constitution was adopted. See *Federalist* No. 46. See also James Jackson Kilpatrick, *The Sovereign States* (Chicago: Regnery, 1957).

30. "Weyden Defects on ObamaCare," *Wall Street Journal*, September 3, 2010, A16; Grace-Marie Turner, Alex Cortes, and Heather R. Higgins, "ObamaCare's March Madness," *Wall Street Journal*, March 7, 2011, A13.

31. Marci Hamilton, "Are Federalism and the States Really Anti–Civil Rights?" *FindLaw's Writ*, January 2, 2003, writ.news.findlaw.com/hamilton/20030102.html.

32. "The Supreme Court's Obamacare Decision: Full Text" *The Atlantic*, July 26, 2012.

33. Mark Tapscott, "Conservative State Attorneys General Are Shocking the 10th Amendment Back to Life," *Washington Examiner*, July 29, 2010; Jeff Taylor "States Fights," *American Conservative*, July 2010, 32–35; Tony Blankley, "Repeal the 17th Amendment," *Huffington Post*, January 27, 2010.

34. William Howard Taft, "Recent Criticism of the Federal Judiciary," *American Bar Association Journal*, 1895.

35. Amy Goldstein and Dan Egger, "Senators Deride Justice Reassignments" *Washington Post*, June 22, 2007, A3; Carol Leonnig, "Political Hiring in Justice Division Probed," *Washington Post*, June 21, 2007; Dan Egger and Amy Goldstein, "Broader Privileges Claimed in Firings," *Washington Post*, July 7, 2007, A1.

36. Leonnig, "Political Hiring."

37. In particular, Rousseau's arguments against separation of powers inspired his disciples from the period of the French Revolution until today.

38. Frank Williams, "Abraham Lincoln and Civil Liberties in Wartime," Lecture # 834, The Heritage Foundation, 2004.
39. James Burnham, "The Paradox of Sovereignty," in *Congress and the American Tradition* (Chicago: Regnery, 1959), 34–44. See also Frank S. Meyer, "Lincoln Again," in *The Conservative Mainstream* (New Rochelle: Arlington House, 1969), 474.
40. President Andrew Jackson, Bank Veto Message, Miller Center of Public Affairs, University of Virginia, July 10, 1832, millercenter.org/scripps/archive/speeches/detail/3636.
41. W. James Antle III, "McCain-Feingold and the Duty to Uphold the Constitution," *American Spectator*, March 7, 2011, spectator.org/blog/2011/03/07/mccain-feingold-and-the-duty-t.
42. James Madison, "Notes of the Constitutional Convention, July 17, 1787," in Max Ferrand, *The Records of the Federal Convention 2* (Washington, DC, 1911), 25–96.
43. "If we judge events by their consequences, the great world revolutionary was Wilson rather than Lenin." Lukacs, *The Passing of the Modern Age*, 22. This statement seemed over-the-top when read in 1970 but appears obvious in the early twenty-first century.
44. Wilson, *Congressional Government*, 187. See also Wilson, *Constitutional Government in the United States*, 54.
45. Wilson, *Congressional Government*, 206–7, 91, 97–8, 187, 22–23.
46. Stark, *Discovering God*, 178–86, 233, 366–67.
47. Stark, *One True God*, 228–30.
48. Gabriel, *The Course of American Democratic Thought*, 32–43.
49. *In Defense of Freedom*, 156.
50. Ibid., 5.
51. Devine, *Does Freedom Work?*, 22.
52. Clinton Rossiter, *Conservatism in America* (New York: Knopf, 1955), 258.
53. Hayek, "The Political Order of a Free Society," 3:130–31.
54. See Hunter, *To Change the World*, 111–31.
55. Ibid., 280–82.
56. Stark, *One True God*, 226–40. Pope Pius XII taught tolerance as the authoritative policy for the largest denomination in the encyclical "On the Mystical Body of Christ," June 29, 1943, www.papalencyclicals.net/Pius12/P12MYSTI.HTM. Most Protestants in the U.S. promoted tolerance for other Protestants even earlier and extended it to Catholics and Jews too at least by the presidency of John Kennedy. See Putnam and Campbell, *American Grace*, ch. 15.
57. Meyer, *In Defense of Freedom*, 157–58. It is not so much that freedom is required for virtuous behavior, which can take place even under repression, as that allowing a coercive power like the state to define virtue is deferring the very defining of virtue to an entity of power that has shown no proclivity to be able to do so.
58. Ibid., 158.
59. Brink Lindsey, "Libertarians and Conservatives: Can This Marriage Be Saved? Fusionism Debate," America's Future Foundation, January 25, 2005; Tim Cavanaugh "Divorce Papers," *Reason*, March 29, 2005; and Daniel McCarthy, "Low Tax Liberalism Redux," LewRockwell. com, March 12, 2005. All of the quotations and discussion are based on notes made by the author at the time.
60. Hayek, *The Fatal Conceit*, 136–37.
61. John Dewey, *Democracy and Education* (New York: Macmillan, 1916), esp. ch. 7.
62. Derek Bok, "Democracy in the 21st Century: Easing Political Cynicism with Civic Involvement," in his *The Trouble with Government* (Cambridge, MA: Harvard University Press, 2001), 10–14, 398–402.
63. Myrdal, *Beyond the Welfare State*, 464–65.
64. Tocqueville, "Townships and Municipal Bodies."
65. John J. Chiodo and Lisa A. Martin, "What Do Students Have to Say about Citizenship?," *Journal of Social Studies Research* 1 (2005): 23–32.

66. "Mission Statement of the John Dewey Project on Progressive Education," University of Vermont, www.uvm.edu/~dewey/mission/mission.html.
67. E. J. Dionne Jr., "Tests for an Unbending Pope," *Washington Post*, April 20, 2005, A25.
68. Joseph Ratzinger, "For Electing the Supreme Pontiff," April 18, 2006, www.ewtn.com/pope/words/conclave_homily.
69. This is preceded by an even more explicit statement: "Do you think I came to bring peace on earth? No, I tell you, but division." It is followed by: "They will be divided, father against son and son against father, mother against daughter and daughter against mother, mother-in-law against daughter-in-law and daughter-in-law against mother-in-law" (Luke 12:49–53).
70. Benedict XVI, "Faith, Reason and the University," Regensburg, Germany, September 12, 2006, www.guardian.co.uk/world/2006/sep/15/religion.uk.
71. Ratzinger, *Truth and Tolerance*, 238.
72. See, e.g., Kristine M. Bober and Colleen I. Murray, "A Postmodern Feminist Approach," *Family Relations*, January 2001, 81–86.

Chapter 9: A Constitutional Way Forward

1. Catherine Rampel, "Recession Officially Over," *New York Times*, September 20, 2010, B1.
2. Brad Schiller, "Doing the Math on a Jobless Recovery," *Wall Street Journal*, February 9, 2011, A15; "Jobs and Wages," *Wall Street Journal*, April 2, 2011, A14.
3. Matt Phillips and Justin Lahart, "This Time, Maybe the U.S. Is Japan," *Wall Street Journal*, January 13, 2011.
4. "The New Abnormal," *Wall Street Journal*, October 30, 2010, A16.
5. "As Contractions Go," *Wall Street Journal*, January 31, 2–13, A14; Nelson D. Schwartz, "U.S. Growth Revised Up, but Year-End Slowdown Is Feared," *New York Times*, November 29, 2012; Catherine Rampell, "Growth Accelerates, but U.S. Has Lots of Ground to Make Up," *New York Times*, January 28, 2012, A1; "The Obama Recovery," *Wall Street Journal*, July 30, 2011, A12.
6. Robert J. Samuelson, "Japan's Lost Decades—and Possibly Ours," *Washington Post*, March 12, 2012, A17.
7. The National Bureau of Economic Research, "U.S. Business Cycle Expansions and Contractions," www.nber.org/cycles/cyclesmain.html.
8. John F. Cogan and John B. Taylor, "Stimulus Has Been a Washington Job Killer," *Wall Street Journal*, October 4, 2011, A21.
9. Benn Steil, "Why We Can't Believe the Fed," *Wall Street Journal*, February 22, 2012, A13.
10. Robert J. Samuelson, "America Hunkers Down," *Washington Post*, June 13, 2011, A17.
11. "Modest Growth Pick-Up in 2013 Projects IMF," *IMF Survey Magazine*, January 23, 2013, www.imf.org/external/pubs/ft/survey/so/2013/NEW012313A.htm.
12. George H. Nash, *The Conservative Intellectual Movement in America Since 1945* (New York: Basic Books, 1976), 178; Lee Edwards, *William F. Buckley Jr.: The Maker of a Movement* (Wilmington, DE: ISI Books, 2010); Kevin J. Smant, *Principles and Heresies: Frank S. Meyer and the Shaping of the American Conservative Movement* (Wilmington, DE: ISI Books, 2002), ch. 3.
13. Meyer, *In Defense of Freedom*, 14–15.
14. William F. Buckley Jr., *Up from Liberalism* (New York: McDowell, Obolenski, 1959), 202–3, 197, 123–24, 189.
15. William F. Buckley Jr., *Did You Ever See a Dream Walking?: American Conservative Thought in the Twentieth Century* (Indianapolis: Bobbs-Merrill Books, 1970), xxxiii.
16. Ronald Reagan, "Address to the Conservative Political Action Conference," March 20, 1981, www.conservative.org/acuf/our-philosophy/.
17. Ibid.
18. Veronique de Rugy, "President Reagan, Champion Budget-Cutter," AEI.org, June 9, 2004, www.aei.org/papers/economics/fiscal-policy/president-reagan-champion-budget-cutter.

19. Hahm Sung Deuk, Mark S. Kamlet, David C. Mower, and Tsai-tsu Suy, "The Influence of the Gramm-Rudman-Hollings Act on Federal Budgetary Outcomes, 1986–1989," *Journal of Policy Analysis and Management* 11, no. 2 (1992): 207–34.

20. Office of Management and Budget, "Composition of Outlays 1940–2015," *Budget of the United States Government, Fiscal Year 2011*, Historical Table 16.1, www.whitehouse.gov/sites/default/files/omb/budget/fy2011/assets/hist06z1.xls.

21. "Reaganomics at 25," *Wall Street Journal*, August 12, 2006, A8.

22. George F. Will, "Beyond Reagan: How Optimism Brings Big Government," *New York Post*, February 11, 2007, A27.

23. Aristotle, *Politics*, trans. Benjamin Jewitt (London: Oxford University Press, 1885), bk. 4, p. 4.

24. John Patrick Diggins, *Ronald Reagan: Fate, Freedom, and the Making of History* (New York: W. W. Norton, 2007), xvii, 25–26.

25. Ibid., 27, 37, 47, 183; Will, "Beyond Reagan."

26. William Grimes, "John P. Diggins, 73, Historian, Dies," *New York Times*, January 29, 2009, B9.

27. See also C. B. Macpherson, *The Political Theory of Possessive Individualism* (London: Oxford University Press, 1962). Diggins mentioned that Reagan was very influenced by the free-market economist Frédéric Bastiat, but he just could not help adding that Marx called Bastiat the "modern bagman of free trade," as if it is obvious that a rationalist bon mot is enough to dismiss a thinker. See Diggins, *Ronald Reagan*, 15.

28. Diggins, *Ronald Reagan*, 33–34.

29. See James Ceaser, "Creed versus Culture," Lectures on Political Thought, The Heritage Foundation, March 10, 2006, www.heritage.org/research/lecture/creed-versus-culture-alternative-foundations-of-american-conservatism.

30. Ronald Reagan, "Remarks at the Dedication of the James Madison Memorial Building of the Library of Congress," *The Public Papers of Ronald Reagan*, Reagan Presidential Library, November 20, 1981.

31. Rothbard, "Frank S. Meyer: The Fusionist as Libertarian Manqué."

32. Joseph Baldacchino, "Freedom Requires Restraint," *Epistulae*, National Humanities Institute, December 2, 2010, 5.

33. Meyer, *In Defense of Freedom*, 84.

34. Ibid., 85.

35. Michael J. Gerson, "Open-Arms Conservatism," *Washington Post*, October 31, 2007. See also his *Heroic Conservatism* (New York: HarperOne, 2007), 161–63.

36. Hunter, *To Change the World*, 274, 279, 282, although he uses the term *power* to cover many actions Meyer would consider not coercion but acceptable social pressure (see page 191).

37. Gerson, *Heroic Conservatism*, 8–9.

38. Pope Pius XI, *Quadragessimo Anno*, Paulist Press trans. (New York: Paulist Press, 1939), sec. 79.

39. John Paul II, "State and Culture," *Centesimus Annus*, Rome, 1991, vol. 5, sec 48, www.vatican.va/holy_father/john_paul_ii/encyclicals/documents/hf_jp-ii_enc_01051991_centesimus-annus_en.html.

40. Gerson, *Heroic Conservatism*, 162, claims that a centralizing principle of "solidarity" trumps subsidiarity. For a critique of this position, see Devine, *Does Freedom Work?*, 151–55, and "Social Doctrine in the National Catechetical Directory," *Homiletic and Pastoral Review* (August–September 1977).

41. Wilson, "The Science of Administration," 10.

42. Herbert Croly, *Progressive Democracy* (New York: Macmillan, 1914), 241–44, 399–405.

43. Peter F. Drucker, "The Effective Decision," *Harvard Business Review*, 1967; and Rick Wartzman, "Toyota's Management Challenge," BusinessWeek.com, March 5, 2010.

44. James R. Haggerty, Gina Chon, and Anupreeta Das, "ITT to Break Up as Bigness Loses Favor," *Wall Street Journal*, January 13, 2011, B1.

45. Small Business Administration, web.sba.gov/faqs/faqindex.cfm?areaID=24.

46. Mises had explained why long before, in his book *Bureaucracy.*
47. Perry Bacon Jr., "Obama Becomes a Cheerleader for U.S. Business," *Washington Post*, February 1, 2011, A3.
48. Robert Samuelson, "Schumpeter: The Prophet," *Newsweek*, November 9, 1992.
49. Hayek, "The Uses of Knowledge in Society."
50. Thomas L. Friedman, *The Lexus and the Olive Tree: Understanding Globalization* (New York: Random House, 1999), 11, 435, 373, 236–37, 362–63.
51. Ibid., 372.
52. Ibid., 337.
53. Robert M. Solow, "The Serfdom Scare," *The New Republic*, December 6, 2012.
54. E. J. Dionne Jr., "Some Aid for the Saints," *Washington Post*, January 31, 2001, A17.
55. Edward Feser, "What Libertarianism Isn't," LewRockwell.com, December 22, 2001, www.lewrockwell.com/orig/feser2.html.
56. Ibid., 2–3, 9. See also Linda Raeder, "The Liberalism/Conservatism of Edmund Burke and F. A. Hayek," *Humanitas* 10, no. 1 (1997).
57. Meyer, *In Defense of Freedom*, 129.
58. Donald Devine, "Wildavsky's Typology and Beyond," in Fred Smith and Alex Castellanos, eds., *Field Guide for Effective Communication* (Washington, DC: Competitive Enterprise Institute, 2004), 40–46.
59. Alexis de Tocqueville, *Democracy in America* (New Rochelle, NY: Arlington House, Heirloom Edition, n.d.), 2:2, 5:114.
60. Robert Putnam, *Bowling Alone: The Collapse and Revival of American Community* (New York: Simon & Schuster, 2000), 30–33, 45–55, 66–80, 94–98, 200–246.
61. Ibid., 386–87.
62. See also Charles Murray, *In Pursuit of Happiness* (New York: Simon & Schuster, 1988), 274–79. Displacement does not have to be total for it to have negative effects; see Arthur C. Brooks, "Can Governments Kill Nonprofits with Kindness?" *Fraser Forum*, December 2004/January 2005, 5–6.
63. "Father Flanagan H.S. to Close," *Washington Post*, March 21, 1997.
64. Charles Murray, *In Our Hands* (Washington, DC: American Enterprise Institute, 2006).
65. Devine, *Does Freedom Work?*, 112.
66. The Pew Partnership for Civic Change, survey conducted October 25 through November 18, 2001.
67. Richard C. Cornuelle, *Reclaiming the American Dream* (New York: Random House, 1965); Hayek, "The Political Order of a Free Society," 50–55.
68. Everett Carll Ladd, *The Ladd Report on Civic America* (New York: Free Press, 1999).
69. World Values Study, "Members of Voluntary Associations," NationMaster.com, www.nationmaster.com/graph/lif_mem_of_vol_org_cha-lifestyle-members-voluntary-organisations-charity.
70. Giving USA Foundation and the Center on Philanthropy, *Giving USA 2010* (Glenview, IL: Giving USA Foundation, 2010).
71. Charities Aid Foundation, *International Comparison of Charitable Giving, 2006* (Kent, UK: CAF, 2006), 6.
72. Patrick F. Fagan, "The Family GDP: How Marriage and Fertility Drive the Economy," *The Family in America: A Journal of Public Policy* 24, no. 2 (2010): 135–49; Everett Carll Ladd, "This Century Has Seen Extraordinary Change—Most of It Outside of Politics," *The Public Perspective*, February/March, 1999, 1–2; "Religious Beliefs Underpin Opposition to Homosexuality," The Pew Forum on Religion and Public Life, November 18, 2003, pewforum.org/Gay-Marriage-and-Homosexuality/Religious-Beliefs-Underpin-Opposition-to-Homosexuality.aspx; Michelle Boorstein, "God in Government: Poll: Support Strong for Gay Rights, Not Marriage," *Washington Post*, May 27, 2009.
73. O'Toole, *The Best-Laid Plans*, part three.

74. Adam Smith, *The Wealth of Nations*, 5:1, 3, 1, 689; Hayek, *Constitution of Liberty*, 341; Hayek, "The Political Order of a Free People," 43–46; and Milton Friedman with Rose D. Friedman, *Capitalism and Freedom* (Chicago: University of Chicago Press, 1962), 30ff.

75. Garrett Hardin, "The Tragedy of the Commons," *Science* 162 (1968): 1243–48.

76. Hayek, "The Political Order of a Free Society," 3:146–47.

77. Charles M. Tiebout, "A Pure Theory of Local Expenditures," *Journal of Political Economy*, October 1956, 416–424. See also James M. Buchanan and Gordon Tullock, *The Calculus of Consent* (Ann Arbor: University of Michigan Press, 1965), 113–14; and cf. U.S. Advisory Commission on Intergovernmental Relations, *The Organization of Local Public Economies* (Washington, DC: GPO, 1987), 38–39.

78. Hayek, "The Political Order of a Free Society," 43–46.

79. James M. Buchanan, "Federalism and Individual Sovereignty," *Cato Journal* 15, nos. 2–3.

80. Devine, *Does Freedom Work?*, 56–59.

81. Hayek, *The Fatal Conceit*, 33.

82. Wilson, *The Study of Administration*, 18.

83. John C. Bollens and Henry J. Schmandt, *The Metropolis* (New York: Harper & Row, 1965), 154–82.

84. Donald Devine, *Restoring the Tenth Amendment* (Fort Lauderdale, FL: Vytis, 1996), ch. 8.

85. U.S. Census Bureau, *Historical Statistics of the United States* (Washington, DC, 1975), 1086.

86. Ibid., and U.S. Census Bureau, *Statistical Abstract of the United States* (Washington, DC, 1999), 309; U.S. Department of Education, *Digest of Educational Statistics*, 1927.

87. Donald Devine, "A Free Market in Government," *National Review*, October 27, 1989, 40–41.

88. Jane Jacobs, *The Death and Life of Great American Cities* (New York: Vintage, 1961), ch. 21, 13.

89. O'Toole, *The Best-Laid Plans*, esp. ch. 9.

90. Contrary to the financial crisis inquiry report, see "Culprits from Beltway Casting," *Wall Street Journal*, January 28, 2011, A18.

91. U.S. Advisory Commission on Intergovernmental Relations, *The Organization of Local Public Economies* (Washington, DC: Government Printing Office, 1988), 18–20, 32–33, 55.

92. Vincent Ostrom, *The Intellectual Crisis in American Public Administration*, 3rd ed. (Tuscaloosa: University of Alabama Press, 2008), 160–63.

93. Bollens and Schmandt, *The Metropolis*.

94. Rousseau, *The Social Contract*, vol. 3, bk. 1, p. 223.

95. Schumpeter, *Capitalism, Socialism, and Democracy*, 138.

96. See William D. Eggers, "City Lights: America's Boldest Mayors," *Policy Review*, Summer 1993; William D. Eggers and John O'Leary, *Revolution at the Roots* (New York: Free Press, 1995), esp. 81–82; and George W. Liebmann, "A Contrast to Regionalism: Reversing Baltimore's Decline through Neighborhood Enterprise and Municipal Discipline," *Calvert Issue Brief*, May 2000.

97. Robert A. Nisbet, *The Quest for Community* (New York: Oxford University Press, 1953, revised 1970), ch. 11.

98. Hayek, "The Political Order of a Free Society," 146.

99. Joel Garreau, *Edge Cities* (New York: Doubleday, 1991), 5.

100. George W. Liebmann, *Neighborhood Futures* (New Brunswick: Transaction Publishers, 2004).

101. Ostrom, *The Intellectual Crisis in American Public Administration*, 154–58.

102. Ronald Reagan, "Remarks at the Annual Legislative Conference of the National Association of Counties," *The Public Papers of Ronald Reagan*, Reagan Presidential Library, March 4, 1985; and Buchanan, "Federalism and Individual Sovereignty."

103. Approximately 60 million Americans live in 315,000 RCAs and 22 million live in the 24 central cities with more than 200,000 population: "National Survey Affirms HOA Success," Communities Associations Institute, April 30, 2012, www.caionline.org/about/press/Pages/NewNationalSurveyAffirmsHOASuccess.aspx. See also U.S. Advisory Commission on Intergovernmental Relations, *Residential Community Associations, Private Governments in the*

Intergovernmental System (Washington, DC: Government Printing Office, 1989), 1; *Statistical Abstract of the United States*, 46; and Liebmann, *Neighborhood Futures*, 39

104. Devine, *The Political Culture of the United States*, 167–72; "Americans Trust Local Government," Gallup, September 18 2008, www.gallup.com/video/110461/Americans-Trust-Local-Govt-Much-More-Than-National.aspx; "Poll Finds Trust of Federal Government Low," CNN/Opinion Research Corporation, February 23, 2010, articles.cnn.com/2010–02–23/politics/poll.government.trust_1_new-national-poll-government-cnn?_s=PM:POLITICS.
105. This and the following quotations are from Joseph Rago, "Interview: William F. Buckley Jr.," *Wall Street Journal*, November 12, 2005.
106. Indeed, this deradicalization was planned. The two most recent editors both told the author separately that they would aim at making *National Review* into the American version of the staid British magazine *The Economist*.
107. See, for example, "The Week," *National Review*, December 18, 2006, 6; and Rich Lowry, "The Myths of '06," *Washington Times*, November 18, 2006, A13.
108. See, for example, "The Week," *National Review*, November 7, 2005, 4.
109. Rago, "Interview: William F. Buckley Jr."
110. Max Weber, *Theory of Social and Economic Organization*, 3:iv, v.
111. Michael Thompson, Richard Ellis, and Aaron Wildavsky, *Culture Theory* (Boulder, CO: Westview Press, 1990), 5–11.
112. Devine, "Wildavsky's Typology and Beyond."
113. Thompson et al., *Culture Theory*, 26–29.
114. Ryan Sager, *The Elephant in the Room* (Hoboken, NJ: John Wiley & Sons, 2006).

Chapter 10: History's Most Exciting Adventure

1. Editorials, "Mr. Obama Reboots," *Washington Post*, January 22, 2013, A8.
2. Editorials, "Small Politicians at the Cliff's Edge," *Washington Post*, December 31, 2013, A14.
3. David Ignatius, "Obama Missing in Action," *Washington Post*, January 2, 2013, A15.
4. Robert Samuelson, "Why the Recovery Lags," *Washington Post*, November 26, 2012, A17; and Arthur Laffer and Stephen Moore, "Obama's Real Spending Record," *Wall Street Journal*, June 12, 2012, A13.
5. "The Amazing Obama Budget," *Wall Street Journal*, February 14, 2011, A18.
6. Sudeep Reddy, "Tepid Job Growth Fuels Worry," *Wall Street Journal*, January 5, 2013. A1; "The Vanishing Workers," *Wall Street Journal*, May 5, 2012, A14; Michael A. Fletcher, "Since End of Recession, Household Income Has Fallen 4.8%," *Washington Post*, August 24, 2012, A10.
7. Government Accountability Office, "Multiple Employment and Training Programs," GAO 11–92, January 2011; Tom Coburn, "Less Could Be Better," *American Spectator*, September 2010, 8.
8. "Independent Payment Advisory Revolt," *Wall Street Journal*, March 9, 2012, A14.
9. Clyde Wayne Crews, *Ten Thousand Commandments: An Annual Snapshot of the Federal Regulatory State* (Washington, DC: Cato Institute, 2010).
10. "Regulation for Dummies," *Wall Street Journal*, December 14, 2011, A20.
11. "The Dodd-Frank Layoffs," *Wall Street Journal*, September 13, 2011, A16.
12. L. Gordon Crovitz, "Exporting Wall Street," *Wall Street Journal*, February 28, 2011, A17.
13. "The Diviner of Systemic Risk," *Wall Street Journal*, September 4, 2010, A14; "The Ruling Ad-Hocracy," *Wall Street Journal*, January 21, 2011, A12.
14. Notice that even seemingly more upbeat interpretations come to the same conclusion. See, for example, Bruce Bartlett, "The Real Tax Gap: Paying for Unfunded Benefits," *Huffington Post*, August 20, 2010, www.thefiscaltimes.com/Issues/Health-Care/2010/08/20/Tax-Burdens-of-Unfunded-Benefits.aspx.

15. Between August 2007 and April 2010, the Federal Reserve was also quietly lending money to private U.S. and foreign banks, reaching a peak of $1.2 trillion in 2008 but continuing throughout the period. These transactions were not revealed until an act of Congress forced discovery in 2011. Bradley Kroun and Phil Kuntz, "Analysis: $1.2 Trillion in Secret Loans to Wall Street," *Washington Post*, August 23, 2011, A13.

16. Alan Reynolds, "Ben Bernanke's Impossible Dream," *Wall Street Journal*, November 9, 2010, A19.

17. Neil Irwin, "Obama Defends $600 Billion Move," *Washington Post*, November 9, 2010, A10.

18. Allan H. Meltzer. "Assessing TARP," Testimony before Congressional Oversight Panel on TARP, March 4, 2011.

19. David Ignatius, "Miscast as Fiscal Heroes," *Washington Post*, July 22, 2012, A19.

20. Irwin, "Obama Defends $600 Billion Move."

21. Robert J. Samuelson, "What the Debt Panel Missed," *Washington Post*, December 6, 2010, A23.

22. Alexander Bolton, "Pelosi, Political Left Rip Report from Debt Commission Chairmen," *The Hill*, November 10, 2010, A1.

23. Holman W. Jenkins Jr., "Lost Decade, Revisited," *Wall Street Journal*, January 2, 2013, A15.

24. Tony Blair, *A Journey* (New York: Knopf, 2010), 657–58.

25. Samuelson, "Bankrupt Economics." That is not to say that no aspects worked; some at least did not make matters worse. But the point is that what was effective was not able to be foreseen beforehand. See Robert Samuelson, "TARP's Success Story," *Washington Post*, March 29, 2011, A17, and Samuelson, "Why the Recovery Lags."

26. Hayek, "The Uses of Knowledge in Society."

27. Holman W. Jenkins Jr., "None Dare Call It Default," *Wall Street Journal*, November 24, 2012, A13.

28. "Palin's Dollar and Zoellick's Gold," *Wall Street Journal*, November 9, 2010, A18. See also Hayek, "The Political Order of a Free People," 148.

29. Hayek, "The Political Order of a Free People," 151.

30. Vincent Ostrom, *The Intellectual Crisis in Public Administration* (Tuscaloosa: University of Alabama Press, 1973), esp. 70–86; Devine, "American Culture and Public Administration."

31. Donald Devine, "Old World Roots of Federalism," The Philadelphia Society, Memphis, Tennessee, October 13, 2012, www.phillysoc.org/DevineMemphis.pdf.

32. Vincent Ostrom and Barbara Allen, "The Continuing Constitutional Crisis in Public Administration," in Vincent Ostrom, *The Intellectual Crisis in Public Administration*, 3rd ed. esp. 154–63.

33. Devine, *Does Freedom Work?*, 56–62.

34. Milton Friedman, "The Role of Government in Education," in Robert A. Solo, ed., *Economics and the Public Interest* (Rutgers, NJ: Rutgers University Press, 1955), 123–44.

35. David H. Petraeus and James F. Amos, "Foreword," *Counterinsurgency* (Washington, DC: U.S. Army Field Manual 3–14/Marine Corps Warfighting Publication 33–33.5, 2006).

36. Hayek, "The Political Order of a Free People," 133.

37. While Buckley used the term *symbiotic* in *Did You Ever See a Dream Walking?* (xxxiii), he used the term *synthesis* from the beginning. See Buckley, *Up from Liberalism*, 193, and William F. Buckley Jr., "The Courage of Friedrich Hayek," 1975, in *Let Us Talk of Many Things* (Roseville, CA: Prima Publishing, 2000), 226. He specifically credited Meyer with having the most likely synthesis in defining American conservatism; see Buckley, *Did You Ever See a Dream Walking?*, xxxiii.

38. Hayek, Meyer, and Reagan were covered above. For Buckley, see *Did You Ever See a Dream Walking?*, xvii–xx.

39. Meyer, *In Defense of Freedom*, 80–98. Again, Catholic social theory calls this the principle of subsidiarity; cf. John Paul II, "State and Culture."

40. Justin Raimondo, *Reclaiming the American Right* (Wilmington, DE: ISI Books, 2008), chs. 10–11; David Gordon's critical essay "Why the Old Right Was Right" in *Reclaiming the American Right*, 313–26.

41. Lukacs, *The Passing of the Modern Age*.

42. Polk did receive a boost from a new book, Robert Merry, *A Country of Vast Designs* (New York: Simon & Schuster, 2009), which did not consider him an ideological nationalist.

43. William Kristol and David Brooks, "National Greatness Conservatism," *Wall Street Journal*, September 15, 1997.

44. Francis Fukuyama, "After Neoconservatism," *New York Times*, February 19, 2006.

45. Irving Kristol, "The Neoconservative Persuasion," *Weekly Standard*, August 25, 2003.

46. Walter A. McDougall, *Promised Land, Crusader State* (Boston: Houghton Mifflin, 2007), 11–12, 172–98, 204–5. He considers meliorism more religious than ideological in nature (205).

47. Ronald Reagan, "Address to the General Assembly of the United Nations," *The Public Papers of Ronald Reagan*, Reagan Presidential Library, June 17, 1982.

48. Martin and Annelise Anderson, *Reagan's Secret War* (New York: Random House, 2009). On the importance of peace in setting American foreign policy, see Angelo M. Codevilla, *Advice to War Presidents* (New York: Basic Books, 2009), 266–67.

49. Ronald Reagan, "First Inaugural Address," *The Public Papers of Ronald Reagan*, Reagan Presidential Library, January 20, 1981.

50. Ibid.

51. Ronald Reagan, "Address to the British Parliament," *The Public Papers of Ronald Reagan*, Reagan Presidential Library, June 8, 1982.

52. Louis J. Freeh, "Khobar Towers," *Wall Street Journal*, June 23, 2006, A10.

53. Ellen C. Carter, "Instances of Use of United States Forces Abroad, 1798–1993" (Washington, DC: Department of the Navy Naval History and Heritage Command, 1993), Congressional Research Service study at the online Naval Historical Center, www.history.navy.mil/wars/foabroad.htm.

54. Ronald Reagan, "Address to the Nation on the Investigation of the Iran-Contra Affair," *The Public Papers of Ronald Reagan*, Reagan Presidential Library, December 2, 1986.

55. Lee Edwards, *The Conservative Revolution: The Movement That Remade America* (New York: Fress Press, 1999), 239.

56. Margaret Thatcher, "Eulogy at the Funeral of Ronald Reagan," Associated Press, June 11, 2004.

57. Ronald Reagan, "Address to Members of the Royal Institute of International Affairs in London," *The Public Papers of Ronald Reagan*, Reagan Presidential Library, June 3, 1988.

58. Doug Bandow, "The Consequences of the Culture of Death," *American Spectator*, June 29, 2009, www.cato.org/pub_display.php?pub_id=10320.

59. Ronald Reagan, "Abortion and the Conscience of the Nation," *Human Life Review*, Spring 1983.

60. Devine, *The Political Culture of the United States*, ch. 1.

61. *Federalist* No. 10.

62. *Federalist* No. 51.

63. Tocqueville, *Democracy in America*, 262.

64. See Kenneth J. Arrow, *Social Choice and Individual Values* (New York: Wiley, 1951).

65. Schumpeter, *Capitalism, Socialism, and Democracy*, ch. 22, p. 269ff.; Donald Devine, *The Attentive Public* (Chicago: Rand McNally, 1970), ch. 1.

66. Schumpeter, *Capitalism, Socialism, and Democracy*, 136–49.

67. Marx and Engels, *The Communist Manifesto*.

68. Gabriel, *The Course of American Democratic Thought*.

69. John Dewey Project on Progressive Education, University of Vermont, www.uvm.edu/~dewey/articles/proged.html.

70. Dewey, *Democracy and Education*, ch. 7.

71. National Center for Education Statistics, U.S. Department of Education, "Highlights from PIRLS 2011: Reading Achievement of U.S. Fourth-Grade Students in an International Context," December 2012, nces.ed.gov/pubs2013/2013010.pdf; National Center for Education Statistics, U.S. Department of Education, "Trends in International Mathematics and Science Study (TIMSS)," nces.ed.gov/timss/results11.asp.

72. National Association of Educational Progress, "The Nation's Report Card," nationsreportcard. gov/reading_2011/summary.asp and nationsreportcard.gov/math_2011/summary.asp. See also Nick Anderson, "National Reading Scores Stagnant," *Washington Post*, March 24, 2010, www. washingtonpost.com/wp-dyn/content/discussion/2010/03/24/DI2010032400938.html.

73. Stephanie Banchero, "Scores Stagnate at High Schools," *Washington Post*, August 18, 2010, A1.

74. Lyndsey Layton and Emma Brown, "Scores on SAT Extend Slide," *Washington Post*, September 25, 2012, A1.

75. Robert Weissberg, *Bad Students, Not Bad Schools* (New Brunswick, NJ: Transaction, 2010), 171–72.

76. John Payton, Roger P. Weissberg, Joseph A. Durlak, Allison B. Dymnicki, Rebecca D. Taylor, Kriston B. Schellinger, and Molly Pachan, *The Positive Effect of Social and Emotional Learning for Kindergarten to Eighth-Grade Students* (Chicago: Collaborative for Academic, Social, and Emotional Learning, 2008), www.lpfch.org/sel/casel-narrative.pdf.

77. Paul Kengor, "Slouching from Gomorrah: Remembering Robert Bork," Center for Vision and Values at Grove City College, January 3, 2013. See also Charles Sykes, "Adult Supervision," *Wall Street Journal*, November 8, 2007.

78. Richard Rorty, *Objectivity, Relativism, and Truth: Philosophical Papers,* vol. 1 (Cambridge: Cambridge University Press, 1991), 109 and part 3.

79. See Thomas Jefferson, Letter to John Adams, September 2, 1813, in Lester J. Cappon, ed., *The Adams-Jefferson Letters* (Chapel Hill: University of North Carolina Press, 1959); John Adams, Letter to Thomas Jefferson, November 15, 1813, in Cappon, *The Adams-Jefferson Letters.*

80. Hayek, "The Political Order of a Free People," 176.

81. Daniel Oliver, "Alphaomegaizing the Conservative Movement," *American Spectator*, June 2010, 36.

82. Charlie Cook, "Why? Why? Why?," *National Journal*, November 6, 2010.

83. Irving Kristol, "The Neoconservative Persuasion."

84. Edwin Feulner, "Mapping Out the Mission," Townhall.com, February 24, 2010, townhall.com/ columnists/edfeulner/2010/02/24/mapping_out_the_mission/page/full/; Lee Edwards, "The Conservative Consensus," *First Principles* No. 8, The Heritage Foundation, January 22, 2007; Chuck Colson, "Limited Government, Mob Rule, or Tyranny," *Two-Minute Warning,* July 12, 2011.

85. Hayek, "The Political Order of a Free People," 146.

86. Lord Acton, "The History of Freedom in Antiquity," 5.

87. Devine, "Wildavsky's Typology and Beyond"; Putman and Campbell, *American Grace*, chs. 3–4, 11; Brian D. Ray, "Research Facts on Homeschooling," National Home Education Research Institute, January 11, 2011, www.nheri.org/research/research-facts-on-homeschooling.html.

88. Bertrand Russell, *The Impact of Science on Society* (London: Routledge, 1952); Richard Weaver, "Impact of Society on Mr. Russell," *In Defense of Tradition*, 134–36.

89. See especially Putnam and Campbell, *American Grace*, chs. 13, 15; "How Important Is Religion?" Gallup 2009, and Zogby International Poll, "Parents Disagree with *National Guidelines for Sexuality and Character Education* issued by the Medical Institute for Sexual Health," February 13, 2003, www.ncfamily.org/pdffiles/zogby_press_release.pdf, and the other citations in ch. 7 above.

90. Meyer, *In Defense of Freedom*, 150, 219–20.

91. Robert D. Novak, *The Prince of Darkness* (New York: Crown Forum, 2009), 367.

92. Michael Reagan, Speech before Bellevue University's Federalist Leadership Center, Raleigh, NC, September 12, 2007.

93. Paul Kengor, *God and Ronald Reagan* (New York: HarperCollins, 2004), 118–20.

94. Reagan, "First Inaugural Address."

95. Devine, *Reagan's Terrible Swift Sword*, 84.

96. John Shaw, "Former Secretary of State Embodies Ideas and Actions," *Washington Diplomat*, April 26, 2011.

97. Elin Woodger and David Berg, *The 1980s* (New York: Infobase Publishing, 2006), 59.

98. Edmund Morris, *Dutch: A Memoir of Ronald Reagan* (New York: Random House, 1999), 91, 184, 428–32.

99. Morris, *Dutch*, 432.

100. James Mann, "Did Reagan Try to Convert Gorbachev?," *Wall Street Journal*, March 7, 2009, W1.

101. Ronald Reagan, "The Agenda Is Victory," *The Public Papers of Ronald Reagan*, Reagan Presidential Library, Conservative Political Action Conference, February 26, 1982.

102. Ronald Reagan, "Remarks on Signing the George C. Marshall Month Proclamation," June 1, 1987, and "Remarks and a Question-and-Answer Session with Economic Editors During a White House Briefing on Tax Reform," June 7, 1985, *The Public Papers of Ronald Reagan*, Reagan Presidential Library. On Hayek and Erhard, see Public Broadcasting System, *The Commanding Heights*, May 15, 2003, ep. 1, chs. 8–9, www.pbs.org/wgbh/commandingheights/shared/minitextlo/tr_show01.html.

103. Lawrence H. White, "The German Economic Miracle: Another Look," *Wall Street Journal*, September 8, 2010, online.wsj.com/article/SB1000142405274870336970457546187341174240 4.html.

104. Reagan, "Remarks at the Dedication of the James Madison Memorial Building of the Library of Congress."

Acknowledgments

———⊰•⊱———

AN AUTHOR OWES MANY OBLIGATIONS on the way to write a book, but he
can blame no one else for its failures. I would especially like to thank
ISI Books, especially editor Jed Donahue; ISI president Chris Long and his
predecessor, Ken Cribb; and academic vice president Mark Henrie. I owe
Eugene Meyer and Robert Luddy much for encouraging and supporting me
in writing the book. Three professors began my journey and have not been
given thanks previously: John Hurley, Charles Crowley, and Francis Cana-
van. Most of all, my wife, Ann, has been secretary and confidante for longer
than she would allow me to say but is appreciated for much more than the
actual years. My children, William, Michael, Patricia, and Joseph, have been
mentioned with great appreciation before, but my grandchildren insisted on
being given recognition this time, so the book has been dedicated to them.
My cup overflows.

Index

INTERCOLLEGIATE
STUDIES INSTITUTE
Educating for Liberty

ISI Books is the publishing imprint of the Intercollegiate Studies Institute (ISI). Since its founding in 1953, ISI has been inspiring college students to discover, embrace, and advance the principles and virtues that make America free and prosperous.

Today ISI has more than 10,000 student members on college campuses across the country. The Institute reaches these and thousands of other people through an integrated program of campus speakers, conferences, seminars, publications, student groups, and fellowships and scholarships, along with a rich repository of online resources.

ISI is a nonprofit, nonpartisan, tax-exempt educational organization. The Institute relies on the financial support of the general public—individuals, foundations, and corporations—and receives no funding or any other aid from any level of the government.

To learn more about ISI,
visit www.isi.org or call (800) 526-7022